GOOD JEW, BAD JEW

*Racism, Anti-Semitism
and the Assault on Meaning*

Steven Friedman

WITS UNIVERSITY PRESS

Published in South Africa by:
Wits University Press
1 Jan Smuts Avenue
Johannesburg 2001

www.witspress.co.za

First published 2023

http://dx.doi.org.10.18772/12023118486

978-1-77614-848-6 (Paperback)
978-1-77614-849-3 (Hardback)
978-1-77614-850-9 (Web PDF)
978-1-77614-851-6 (EPUB)

This publication is peer reviewed following international best practice standards for academic
and scholarly books.

Project manager: Catherine Damerell
Copy editor: Na'eem Jeenah
Proofreader: Lee Smith
Indexer: Margaret Ramsay
Cover design: Hybrid Creative
Typeset in 11 point Minion Pro

GOOD JEW, BAD JEW

CONTENTS

ACKNOWLEDGEMENTS

I could not have written this book without the continuing support of the University of Johannesburg, its Faculty of Humanities in particular, which continues to enable my work by offering me an academic home.

I am also grateful to Wits University Press, which continues to publish my work even when it tackles topics that others may find too risky.

I hope that this book justifies the faith that both institutions continue to show in me.

Racism, one of the ugliest features of human society, is also among its most resilient.

When the African American scholar W. E. B. Du Bois wrote, at the very beginning of that century, that the 'problem of the twentieth century is the problem of the color-line',[1] he summed up a core reality of the next hundred years. But perhaps not even he could have imagined that, two decades into the twenty-first century, it too was on its way to becoming a century whose problem would be 'the color-line'. Focused on the 'relation of the darker to the lighter races',[2] Du Bois could not have expected that the worst racially motivated slaughter during the century would be visited by whites on other white people, not on people of a darker complexion. The Nazi genocide slaughtered six million Jews and between eight and ten million Slavs simply because they had been born into the 'wrong' ethnic group. (If we calculate deaths as a proportion of population size, the most brutal mass murder of the modern era was that of ten million Congolese people at around the time that Du Bois' observation appeared in print; of course, the sheer number of Nazi victims was greater.[3])

While the Nazis slaughtered Slavs and Roma people too, racism directed at Jews was a core element in their ideology of the Aryan 'master race'. The prejudice was not new; active hostility to Jews stretches back to the founding of Christianity and was hardened by the emergence of absolutist states in the Late Middle Ages. But Jewish identity is complicated by the fact that Jews are both adherents of a religion and members of an ethnic group. This is not unique; Sikhs are another well-known example of a religious group which is also an ethnic group. But it is unusual.

Until the French Revolution and the Enlightenment, these two identities were fused (for reasons that will be discussed in chapter 4), and all Jews were effectively forced to adhere to their religion by the reigning authorities. When Jews were allowed to choose whether to practise their religion, those who chose not to were still regarded as ethnically Jewish. This made Jewish identity more complicated than that of most other religious or ethnic groups. It is possible to choose to be Jewish by converting to the religion but the various strains of Jewish religious expression have different requirements for conversion. Those with stricter requirements do not recognise the converts of the more lenient streams, so not everyone who considers themself to be Jewish is accepted as such by the entire Jewish community. Since Jews are also an ethnic group, those who abandon the Jewish religion are still regarded as Jewish but the status of Jews who join another religion has been controversial.[4] There are enough grey areas on the borders of Jewish identity to ensure that the question of who is Jewish and who is not is still hotly debated within the Jewish fold.[5]

What matters for our purpose is that, when restrictions on Jews in Europe began to ease, religious hostility to them as a group became less tenable. In theory at least, Jews could choose not to be Jewish by converting to Christianity, as more than a few did. But bigotry is not that easily ended. Those who were prejudiced against Jews, presumably alarmed that they could now integrate into society, focused not on the religion of the targets of their bigotry but on accidents of birth; they began to insist that Jews constituted a separate and dangerous race. It is no accident that this ideology of racism emerged only in the nineteenth century, after the Enlightenment.

The ideologues of this new racism called it 'anti-Semitism'. The term has remained in usage even though it is inaccurate since Arabs are

Semites too.[6] While anti-Jewish racists often despise Arabs as well, the term was used to describe a prejudice against Jews alone. The bigotry of which Du Bois wrote – against black and Asian people – is also very old. It can be traced back at least to the Atlantic slave trade and the British colonisation of parts of Asia and Africa. The term 'racism' that we use today was, however, originally coined to describe racial prejudice against Jews only.[7] While prejudice against 'the darker races' dominates today in discourse and in practical manifestations of racism, anti-Semitism has not disappeared, as demonstrated by the murder of Jews at synagogues in the United States and Germany in 2018 and 2019.

These two prejudices obviously have different targets but, for decades after Du Bois' prophecy, they have been linked. As the anti-colonial theorist Frantz Fanon pointed out, anti-Jewish racism and prejudice against black people (and Arabs and Asians) usually formed part of a package of bigotries which went together. Anti-Semitism was, in the view of some scholars, a form of white supremacy,[8] though this is less so than it once was. One reason for this change in how anti-Semitism is viewed is that the fight against racism has, justifiably, centred on the relationship between the 'lighter' and 'darker' races of which Du Bois wrote. While prejudices against groups considered 'white' survive, today they rarely – if ever – enable domination over these groups. (Like some other groups regarded as 'white' today, such as Irish and Italian immigrants to the United States,[9] Jews were not always seen as 'white' by the dominant culture.[10]) By contrast, deeply racist attitudes to 'darker' people that were notoriously displayed in reactions to the 2022 Russian invasion of Ukraine[11] do enable domination and the denial of rights. An obvious example is the constant attempt to deny 'darker' people access to countries which enthusiastically welcome white Ukrainians.

But there is another reason why a wedge has been driven into discussions of anti-Jewish racism and of racism against 'black, brown and yellow' people. The Israeli state and its supporters have converted 'anti-Semitism' from a description of anti-Jewish racism to a weapon against their critics, many of whom happen to be Jews who believe that the state's attitudes and practices are racist. In effect, an allegation of racism has been turned into a weapon against anti-racists. This is accompanied by another turnaround: the Israeli state and its supporters seek to turn the campaign against anti-Semitism from a rebellion against white supremacy into an endorsement of white Europeanness. This book discusses how this happened and what it means both for Jewish identity and for our understandings of anti-Jewish racism, both real and imagined. It also discusses how the lessons of this process apply more generally to current developments in South Africa and the world.

Much has been written about the Israeli state's impact on the lives and rights of the Palestinian people. The domination over Palestinians is by far the most insidious effect of the establishment of the Israeli state as an authority that serves only one ethnic group on territory also inhabited by other groups. Less obvious is the impact of the Israeli state's role on Jews and Jewish identity. This is the subject of this book. Its focus does not suggest that the distortions of Jewish identity and the misuse of anti-Semitism to demonise other Jews (often in deeply anti-Semitic terms) are more important than the daily experience of Palestinians. Rather, it argues that the changes wrought to Jewish identity form an important element in the ideology which underpins the Israeli state and that they deserve more attention than they have received.

THE REALITY OF RACE

Why is this of concern to people who are not Jewish and who have no particular interest in how Jews understand themselves and in the problem of anti-Jewish racism?

Du Bois was, in essence, correct. Racism remains the core fault line between human beings. This relates not only to the 'color-line' but also to the bigotry that some of the same 'race' harbour against others who are seen to be culturally or ethnically different. It was the central divide through the twentieth century, as Du Bois had foretold, and remains so now. This is not to deny the importance of other divisions. But human identities – race, religion, language, ethnicity, gender – have more power to mobilise people, and to divide them, than any other of the divisions that set one person off from another. These identities also remain the chief rationale for the domination of some human beings over others.

To claim this is to challenge some firmly held beliefs across the political spectrum. On the left, it has long been argued that race and other identities are not the 'real' issues which divide society, even when people believe that this is what sets them apart. These divides are seen as symptoms of – and often as justifications for or deflectors of attention from – the division of people into social classes: those who own the means to produce goods and services and those who are forced to sell their labour to the owners.[12] But it was slavery, a system of racial domination, which provided the material basis for the development of prosperous capitalist societies, a reality often ignored by theorists of class.[13] If a classless society did emerge, it might end bigotry and an emphasis on identities. But since none ever has and there are no signs that one is on the horizon, this remains hypothetical. It is very apparent in our present reality that, as the scholar Ashutosh Varshney pointed out, people who are dominated by others are more likely to mobilise behind identities than any other form of difference. Mobilisation against poverty is likelier, he suggests, if the poor share a common identity. 'Not only is it easier to mobilize the poor as members of ethnic communities, but that is also how they often vote – along lines of ethnicity, not class.'[14]

It is common among both liberals and conservatives in societies with a history of racial domination to insist that the extension of rights to everyone has dissolved racial differences and that racial tensions are kept alive solely by small, politicised groups. In South Africa, survey data is interpreted to support claims that people do not see racial issues as a priority.[15] But these claims fly in the face of observed reality since race remains a powerful source of identity and division which shapes most political debates, even when people are ostensibly talking about something else. They also ignore the probability that, where racial identity is a pervasive reality in society, interviewees who identify seemingly race-free priorities such as jobs or better education may also be making a statement about the prevailing racial power balance and on how, depending on the speaker's identity, it could be preserved or changed.

Liberals and conservatives harbour their own versions of the leftist claim that racial divisions are simply a reflection of economic realities. They portray the marketplace as an identity-free zone that is free of race and gender prejudices. Investors and companies, they insist, cannot afford racial biases because these would eat into their profits. This ignores the extent to which economic activity, since it is conducted by human beings who do not place their preferences and prejudices aside when they enter the world of commerce, may reflect racial and other biases. Two American activists, Tema Okun and Keith Jones, argue that the cultures of businesses and other organisations which seem entirely blind to identities actually privilege whites. 'The belief that traditional standards and values are objective and unbiased; the emphasis on a sense of urgency and quantity over quality, which can be summarized by the phrase "the ends justify the means"; perfectionism that leaves little room for mistakes; and binary thinking,' are all, in this view, expressions of a dominant culture to which people who are neither white nor male must conform if they want to get on in the world.[16] Whether we agree on the list or not, there are ways of doing things and patterns of beliefs in businesses and other organisations that perpetuate racial hierarchies.

It is often argued that race is purely a 'social construct',[17] that it is a creation of society because there are no biological differences between races. Science supports this view; there are no biological differences between people of different races which are any more significant than, say, the differences between brown- and green-eyed people. There are biological differences between men and women but that does not mean that either is programmed at birth to play their traditional roles. But when it is advanced to support the claim that identities do not really matter, this argument misses an important point: how human beings think and act in society is shaped not by biology but by the meanings which they construct. 'Social constructs' are, therefore, what shape society and the way in which it operates. The fact that white people are clearly not biologically superior to other people is as unlikely to dissuade a white supremacist as the news that gender relations are learned is likely to alter patriarchal attitudes among men.

If we are to understand race, it is crucial, as the theorist Stuart Hall argued, that we see it as an instrument of domination. Race, Hall wrote, 'is the centerpiece of a hierarchical system that produces differences'.[18] In other words, some use it to 'produce' differences because this enables them to wield power over others. The fact that they have to invent biology to do that does not alter the reality that it enables their domination. The anti-racist scholar Alana Lentin insists that race must be understood 'as a political project with ongoing effects'.[19] It is used to create 'power imbalances and inequality'[20] and has 'ongoing effects' because it continues to keep these alive. It is not rooted in biology but it has biological consequences: it 'can have a physical impact on the individual's racialised body as well as a psychological effect on the mind'.[21] That race is a social construct does not make it any less powerful a shaper of behaviour in society.

APPLYING THE CASE MORE WIDELY

The changing uses to which anti-Jewish racism are now being put shed light on other ways in which race currently divides human beings. The attempt to morph anti-Semitism from a protest against racial domination into a justification of it is part of a new racism of the sort that concerned Du Bois, the kind of racism that some lighter-skinned people inflict on those who are darker.

Anti-Semitism is not the only bigotry that has undergone a metamorphosis in the hands of those who wish to preserve the historic domination of some over others. There are echoes in current responses to the domination of white people over others. As we will see, allegations that the dominated groups are guilty of prejudice have become a powerful weapon in the hands of those who seek to shore up racial hierarchies. This probably began to emerge publicly about half a century ago when white men used the courts in the United States to challenge affirmative action and its attempts to undo the effects of racism by claiming that they were victims of racial discrimination. In the past decade, it has expanded into much broader claims that those who challenge racial hierarchies are the racists, not those who are being challenged. The case of weaponised anti-Semitism offers an insight into how this has occurred.

These claims have been particularly common in South Africa since majority rule was achieved in 1994. Anyone who observes that racism survived the end of apartheid is routinely accused of playing 'the race card' – using race to advance their own agendas. One example is that of a former government minister who observed that 'our non-racial dream is not embraced by the majority of white South Africans' and who was then accused of stoking racial distrust.[22] White people often assume, despite evidence to the contrary, that they are being denied jobs and opportunities – including selection to national sport teams – because they must make way for poorly qualified black people. More generally, it is often claimed or implied that when black people occupy positions in society that were previously monopolised by whites, race, not merit, is being rewarded.

These claims are always phrased as a call for 'non-racial merit' but they assume that only white people have merit, which is, of course, a deeply racial bias. While the prejudiced used to stress the need to recognise that races differ from each other, they now seek to portray those who campaign against racial privilege and power as bigots who invent racial differences where none exist. The parallel with branding opponents of the racist behaviour of the Israeli state as anti-Jewish racists should be clear. This book's discussion of the ways in which claims of anti-Semitism are used to deflect charges of Israeli state racism also invites attention to the way in which professed anti-racism has become a weapon in the hands of racial supremacy – particularly since many of those who peddle the former are also prone to propagate the latter.

Attempts to change the meaning of anti-Jewish racism also say something important about the challenges that face dominated groups and, more particularly, the need to guard against unwittingly reinforcing the attitudes that produce domination while seeking to challenge it. The use of anti-Semitism to browbeat Israeli state opponents is part of a larger reality in which those who do this seek to change the nature of Jewish identity by distinguishing between 'real' Jews and the rest (at least some of whom may find themselves accused of being anti-Semites). They also seek to 'flatten out' Jewish identity. Jews are no longer, like every other group, a complicated mix of differing opinions and perspectives. The complexities of being both an ethnic group and a religion, with which Jews have grappled since the Enlightenment allowed them a choice, are obliterated. Instead, there are only 'good' Jews who attach their identity to the Israeli state and 'bad' ones who do not. The journalist and writer Nesrine Malik noted a similar 'flattening' of Muslim identity:

> There was a time when a Muslim was a much more complicated, much roomier thing to be – inflected with local culture and individual circumstances. Today, you can only be a good Muslim or a bad one. Either a 'moderate' or a 'radical'. Either a Muslim who needs to be saved or a Muslim you need to be saved from.[23]

While current Muslim and Jewish experiences are very different, there are important links, even if they are not easily seen. One link is the way in which those who hold power seek to turn a complex identity in which many perspectives may be heard into a hollowed-out label. The historian Avi Shlaim, responding to claims that all 'real' Jews support the Israeli state, observes: 'Ironically, to treat Jews as a homogeneous group is in fact an antisemitic trope. It is antisemites who fail to differentiate between different kinds of Jews, and want to see them all clustered in one place. It is on this basis that Theodor Herzl, the visionary of a Jewish state, predicted that "the antisemites will become our most dependable friends".'[24] As we will see, the 'authentic Jews' turn out to be imitations of those who once visited prejudice on Jews. We will also see that these shifts are directly comparable to attitudes in India where, one of that country's thinkers,

Ashis Nandy, tells us, those who trumpet their authentic 'Indianness' are, in reality, mimics of the colonisers they claim to oppose.

There are important consequences of this discussion for South Africa, where a long-delayed debate on decolonisation and decoloniality continues. This is fuelled by an entirely justifiable demand that the norms of the society, as well as what is taught in schools and universities and what is said in the media, should not reflect an assumption that the countries which once colonised Africa and Asia are the only fonts of wisdom and value. But there is no agreement on what decolonisation and decoloniality is and this raises the danger that some of the 'cures' may simply mimic the 'disease' in the same way as the approaches of Zionists, supporters of a Jewish state, mimic those of anti-Semites. This book will show how understandings of Jewish identity and Indian self-understandings can help to inform the debate on what a really decolonised South Africa might be.

This brief introduction has, hopefully, shown that the uses and abuses of anti-Semitism have much to teach us about race and identity today. But a brief word is also needed on the book's title. It is, as a later chapter will show, inspired by an important book by Mahmood Mamdani, *Good Muslim, Bad Muslim*.[25] The link with the theme of this book is that Mamdani is concerned to explain the phenomenon to which Malik responds – how some Muslims have been demonised by Western power holders while others are accepted. Mamdani wants to show how identities can be imposed on people by a power outside their group, a new coloniser as it were, while this book hopes to show how some within a group can seek to impose an identity on others, inverting our common understanding of racism. But there are parallels between the two that need discussion, not only because they throw more light on the topic but because, at a time when strenuous efforts are being made to place impenetrable walls between Jews and Muslims, the parallels between their experiences can remind us of the common humanity of both groups and so help to break down the wall.

1

Turning Anti-Semitism on its Head

Anti-Jewish bigotry just isn't what it used to be.

On 6 January 2021, demonstrators incited by then president Donald Trump stormed the United States Capitol in an attempt to overturn the result of a presidential election that Trump had lost. Since the event was a festival of white nationalist prejudice, it was perhaps predictable that some demonstrators would be wearing garments bearing the slogan 'Camp Auschwitz',[1] celebrating a death camp in Poland where the Nazis had murdered Jews and others. But the January 2021 event was a little more complicated than it initially appeared. First, one of the participants, apparently a Christian Zionist,[2] proudly waved an Israeli flag. Also, 'another masked protestor sported a black-and-white Israeli flag sown onto his paramilitary vest, beside a pro-police "Thin Blue Line" flag'.[3] News agencies reported that several Israeli flags were waved in the protest.[4] Second, among the participants were Orthodox Jews, who, reportedly, had voted overwhelmingly for Trump.[5]

To anyone familiar with the history of anti-Jewish racism, the event sent very confusing messages. Why would people who cheer the genocidal murder of six million Jews also support a state whose parliament, in 2018, passed a basic law declaring itself the 'nation state of the Jewish people'?[6] What were Orthodox Jews doing on the same side of the barricades as those who hanker for Nazi death camps? What, for that matter, were they doing supporting a president given to repeating and endorsing anti-Jewish slanders and who, in 2016, used an image in his campaign literature that included the Jewish Star of David to brand his (non-Jewish) opponent Hillary Clinton as corrupt?[7] Trump had also told American Jews that the Israeli state was 'your country',[8] repeating the stock prejudice that Jews are not really loyal to the countries in which they live – much like telling South Africans of Indian descent that their country is India. In one view, this 'betrayed his understanding of U.S. Jews as not fully American, in keeping with his overall exclusivist notion of citizenship'.[9] Why would a politician who harbours such prejudices enjoy any Jewish support, particularly from some who enthusiastically embrace their Jewish identity?

The answer to these questions is that the world has moved on in some odd and disturbing ways. Not that long ago, anti-Semitism, bigotry directed towards Jews, was a (reasonably) straightforward matter. Racists directed their contempt, venom and, at times, violence at Jews just as other racists might direct the same poison at black or Asian people. Since anti-Jewish racism can be seen as a type of white nationalism, those who were prejudiced towards Jews often harboured the same biases against blacks or Asians. Anti-Semites disliked all Jews. For their part, Jews might have different views on what to do about anti-Semites. For some, an ethnic Jewish state was the solution; others believed that democracy, not a state for Jews alone, was the best way to fight anti-Jewish racism. But all agreed that anti-Semites were dangerous foes, not friends.

No longer. While the combination of Israeli flags and T-shirts lamenting that the Nazis did not kill more Jews might seem extreme, it was part of a trend – the alliance of anti-Semites and some Jews against other Jews. On the first score, Trump was not the only politician with anti-Semitic leanings to enthusiastically endorse – and be endorsed by – certain Jews (those who happen to run the 'Jewish state'). Hungarian prime minister Viktor Orban is another, despite the fact that he had run a campaign against Jewish financier George Soros that repeated the Nazi stereotype that portrays Jews as wealthy manipulators of white Christians. Orban also refused to condemn a magazine run by his lawyer when it pictured the leader of Hungary's largest Jewish organisation showered in bank notes.[10] Like Trump's campaign image, this Hungarian caricature repeated the standard anti-Semitic claim that 'Jewish money power' manipulates the world. Orban is a great admirer of Miklos Horthy, who ruled Hungary from 1920 to 1944, and was a proud anti-Semite who introduced measures modelled on the Nazis' anti-Jewish laws. Other such politicians include the former Brazilian president, Jair Bolsonaro, who called Hitler a 'great strategist' and suggested that Jews who died in Nazi death camps actually perished from hunger and cold.[11] There is also Polish leader Jaroslaw Kaczynski, whose party proposed imprisoning anyone who suggested that the Polish state had co-operated in the Nazi murders of Polish Jews.[12]

An important source of anti-Jewish hostility is the Christian right, which has held Jews in contempt for centuries.[13] But its religious beliefs also ensure uncritical support for the Israeli state. Many Christian Zionists believe that Jews must control historical Palestine because this is essential to the second coming of Christ when Jews, like all other non-Christians, will either convert to Christianity or be damned.[14] The fact that these allies of the Israeli state see it as an essential means to achieve the death of the Jewish religion, and that hostility to Jews is deeply embedded in their view of the world, does not deter the state and its supporters. In a 2019 state visit to Brazil, then prime minister of Israel, Benjamin Netanyahu, declared, 'We have no better friends in the world than the Evangelical community.' This despite his admission that: 'Anger and vitriolic theories of Jewish control over the United States are … apparent inside the [Evangelical] churches, where old theories about Jewish influence in politics collide with religious views about the crucifixion of Jesus.'[15] The Israeli state has sold arms to anti-Semitic military juntas in Argentina and Bolivia. It also supplied weapons to the Azov brigade, an overtly pro-Nazi and anti-Semitic division of the Ukrainian army, prompting a petition from Israeli human rights activists who urged that it stop these sales.[16] Trump, one analysis notes, 'brought classic antisemitism back into fashion in the United States while being warmly embraced by the prime minister of the Jewish state'.[17]

Orban, Bolsonaro and other right-wing heads of government have paid official visits to the Israeli state where they undertake the obligatory trip to Yad Vashem, the memorial to the Nazis' Jewish victims. Even the architect of the slaughter that the monument commemorates, Adolf Hitler, is now offered a posthumous free pass from a leader of the 'Jewish state'; in 2015, Netanyahu told the World Zionist Congress that Hitler had not wanted to exterminate Jews but had been persuaded to do so by the (Muslim, Arab) Grand Mufti of Jerusalem, Haj Amin al-Husseini.[18] As we will see, the claim is entirely spurious. But it does, of course, let Hitler off the hook. While the Israeli state and its supporters often mobilise horror at the Nazi slaughter for their own purposes, they reserve the right to absolve its perpetrators for reasons of state and because they share other prejudices.

A less bizarre but equally important example is a campaign against 'anti-Semitism' in Britain's Labour Party. We will return to this later but, for now, the important aspect of this purported fight against anti-Jewish racism is that many of those expelled for allegedly harbouring prejudice against Jews are, in fact, Jewish.[19] According to a report by the group Jewish Voice for Labour, which has been a particular target of the 'campaign against anti-Semitism', Jewish members of the party are 20 times more likely to face complaints alleging that they are anti-Semitic than non-Jewish members. It accuses Labour of 'purging Jews from the party'.[20]

How is this justified? The answer is found in an incident during the Labour Party's 'anti-Semitism' saga. Its former leader, Jeremy Corbyn, who was routinely accused of anti-Semitism, was invited by a Jewish group sympathetic to him to attend a Passover meal. He attended, taking some horseradish, which plays a role in the ritual meal, from his garden. But Corbyn's detractors refused to accept that he could not be anti-Semitic if he had joined enthusiastically with Jews in a very Jewish ritual;

they insisted, in a chorus, that the left-wing Jewish group that had invited him was comprised of 'the wrong sort of Jews'.[21] Some of them, including a Labour MP, claimed that Corbyn was deliberately baiting most Jews by hanging out on a Jewish holiday with Jews whose opinions other Jews didn't like. In this Orwellian view, to dine with Jews and share in their festivals is anti-Semitic – if the Jews in question happen to be disliked by the communal power holders. Throwing Jews out of the party Corbyn once led because they are 'anti-Semites' is presumably justified on these grounds, since the offending Jews offend other Jews. Taken to its logical conclusion, this means that associating with a member of any group is a racist act if they happen to be disliked by other members of their group.

Our puzzle becomes even more puzzling. Anti-Semites, it appears, are no longer viewed as enemies by Jews or, more accurately, by those Jews who see themselves, and are seen by much of the world, as mainstream Jewish leaders. But the fight against anti-Jewish racism continues and anti-Semitism, it appears, can be something Jews do – sometimes, in greater numbers than non-Jews do. It can be expressed not by denouncing Jews and their rituals, but by joining with them in participating in them. Hatred of Jews can be expressed not by banning Passover rituals and discriminating against those who take part in them but by observing them with Jews of a particular political persuasion. (A horrified article in the right-wing *Daily Mail* revealed that participants in the Passover meal that Corbyn had attended had denounced capitalism.[22]) Fraternising with 'bad Jews' – or 'the wrong Jews' – is a great deal worse than expressing hostility to all Jews. One of the attractions of the anti-Semitic leaders now beloved of some Jews is that they too distinguish between 'good' and 'bad' Jews and are eager to work with the 'good' ones against the 'bad' ones.

MAKING SENSE OF THE CONFUSION

If you find this confusing, you are paying attention.

Were black leadership across the world to embrace anti-black racists as trusted allies, to insist also that white people who attended events organised by black people which are of cultural and spiritual significance to them were actually insulting blacks by associating with 'the wrong blacks', and if they were to seek to fight racism directed at black people mainly by acting against other black people, this would, to put it mildly, seem odd. But the current attempt by 'Jewish leadership' to redefine anti-Semitism in this way is treated as entirely normal by a range of opinion formers and people of influence in Europe and North America.

To make sense of this, it is crucial to understand that for those in positions of Jewish authority who peddle this attempt to manufacture a reality that seems entirely unreal, anti-Semitism no longer means prejudice against Jewish people. In the English-speaking world, we can date this development to the 1970s when Arnold Foster and Benjamin Epstein, who held leadership roles in the American Anti-Defamation League, published a book titled *The New Anti-Semitism*.[23] This started something of a cottage industry – more books in a similar vein followed. It is noteworthy that the Anti-Defamation League was founded to combat anti-Semitism in the United States, but it has become chiefly a propaganda vehicle of the Israeli state.

These writings did seem partly concerned to identify hostility to Jews, even if its claims bordered on the paranoid. An example of this paranoia was the insistence that the film *Jesus Christ Superstar* (whose director was Jewish) was anti-Semitic; another was the use of opinion poll data to target black Americans as arch anti-Semites, a claim that became a theme in much of the writing on the 'new anti-Semitism'. In France, branding black people and Arabs anti-Semitic is a strong focus of the right wing.[24] But much of this kind of claim was entirely detached from anything that a reasonable person might identify as anti-Jewish racism. The 'new anti-Semitism', one tract complained, had created an environment in which 'war is getting a bad name and peace too favorable a press'.[25] This tendency to find anti-Semitic intent in strange and marvellous places has spread to other parts of the globe. In Britain, opposition to capitalism was branded anti-Semitic;[26] even more weirdly, so was a motion of no confidence in the leader of the Labour Party on the grounds that he had failed to keep a promise to unite the party.[27] In South Africa, calls for affordable housing in the Cape Town inner city were branded anti-Semitic,[28] presumably because one of the pieces of land that campaigners wanted earmarked for the housing project had been set aside for a Jewish school but was not, in fact, used to build one and so was unused.

Taken together with the pattern in which anti-Semites are Jews of a particular persuasion, not non-Jews who have shown hostility to Jews, these examples show that the term 'anti-Semitism' has become detached from its moorings. It no longer means racism directed at Jews; it means holding left-wing or egalitarian opinions, which often seems to include being opposed to the white supremacy of which anti-Semitism was once a part. The new Jew – or victim of anti-Semitism – is no longer a member of a particular ethnic group. It is a right-wing person, Jewish or non-Jewish, who supports the economic status quo and the racial hierarchies that have reigned in the West for centuries. The new anti-Semite is not a person who hates Jews. It is a person, Jewish or non-Jewish, who embraces egalitarian values. Jewish people are no longer victims of prejudice as a group; they are now divided into two groups – one 'good', the other 'bad' – and 'bad Jews' are one of the groups most likely to be accused of anti-Semitism. This is so because of, and not despite, the fact that the 'bad Jews' who are stigmatised as 'anti-Semites' tend to be anti-racists.

How did this come to be?

THE ROOTS OF THE 'NEW ANTI-SEMITISM'

The first – and perhaps the most important – reason for this trend is the state of Israel in general and the ascendancy of the Israeli right wing in particular. As the (Jewish) American activist and academic Norman Finkelstein points out, the original purpose of the authors who claimed to have discovered a new type of anti-Semitism was to insist on unquestioning support for the policies and actions of the Israeli state, whatever their effects on the lives of Palestinians.

Sustaining the State

The American 'new anti-Semitism' writing may seem unworthy of much attention because it appears to be a fringe view among a small group of Americans. It was anything but that. It was a product of the Israeli state and has now become not only a core position among the state's defenders but 'one that characterises the mainstream of most of western politics'.[29]

The claim that hostility to the Israeli state was born of anti-Jewish hatred had emerged in that state years before the Americans claimed to have found a new and dangerous anti-Semitism. 'A significant intellectual milestone was in the late 1960s when Israeli researchers began to develop the concept of "new antisemitism". Their view was that the old anti-Jewish sentiment that had taken shape and changed form over the centuries was now directed first and foremost against the Jewish political enterprise of Zionism and Israel.'[30] Two Israeli academics who were influential advocates of this position were Robert Wistrich, author of a much-quoted book on anti-Semitism,[31] and Dina Porat, whose Tel Aviv University research institute was funded by the Israeli state.[32] But a recently published study shows that it was the Israeli state itself which had started the ball rolling; the term had been used at a series of seminars organised by the office of the Israeli president in the late 1980s.[33] This view soon became deeply embedded in the state's ideological battle with its critics.

Zionism, the ideology that advocates a state for Jews in historic Palestine, had originally claimed to be an antidote to anti-Semitism. Jews, it had declared, were disliked because, unlike other ethnic groups, they did not have a state. Once they had one, the Jews' detractors would realise that they were normal (because normal groups have a state) and would abandon their prejudices. Their main hope had been that Europeans would react in that way. However, even people who were not European would, it seems, admire the Jews if they had a state. This was illustrated in the novel *Altneuland*, written by Theodor Herzl, the key ideologue of Jewish statehood, in which a fictional Arab (Palestinian) called Rashid Bey welcomes Jewish settlement because it brings development.[34]

Not surprisingly, these hopes were misplaced. Creating a state for one ethnic group on territory which was home to another did not end anti-Semitism. Nor did it win the Palestinian acceptance which Herzl had predicted. So it did not end conflict for those Jews who lived in the state – rather, it created a new source of tension. Real Palestinians – not those who featured in Herzl's novel – did not agree that they should lose their lands and freedoms; they therefore resisted and inevitably attracted support. While some who rejected the displacement of Palestinians disliked Jews, most were motivated by support for human rights and their political views were liberal or left wing; many were – and are – Jews. Opposition to the state and its actions did not target Jews; it was aimed at the Israeli state and, in some cases, the ideology that underpinned it. But central to Zionism's understanding of itself was the claim that it was the vehicle of all Jews, not merely those Jews who supported the idea of a Jewish state. To reject the state – or even to criticise what it did – was to show hostility to the Jews, even if you happened to be Jewish. The logic was false, of course, just as to oppose apartheid in South Africa was not an expression of prejudice against white people. But it served the purpose of Zionism and its allies.

For the ideologues of Zionism, their 'Jewish state' quickly turned from a cure for anti-Semitism to its cause when it was faced by the reality of Palestinian resistance. The Palestinians who wanted their land back were labelled the 'new Nazis'. Hence Netanyahu's false claim that it was Mufti al-Husseini, not Hitler, who devised the mass murder of European Jews. This was not a personal quirk – Netanyahu was following the lead of Malcolm Hoenlein, an American Jewish leadership figure and vocal supporter of the Israeli state, who told a 2004 meeting in Toronto, Canada, that Hitler had reluctantly 'followed the wishes of the Mufti' when he had decided to try to kill all Jews.[35] This invention served a purpose: it conveniently portrayed Palestinians not as victims of the power of the Israeli state but as powerful Jew-haters whose enmity was even greater than that of the Nazis. It follows, of course, that if Palestinians are Nazis, those who support their cause are too. An Israeli scholar notes that 'any substantial criticism of Israel and Zionism is perceived in public opinion, and especially among national and international political and cultural institutions, as an ideological continuation of the [Nazi] Holocaust'. The primary effect, he argues, is to 'delegitimise the Palestinian cause and to practically remove once and for all the Palestine issue from the international agenda'. [36]

The claim that the Israeli state is a victim of anti-Semitism is deeply embedded in the thinking of its mainstream population, including that of 'liberal' Zionists. In 2022, when Amnesty International released a report declaring that Israel was an apartheid state, the (liberal) Israeli journalist Gershom Gorenberg tweeted a quote from the (liberal) Israeli novelist Amos Oz's 2002 book *A Tale of Love and Darkness*: 'Out there, in the world, all the walls were covered with graffiti: "Yids [Jews], go back to Palestine", so we came back to Palestine, and now the world at large shouts at us: "Yids, get out of Palestine".'[37]

Neither claim was true. It was not 'the world' which told the Jews to 'go back to Palestine' – it was some Jews in the Zionist movement. They were initially frustrated because 'the world' did not share their enthusiasm. Even after the British, in 1917, accepted the principle of a Jewish 'national home' in Palestine, one of the constant Zionist complaints before the state's founding in 1948 was that the British authorities imposed controls on Jewish immigration to the territory. Getting Jews to settle in Palestine was not the goal of anti-Jewish bigots and it was certainly not that of the democracies in which Jews enjoyed citizenship rights. Nor do Amnesty International or other critics of the Israeli state want Jews to get out of Palestine. There is little support among the Israeli state's critics for the notion that Jews should leave the territory; their demand is that it recognises Palestinian rights. Some favour separate states for Jews and Palestinians (the famed or infamous 'two-state solution'), others a shared state with equal rights for all. None of them suggests that Jews should leave. Oz's claim – which is a mainstream view among supporters of the Israeli state – mirrors that of white South Africans during apartheid that a non-racial democracy would spell the end of whites in general and white Afrikaners in particular.

The claim may be false, but it remains the mainstream view because, as noted above, it is convenient to the Israeli state and its supporters. It is meant to justify any action the state chooses to take, including violence. Their logic is that since Jews were victims of racist mass murder, they are entitled to do anything that some politicians claim will prevent a recurrence. ('They' in this context refers to the Israeli state, which presumes to speak for every Jew despite all evidence to the contrary.) The Nazi genocide was not a warning against racism but an excuse to continue it. As Israeli journalist Gideon Levy explains it, 'Gaza is permitted because of Auschwitz.'[38] Assertions such as Oz's have important impacts on Jewish identity too, which work in the state's favour even as they distort who Jews are.

The most important of these impacts is that the assertions are repeatedly used to demonise Jews who are considered even mildly sympathetic to Palestinian concerns. This includes fervent supporters of the state who might anger the right wing by seeming to be 'soft' on Palestinians. A popular right-wing Israeli singer has claimed that he would have been happy to see Oz killed in Treblinka, the Nazi death camp in Poland. The reason was that Oz was a liberal Zionist who hoped that an ethnic Jewish state could somehow coexist with Palestinians. When prime minister Yitzhak Rabin and foreign minister Shimon Peres, both pillars of the Zionist establishment, signed the Oslo Accords with the Palestinian leadership in the early 1990s, the right wing depicted them in Nazi uniforms with Hitler moustaches.[39] Rabin was subsequently assassinated by a right-wing Zionist. Any Jew who is considered, however tenuously, to want an accommodation with Palestinians becomes not a political opponent but a Nazi; anti-Semitism becomes not hatred of Jews but opposition, real or perceived, to Israeli state racism.

The Uses of Hysteria

This tendency to target even mainstream Zionists who are not considered sufficiently rabid in their nationalism is also evident outside the state.

Gabriel Schoenfeld, the senior editor at the right-wing American journal *Commentary*, identifies Jewish public figures who he considers to be anti-Semitic. While some on his list are obvious left-wingers and non-Zionists, it includes the journalist and commentator Leon Wieseltier, a vocal and uncritical supporter of the Israeli state. His crime, according to Schoenfeld, is that he dismissed claims that anti-Semitism was sweeping Europe; he called it 'ethnic panic' and assured European Jews that 'Hitler is dead'.[40] So it is not enough for Jews who wish to avoid the charge that they are anti-Semites to support the Israeli state – they have to do this with the requisite degree of hysteria.

This is so because hysteria is a necessary ingredient in the fight against the 'new anti-Semitism'. Just as branding Palestinian resistance as a form of Nazism buttresses the Israeli state, so does the claim that Jews who live outside it are constantly under threat because only the state can save Jews from a world filled with people who hate them. Their writings, within Israel and outside it, are awash with claims that America and Western Europe are engulfed by virulent anti-Jewish racism and a resurgent Nazism whose supporters are said to include much of the Western media and even Israeli intellectuals.[41] As Wieseltier's case shows, anyone who questions the claim that anti-Semitism is escalating is viewed as weakening an instrument of the Israeli state and so is also anti-Semitic, even if they happen to be fervent Zionists. The inventors of the 'new' anti-Jewish racism are explicit about this. According to Phyllis Chesler, a zealous denouncer of those branded as 'new anti-Semites', anyone who denies that the mainstream media and certain Israeli professors are anti-Jewish bigots 'is also an anti-Semite'.[42] This tends to set up the sort of paranoid infinite regress that is typical of totalitarian thinking: you are against us not only when you say you are against us but also when you question our claim that everyone is against us. Similarly, you are anti-Semitic not only when you express prejudice against Jews but also when you question our claim that others do.

Portraying the threat to Jews in stark terms is meant to create a sense of crisis, uniting Jews around a common fear that they are once again staring discrimination (and worse) in the face. Wieseltier's crime was pointing out the obvious: that a new Nazi genocide was not around the corner. He was unwittingly undermining a tactic which is deeply embedded in the thinking and the survival strategies of the Israeli state: threats to Jews must be exaggerated or created because this justifies the claim that an ethnic state in historic Palestine is Jews' only key to survival in a hostile and hatred-filled world. But, while this is ostensibly designed to achieve unity against a common threat, it can, of course, succeed only if it sows division by vilifying Jews who do not feel threatened. It is, therefore, partly responsible for creating the division between 'good Jews' and 'bad Jews' because only the Jews who agree that all critics of the Israeli state are dangerous anti-Semites are accepted as 'real Jews'.

Similarly, comparing anti-Jewish racism to any other form of racial bigotry is now branded anti-Semitic because it is said to reduce the significance of Jewish suffering – which is the justification for the state. This is not, however, a right-wing monopoly. Deborah Lipstadt is a historian whose successful legal battle with a writer who denied that the Nazis had murdered millions of Jews attracted international attention. As US president Biden's special envoy to combat anti-Semitism, she has insisted that hatred of Jews is both eternal and unlike any other form of discrimination or bigotry. The Nazi genocide is also, in her view, unlike any other event. 'Beginning with her earliest work, which argues that the Holocaust was a unique, incomparable event, Lipstadt has tended to exceptionalize antisemitism as the most ancient, enduring form of prejudice – a constant transhistorical force, resurfacing across eras and continents.'[43] While this stance was originally aimed at German scholars who sought to minimise the Nazi genocide by comparing it to Soviet violence, it now acts as a weapon against anyone, including Jews, who argue that all racisms are alike and that Jews, as victims of bigotry, should ally themselves with racism's other victims (including Palestinians). One effect of this stance is to let much contemporary racism off the hook because it is not the Nazi genocide.[44] The American Jewish Studies scholar Barry Trachtenberg observes: 'If one accepts antisemitism to be eternal, and not a consequence of social or historical factors, then it is a fact of life that will forever push Jewish people into defensive postures. It will make us more nationalist, more reactionary, more militaristic, and more closed off from the rest of the world.'[45]

Labelling a lack of hysteria as 'anti-Semitic' also helps to police the boundaries of who is accepted within the Jewish fold and who is not. Requirements for membership include not only uncritical support for the Israeli state but also a willingness to allow it and its vocal supporters to declare what and who is anti-Semitic and how great the threats to Jews are, even when the evidence shows that there is no threat at all. One victim of this was past president Jimmy Carter's former national security advisor, Zbigniew Brzezinski, after he commended Barack Obama and his secretary of state, John Kerry, for ensuring that 'Congress is finally becoming embarrassed by Netanyahu's efforts to dictate US policy'. Jeffrey Goldberg, a journalist and eager policer of boundaries on behalf of the Israeli state, insisted that Brzezinski was saying that 'Jews run America'. A representative of J Street, a liberal Zionist lobby in Washington, responded: 'He doesn't say or even imply that. Willingness to accuse everyone of anti-Semitism makes it impossible to respect you.' Goldberg replied: 'I continually defend [J Street's] place inside the Jewish tent. But the behavior of its employees makes such defenses difficult.'[46] So Jewish identity is not a matter of belief, birth or cultural affinity; a 'place inside the tent' depends on one being a 'good Jew' in the eyes of the Israeli state's most vocal and uncritical supporters. Supporting the state is necessary but not enough, since J Street does support it. It is also necessary, as Wieseltier discovered, to possess a willingness to imagine hostility to Jews even where none exists.

There is an irony in this. The Israeli state is an ethnic nationalist project and ethnic nationalists want to unite their group by pointing to an external threat. This inevitably triggers hostility to non-members of the group. Thus the (Jewish) Israeli historian Irit Kenyan warns that Jewish (or, more accurately, Zionist) 'collective victimhood is closely associated with ingroup cohesion and unity', which 'often comes at the expense of relations with the outgroup'.[47] But the state stresses the 'cohesion' of the group precisely because some members do not agree that the supposed threat is real. The state would not need to emphasise group cohesion in this way if everyone in the group agreed that they felt threatened. Thus, the only way it can 'unite' the group is to divide it by insisting that those who do not agree are not authentic members. It is in this irony that the distinction between 'good' and 'bad' Jew is born.

The distinction becomes particularly stark when Jews break one of the core taboos of Jewish ethnic nationalism – making Jewish identity a topic for rational discussion with people who are not Jewish. In late 2020, Peter Beinart, for many years America's most quoted liberal Zionist who, by then, had publicly ended his support for an exclusively Jewish state, was invited to be a panellist in a discussion on anti-Semitism. Two of his invited fellow panellists were Rashida Tlaib and Marc Lamont Hill. Tlaib is a Palestinian-American member of the US Congress who is outspoken in her support for Palestinian rights; Lamont Hill is a black American academic and broadcaster whose contract with CNN had been terminated when he had publicly rejected the idea of a state for Jews only. Both had been branded anti-Semitic because of their opposition to the Israeli state and Beinart wanted to signal that there was a difference between anti-Semitism and anti-Zionism and that he viewed his fellow panellists as anti-racists who were, therefore, eminently qualified to discuss racism directed at Jews.

Predictably, Beinart's participation alongside Tlaib and Lamont Hill enraged supporters of the Israeli state and prompted this reaction from Dani Dayan, its former ambassador to the United Nations: 'If you are non-Jews who like to tell Jews what is and what isn't antisemitism, you are most probably antisemites. If you are a Jew collaborating with them, you are most probably their useful idiot.'[48] In the ethnic-nationalist mind, a panel of anti-racists discussing anti-Jewish racism transforms into an anti-Semitic act because it breaks the – deeply racist – taboo that people who are not members of the group have no right to discuss what anti-Semitism is, particularly when they are critics of the Israeli state. The Jew who agreed to be their co-panellist became a very bad Jew indeed. The anger is prompted by the assumption that only ethnic nationalists, Zionists, can decide what anti-Semitism is because only they are the 'real' Jews.

A Question of Power

At stake is power – the power to decide what Jewish identity is and what hostility to it is. There are strong echoes of a famous passage in Lewis Carroll's *Through the Looking-Glass*:

> 'When *I* use a word,' Humpty Dumpty said in rather a scornful tone, 'it means just what I choose it to mean – neither more nor less.' 'The question is,' said Alice, 'whether you *can* make words mean so many different things.' 'The question is,' said Humpty Dumpty, 'which is to be master – that's all.'[49]

The Israeli state and its allies are 'master' when they decide what anti-Semitism means. To allow others to do so would be to surrender the power to decide not only what Jewish identity is but what hatred for it is too. If the meanings of words must be bent entirely out of shape to do this, and if Jews who insist on retaining the meaning are to be demonised as haters of themselves and all other Jews, so be it. The 'mastery', not truth, is the priority.

There is another irony in this notion that the state is surrounded by anti-Semites, many of whom are Jewish. If true, it would mean that 'Zionism is ironically a failure' because it provokes anti-Semitism rather than, as promised, ending it. 'The project of normalization within the state of Israel was supposed to procure normalization for Jews everywhere. Normalization meant that Jews would no longer see themselves primarily – certainly not exclusively or preternaturally – as victims of history but rather as part of it. That re-entering history didn't only mean power but also a belief that Jews were basically like everyone else.'[50] The claim that the state's foundation worsened anti-Semitism means that it had failed to perform its task.

Despite this, the groundless claim that the Israeli state is the victim of a new form of anti-Semitism has become a central theme of its apologists. It is, they insist, now 'the Jew of the nations', a phrase which is embraced by a range of authors devoted to the defence of the state.[51] By this they mean that it is now the target of the same bigotry to which Jews as an ethnic group had been subjected. While this would no doubt have shocked Zionism's founders, it provides a justification for why anti-Semitism has, for the state and its supporters, become something other than racial bigotry directed at Jews. If the state is now the Jew, an anti-Semite is now someone who is critical of or opposed to the state and so a supporter of the state could not be an anti-Semite even if they were prejudiced against Jews as an ethnic group. This too underpins the division of Jews into the 'good' ones who support the state and the 'bad' ones who do not. And it explains why the rest of humanity is judged by its attitude to the Israeli state, not by its attitudes to Jews.

Like Netanyahu, the peddlers of the 'new anti-Semitism' knew that the Christian Zionists in the US were anti-Semites, but they supported the Israeli state and so they were friends of the Jews. They were, they said, more comfortable with fundamentalist preachers who said that God did not hear the prayers of Jews than with liberal clergy who endorsed the rights of all. After all, the anti-Semites supported the Israeli state. 'Fundamentalist intolerance is currently not so baneful as its friendship for Israel is helpful,' they declared.[52] An anti-Jewish bigot who was 'helpful' to the Israeli state was a friend, no matter how much they might dislike Jews.

Just as the notion of the 'new anti-Semitism' was not a fringe position among allies of the Israeli state, its authors were not fringe figures in American Zionism. Arnold Foster, Benjamin Epstein and Nathan Perlmutter all held senior posts in the Anti-Defamation League. Hoenlein, who inspired Netanyahu to blame a Palestinian for the Nazi genocide, was also prominent in 'official' American Jewish organisations that were solidly in the camp of the Israeli state. They regularly visited Israel and

2

Making 'Good Jews' White and European

The claim that opposition to the Israeli state is 'anti-Semitism' has become the official view in Western Europe and North America; in some US states, opposition to the Israeli state has been criminalised.

Deborah Lipstadt, mentioned in chapter 1, exemplifies this distortion of the term 'anti-Semitism'. She claimed that the founders of the Boycott, Divestment and Sanctions (BDS) movement, which uses non-violent pressure on the Israeli state to further Palestinian demands, are anti-Semitic because they endorse the right of Palestinian refugees to return to the homes of which they had been dispossessed 'and [they] therefore [advocate] the end of Israel as a Jewish state.'[1] For her, to demand that refugees be allowed to return to their homes expresses anti-Jewish hatred. The American government agrees, hence her appointment as its arbiter of anti-Semitism. It is not alone. That anti-Semitism means not hatred of Jews but opposition to the Israeli state is now the mainstream position throughout the West. Western governments have a new-found enthusiasm for rooting out 'anti-Semitism', which, in reality, is a thinly disguised assault on critics of the Israeli state.

There is an irony to this. The American Jewish comedian Groucho Marx famously withdrew his membership from a tennis club. On being asked the reason, he responded that he would not belong to any club that would have him as a member.[2] The remark was, it is said, not meant to make a political point. He wanted to resign from the club in favour of another, but it refused to let him go. His witty response secured his exit. But his statement could be seen as an unconscious reaction to the situation of the Jew in polite Western society where, since the Enlightenment, Jews were tolerated but still seen as outsiders, excluded from the places where 'real' Westerners gathered. The metaphorical clubs that they wanted to join would not have them as members. Western embrace of the claims of a 'new anti-Semitism' makes some Jews – those who endorse the Zionist enterprise – welcome in the Western club that had once barred them.

This partly explains the success of Israeli state propaganda in the West. Nazism deprived anti-Semitism of legitimacy among Western elites and the Israeli state has used charges of anti-Semitism as a stock weapon in the propaganda war. An Israeli politician suggests that this is a cynical ploy. Shulamith Aloni, who led Meretz, a liberal Zionist opposition party, and was both a cabinet minister and the leader of the opposition, said of the use of anti-Semitism allegations to smear the Israeli state's critics:

> It's a trick, we always use it. When somebody from Europe is criticising Israel then we bring up the Holocaust. When in this country [the US] somebody is criticising Israel then they are antisemitic ... It's very easy to blame people who criticise certain acts of the Israeli government as antisemitic and to bring up the Holocaust and the suffering of the Jewish people ... that justifies everything we do to the Palestinians.[3]

The European Union's (EU) constant assumption that anti-Semitism is hostility to the Israeli state, not to Jewish people, may be partly a product of one such 'trick'. Its working group on anti-Semitism barred a Jewish group that opposes Israeli state policies. The working group, one analysis says, was a response to a 2003 poll among citizens of EU states in which nearly 60 per cent of respondents saw Israel as the foremost threat to world peace. While common sense would see this as an indictment of the Israeli state, its supporters persuaded the EU that it indicated rampant anti-Semitism in its member states.[4] The EU has acted accordingly ever since.

A DAMAGING DEFINITION

In Western Europe and the United States, the focal point of this project is the definition of anti-Semitism adopted by the International Holocaust Remembrance Alliance (IHRA), which was initiated in 1998 by former Swedish prime minister Göran Persson.

IHRA claims a membership of 35 governments (including all major Western powers) and is meant to 'combat growing Holocaust denial and antisemitism'.[5] Its definition of anti-Semitism has become an article of Zionist faith and is repeatedly portrayed by Zionists as 'what the Jewish community wants'. Its advocates offer no evidence that the Jewish community really does want it and make no attempt to defend its merits.[6] The definition is not designed to resist the kind of bigotry that prompted the Nazi genocide but is a bludgeon to suppress opposition to a state whose legislation reveals it as a source of racism.

According to the IHRA, 'anti-Semitism' includes: 'claiming that the existence of the State of Israel is a racist endeavor'; 'accusing Jewish citizens of being more loyal to Israel ... than to ... their own nations'; 'drawing comparisons of contemporary Israeli policy to that of the Nazis' and 'holding Jews collectively responsible for actions of the state of Israel'.[7] The first-mentioned clause, denying that the Israeli state is a racist endeavour, rejects criticism of the racist character of a state – even when it passes a law declaring itself the state of only one ethnic group among many to which its citizens belong. In 2020, a statement by over 100 Palestinian and Arab academics noted that this clause 'did not bother to consider' that the Israeli state had given itself 'the right to create a Jewish majority by way of ethnic cleansing ... The IHRA definition potentially discards as antisemitic all non-Zionist visions of the future of the Israeli state, such as the advocacy of a binational state or a secular democratic one that represents all its citizens equally'.[8]

The definition, which purports to outlaw a form of racism, instead demonises anyone who refuses to accept the premise of the Israeli Nation State Law, that the Israeli state is the property of only one ethnic group.[9] It is therefore not surprising that an Oxford University study found that the definition was largely drafted by advocacy groups which support the Israeli state, not by scholars of Jewish history.[10] According to a recent book, the pressure to adopt the IHRA definition was the product of a political project by the Israeli state that had been designed to demonise and silence its critics.[11] The IHRA definition is a victory for a state seeking to deflect anti-racist criticism.

To equate an ethnic group with a state is never accurate. In this case, the invalidity is enhanced by the fact that widespread Jewish support for a Jewish state is very recent and not, as its supporters claim, an age-old aspiration. Zionists claim that Jews have been largely united in their desire for a state throughout the ages. Ironically, secular Zionists quote the Hebrew Bible (in which they do not believe) in defence of this claim because it is said to show that Jews had inhabited the land millennia ago[12] and that they yearned to return when they had been exiled. But historical narratives in religious texts are rarely meant to be taken literally; they convey spiritual messages, not a historical chronicle.[13] For most Jews, references to Zion and Jerusalem express a spiritual longing for a redeemed world, not a political project. This is why traditionalist Orthodox Jewish sects vehemently oppose Zionism and the Israeli state.[14] Rabbi Joel Teitelbaum, who headed a community of strictly observant Orthodox Jews,[15] described Zionism as a greater sin than the golden calf.[16] When the Zionist movement was formed in the nineteenth century, it did not command much Jewish support. 'For the first decades of its existence, Zionism was a marginal movement in Jewish life.'[17] At most, it has commanded majority Jewish support since the Nazi genocide. This hardly qualifies it as an ages-old core Jewish belief.

If the IHRA clause about denying that a particular state is a racist endeavour was applied to South Africa, it would have declared the struggle against apartheid a racist, anti-white movement. It would also have endorsed an important strand in apartheid ideology. Although white domination was broadly supported by virtually all whites, apartheid was originally an expression of Afrikaner nationalism,[18] a movement born out of a revolt against British colonialism and the brutal suppression of the white Afrikaners. During the war between the British and white Afrikaners at the turn of the twentieth century, the British placed Afrikaner women and children in concentration camps. This and other forms of British discrimination prompted white Afrikaners to mobilise to win control of the state. They succeeded in 1948, after which they tightened and systemised white domination by creating apartheid. One of apartheid's premises, as a cabinet minister pointed out in the 1970s, was to ensure that there would be 'no black South Africans'.[19] During apartheid's heyday, it was common for government ideologues to insist that apartheid's destruction would mean the destruction of white Afrikaners. If the IHRA definition had been applied to South Africa, it would have implied that it would be a racist endeavour to work for the end of a system of racial domination whose stated aim was to reduce 90 per cent of the population to foreigners in the land of their birth.

The other two clauses mentioned earlier seem at first glance more reasonable. But, while comparing the Israeli state to the Nazi regime may be inaccurate, it is hard to see how it is anti-Semitic. If it is, Major General Yair Golan, who served as deputy chief of staff of the Israel Defense Forces from 2014 to 2017, is an anti-Semite. He told a ceremony to honour victims of the Nazi genocide: 'If there is one thing that frightens me about the memory of the Holocaust, it is identifying the revolting trends that occurred in Europe as a whole, and in Germany in particular ... and finding evidence of those trends here, among us, in 2016.'[20] While Golan's remarks were denounced by government representatives, no one accused him of anti-Semitism, presumably because the label would have seemed ridiculous when applied to a senior Israeli general. Similarly, the philosopher Yeshayahu Leibowitz, who was a devout Orthodox Jew and proud Zionist, described the right-wing Zionists, the forebears of those shaping the policies of the Israeli state in the early 2020s, as 'Judeo-Nazis' because he wanted to 'liken the State's policies toward Palestinians to the Nazis' genocidal policies towards the Jews'.[21] He too was not labelled an anti-Semite.

If holding Jews collectively responsible for the actions of the Israeli state is anti-Semitic, it and its supporters must be anti-Semites because Jews who do not support the state are demonised as 'self-hating' traitors, 'the wrong sort of Jews' or not really Jewish at all. The IHRA and its participating governments do not consider this attempt to force all Jews to associate with the state's actions as anti-Semitic. Nor do they acknowledge that, by labelling opposition to the state as hostility to Jews, their definition violates this clause. Thus the IHRA definition itself becomes anti-Semitic and, consequently, the Western states that endorse and apply it are keeping alive a shameful history of anti-Jewish racism.

One analysis argues that to equate Jews with the Israeli state, as its leaders and supporters do, is 'inherently anti-Semitic' since it 'treat[s] Jews as synonymous with Israel's acts of aggression'.[22] To assume that a state and an ethnic group are one is to associate the group with every action of the state, even if many of its members do not live in that state and have no control over its actions. By substituting a state for an ethnic group, the zealotry of the 'new anti-Semitism' approach, like all bigotries, implicates all members of a group in the actions of only some. It also helps to strengthen an anti-Semitic prejudice – that Jews living outside the Israeli state harbour dual loyalties and that their support for the Israeli state weakens their loyalty to the state in which they live.[23]

IHRA illustrates the extent to which opposition to a state has been conflated with hostility towards Jews. One of many illustrations of this is the role of the Simon Wiesenthal Center (SWC), one of the organisations that influenced the definition. The SWC was founded to research the Nazi genocide and to hold its perpetrators to account. It still claims that it 'confronts anti-Semitism … [and] hate'.[24] But it now defines 'anti-Semitism' and 'hate' as opposition to the Israeli state: 'Amongst the "most notable antisemitic incidents" listed by the SWC in recent years were Airbnb's 2016 decision to delist Israeli rental properties located in the territory occupied by the state in 1967 (decision reversed in 2019); UN Resolution 2334 condemning Israeli settlements; and the 2021 International Criminal Court ruling that it had jurisdiction in Palestine.' In January 2022, SWC's 'Global Antisemitism Top Ten' included the BBC, 'the entire state of Germany' and Jewish Voice for Peace, resulting in the EU criticising it for having 'gone too far'.[25]

The British Jewish author Robert Cohen points out that, by defining hostility to Jews in a way which substitutes a state for an ethnic group, the IHRA definition also defines 'what it is to be Jewish':

> By that reckoning, to be Jewish is to deny the possibility that Zionism has played out in racist ways, despite the overwhelming evidence to the contrary. And to be Jewish is to believe that the State of Israel is a democratic nation like any other, despite Israel's own constitutional laws defining it as the nation state of the Jewish people rather than the state of all its citizens ... To be Jewish, according to the IHRA, is to deny the truth, ignore reality, and defend the indefensible.[26]

The IHRA definition has been mobilised to stigmatise political expression and shut down free speech in the United States and Western Europe. It has been adopted by several Western governments and by universities pressured by those governments.[27] It has been wielded against academics who campaigned for Palestine to deprive them of their jobs and to suppress campaigns against the Israeli state, in particular the BDS movement.[28] A summary of the repression of BDS activists and the suppression of their activities was published by the Palestine BDS National Committee;[29] the list of attempts to shut down this legitimate form of expression has grown since then.

In France, an 1881 law which allows the punishment of anyone who calls for the boycott of goods from a country whose policies they criticise has been used to prosecute campaigners for Palestinian rights. Activists faced criminal charges because they participated in non-violent BDS advocacy; at least one was arrested for wearing a BDS T-shirt. In October 2015, France's highest appeals court ruled that the call to boycott Israeli products on the basis of their origin was illegal. Police used this ruling to try to prevent BDS demonstrations.[30] Germany has been particularly strident in restricting support for Palestinians, which is routinely labelled anti-Semitic,[31] a charge to which the German mainstream is understandably sensitive in the light of that country's Nazi past. In the US and Britain, legislation inspired by the IHRA definition is used to penalise companies and local governments which avoid trade with the Israeli state.[32] In 2021, some US states used these laws to penalise the ice cream company Ben and Jerry's and its parent company, Unilever, after it announced that it would not trade in the territories occupied by the Israeli state since 1967.[33]

The IHRA definition is also the basis on which the post-Corbyn British Labour Party instituted disciplinary charges against Diana Neslen, a Jewish woman in her eighties and a regular synagogue attendee who, unlike many officials and supporters of the Israeli state, also observes Jewish religious dietary laws. Her crime was a tweet: 'The existence of the state of Israel is a racist endeavour and I am an antiracist Jew.'[34] This makes her an anti-Semite according to the IHRA definition, which Labour has embraced.[35] (The charges were dropped when Neslen took legal action, asserting that anti-Zionism was a protected belief under British law.)[36] It also inspired the campaign which cost the (Jewish) British academic David Miller his job. *The Jewish Chronicle*, a strident praise-singer for the Israeli state, responded to the Miller case with a demand that all British academics who opposed Zionism be deprived of their posts.[37] Again, 'anti-Semitism' was used to target anti-racist Jews and close down the freedoms that citizens of Western states are supposed to enjoy.

The IHRA definition's lead drafter, Kenneth Stern, insists that it was never intended to silence critics of the Israeli state. Responding to an executive order by then US president, Donald Trump, which sought to silence critics on college campuses, Stern wrote that the definition was 'created primarily so that European data collectors could know what to include and exclude' when they monitored anti-Semitism; it was never meant to silence anyone. He worried that it would be used to stifle free speech and to hunt down opponents of the Israeli state on university campuses. 'I'm a Zionist. But on a college campus, where the purpose is to explore ideas, anti-Zionists have a right to free expression.'[38]

Avi Shlaim notes that the document from which the definition is drawn contains a statement defining anti-Semitism – in which criticism of the Israeli state is not mentioned – and 11 'illustrative examples' which do mention it. Within the IHRA, there were two opinions: one group wanted criticism of the Israeli state to be included in the definition and the other did not. Consensus between the groups could be achieved only by separating the examples from the definition. 'Pro-Israel partisans, however, have repeatedly conveyed the false impression that the examples are an integral part of the definition. They also habitually omit the qualifier that this is only a draft – a "working definition".'[39]

While this does not alter the reality that the working definition is 'poorly drafted, internally incoherent, hopelessly vague (and) vulnerable to political abuse',[40] it does show that even this deeply flawed document has been misrepresented to create a false equivalence between rejection of the Israeli state and hostility to Jews. Stern's reservations were shared by David Feldman, director of the Institute for the Study of Antisemitism at Birkbeck, University of London, who warned that it was not clear what the IHRA definition meant. It would inevitably be used to target critics of the Israeli state, he argued: 'The chilling impact on students, on academic and professional staff and on institutions dedicated to debate and robust discussion, will be corrosive and long-lasting.'[41] Mainstream Jewish scholars of anti-Semitism see the definition's dangers; major Western governments do not.

Because the IHRA labelled anti-racist political speech as racist, its examples were always sure to be used as far more than a misguided guide to researchers. The problem lies in the distortion which labels opposition to a state accused of racism as racist. Whatever the drafters' intention, the definition 'shift[s] the focus from real antisemitism to the perfectly respectable and growing phenomenon of anti-Zionism'.[42]

The Israeli state and like-minded Western governments strenuously resist the claim that their endorsement of this position allies them with white supremacy. But it does. It brands anti-racists as racist and enables the racists who they oppose to adopt a spurious anti-racist mantle.

THE RIGHT AND THE TRUE

If Western governments do not know that the 'new anti-Semitism' approach allies them with the global right wing, its architects do. It is an alliance about which they have no regrets.

An important reason for the 'new anti-Semitism' framework is a growing shift to the right by supporters of the Israeli state and an antipathy to anyone who suggests that inequality, racial or social, is a problem. Phyllis Chesler wrote: 'What's new about the *new* anti-Semitism is that for the first time it is being perpetrated in the name of anti-racism, anti-imperialism, and anti-colonialism'.[43] Her words reflect a reality even as they distort it. Real anti-Semitism – hostility to Jews – was closely allied to white supremacy. Anti-Semitism was largely associated with the right, though it was not a disease to which the left was immune, hence the widespread reference, especially among Germans, to left anti-Semitism as 'the socialism of fools', a phrase often attributed to German socialist politician August Bebel but more likely coined by the Austrian politician Ferdinand Kronawetter.[44] Opposition to racism, imperialism and colonialism was not, in the main, accompanied by prejudices against Jews. But the establishment of the Israeli state in 1948 complicated this.

The founders of the state were labour Zionists who identified with the European left and hoped to be seen as an anti-colonial movement.[45] But labour Zionism has been declining since the Israeli right won its first national election in 1977. Today it barely exists. At the time of writing, the Labour Party held only 4 out of 120 seats in the Knesset, the Israeli parliament. The politics of the state has moved ever rightward as the contradiction between left-wing or liberal ideas and ethnic nationalism became apparent.

While the Israeli right is deeply hostile even to mildly liberal ideas among Jews within the Israeli state, its antipathy is much greater to anyone elsewhere who expresses them. The growing influence of the apostles of the 'new anti-Semitism' mirrors the rightward shift in Israeli society. This shift is sometimes portrayed as a tragic departure from Zionism's original ideals but it was inevitable since the Zionist 'left' was as eager as the right to establish ethnic nationalist control over Palestinian lands.[46] The proponents of the 'new anti-Semitism' are no longer interested in portraying the domination of Palestinians as a liberal or left-wing project. This has brought them into inevitable conflict with the left and some liberals who rejected the denial of rights to Palestinians by using terms framed in the language of human rights and anti-colonialism. Zionism's ethnic nationalism meant that the hope of an alliance with the left and even many liberals was never realistic. For Israel, the global hard right is, therefore, 'now a natural and perhaps inevitable choice'.[47]

The language of white nationalism has become part of the currency of figures in the Israeli state. Former general Effie Eitam, for example, told an interviewer that land settled by Palestinians was 'the Jewish people's vital space'.[48] While he may have been unaware that the term 'vital space' was at the core of Nazi ideology, the fact that he sees the world in much the same way as other racial ideologues illustrates the affinity between the state's ethnic nationalism and the global right. Eitam is hardly a marginal figure; he was, ironically, nominated by Netanyahu to chair Yad Vashem, the memorial to Nazi victims, although he was not appointed after protests within the Israeli state and abroad.[49]

The rightward shift within the state is, inevitably, echoed by its supporters elsewhere and reflected in the claims of a 'new anti-Semitism'. To some commentators, this is also a product of a rightward shift among Jews in Western countries, particularly the United States. In this view, Jews tended initially to identify with egalitarian politics since they had been victims of racism and had been forced to live in poverty. But once they prospered in liberal democracies, they moved rightward.[50] This does seem to be true of Britain where most Jewish voters originally supported the Labour Party but now vote Conservative.[51] But it is not true of the United States where a comfortable majority of Jews support the Democrats and remain firmly to the left of centre.[52] And, while it is one of the enduring American myths that politicians kowtow to Israel because they need to court the Jewish vote, one study found that only four per cent of Jews in the US see their president's stance on Israel as a priority issue.[53] Painting liberals and left wingers as anti-Semites is a pre-occupation of elites, not of the Jewish public.

But it does impress the right wing across the globe. Referring to white supremacist groups that 'hate Jews and love Israel', the American non-Zionist group Jewish Voice for Peace noted: 'Depending on their spe-cific ideology, they may admire Israel as a model ethnic supremacist state, share its Islamophobic and anti-Arab views, and/or want Jews to be corralled in their own state far away from the US'.[54] The right loves Israel. Not only was it founded on a notion of ethnic purity that they find appealing, it also defends it with a disregard for international norms that they find even more to their taste.[55] They overlook the fact that the state is governed by Jews because it does everything they want to do and always gets away with it. Those on the right who are anti-Semitic, and most are, also seem comfortable with a distinction between good and bad Jews although, given their proclivities, they may also prefer to distinguish between Jews and (Jewish) Israelis, retaining a scorn for the former but respecting the latter. Since, as we will see, Israeli Zionism assumes that Jews who are not Israelis are an inferior breed, this too would cement the bond between right-wing anti-Semites and the Israeli state and its admirers.

This is why the appearance of the Israeli flag alongside anti-Jewish slogans at a demonstration is part of a pattern. The flag also flew alongside the Confederate flag, the banner of US slave-holding states in the nine-teenth century, at a 'Straight Pride' parade in Boston, and in a pro-Trump car caravan. 'Different parts of the U.S. right use the Jewish state as a canvas to project their own fantasies of nationalist chauvinism, Christian redemption, white pride, and antisemitic conspiracism,' writes Ben Lorber. They celebrate it 'as a front-line defender of Western civilization in its crusade against radical Islam. It is viewed as a nation that embodies the strong arm of xenophobic nationalism and militarized masculinity, unapologetically pushing back invading ethno-religious Others ... and protecting its heritage in bold defiance of a chorus of liberal outcry.'[56] For the white supremacist right wing, the Israeli state is a role model – even if it is run by Jews.

One of many examples of fusing right-wing positions with support for the Israeli state is the case of Maram Salem, a Palestinian journalist working in Germany who was fired by the state-owned broadcaster Deutsche Welle after one of her Facebook posts was denounced to her employer as anti-Semitic and 'anti-Israel'. It contained no reference to Jews or the Israeli state, but decried threats to freedom of expression in Europe.[57] This suggests that if a Palestinian cares about freedom of speech in Europe, it must be because she wants to express anti-Semitic or anti-Zionist views. This assumes that freedom of expression leads to anti-Semitic or anti-Zionist views. But it is also an example of the infinite regress; all critics must be silenced by labelling them anti-Semitic and anyone who complains about the silencing must also be an anti-Semite. That Salem was targeted for defending freedom of speech illustrates that the hard right easily labels as 'anti-Semitic' those values that it dislikes, such as defence of the right to express views which are outside the European mainstream.

Support for the Israeli state has increasingly been accompanied by familiar right-wing attitudes. This too is not new; the 'new anti-Semitism' brigade illustrates how neat the fit is between support for the Israeli state and other right-wing stances. Chesler's list of anti-Semites includes the United Nations, 'Western-based international human rights organizations, academics, intellectuals', activists who are 'anticapitalist, antiglobalist, pro-environment, antiracist and antiwar', as well as 'progressive feminists', 'Jewish feminists' and 'European, and left and liberal American media'.[58]

But it is the Perlmutters who give the game away – they reveal that 'anti-Semitism' amounts to nothing more than taking liberal or left-wing positions. They acknowledge that 'real anti-Semitism' (the title of their book) may be perpetrated by people who bear no ill will towards Jews at all. It is, rather, advocating policies or positions that threaten (what they believe to be) Jewish interests.[59] It is, according to them, anti-Semitic to campaign for the end of America's electoral college, to call for cuts in the military budget or to oppose nuclear power – all of which are left-of-centre views.[60]

Why are these issues the targeted ones? Because the electoral college, which distorts democracy by giving a disproportionate say to voters in smaller states, purportedly gives Jews influence 'over Middle East policy' since, according to the Perlmutters, they are concentrated in 'swing states' that decide the fate of elections. Larger military budgets mean there are more funds for the Israeli state's war machine, and phasing out nuclear power would increase the role of oil and thus advantage Middle Eastern countries which were, at the time of their writing, considered hostile to the Israeli state.

Much of this reasoning is false or out of date. American Jews are not concentrated in 'swing states' that decide the fate of national elections but in states such as New York and California,[61] which usually elect Democrats by large margins and whose residents' votes count for less than those of voters in small states. The electoral college advantages the American right by giving a disproportionate say to small, mostly rural states in which the right dominates. The fact that the Perlmutters confuse the interests of the right with those of American Jews accurately reflects their prejudices. Their assessment of energy politics ignores the likelihood that renewables rather than oil would be seen as an alternative to nuclear power – and was written well before some key oil-producing states decided, at the prompting of the Trump administration, to end their (often-feigned) opposition to the Israeli state. But right wingers are as hostile to alternative energy as they are to majority rule. Again, they confuse the preferences of the right with the interests of Jews.

A more democratic United States of America, reduced funding for war and a shift to energy sources other than nuclear power may well benefit many Jews and would, polls suggest, command widespread Jewish support. But they would, in the view of the proponents of the 'new anti-Semitism', make life more difficult for the Israeli state. 'Anti-Semitic' for them means 'not in the interests of the Israeli state'. Given how that state defines its interests, it is no surprise that it also means left of centre. This has polarised Jewish opinion by alienating many Jewish liberals and left wingers.[62]

The IHRA definition, and the thinking which justifies it, is also being used to undermine democratic principles such as academic freedom and freedom of speech. One activist warned that spurious anti-Semitism claims by a British Jewish establishment that is committed to advancing the goals of the Israeli state are being used to further right-wing goals such as suppressing protest.[63] They are also being used to remove politicians whose views they dislike such as former Labour Party leader Jeremy Corbyn.[64]

The Labour Party's purge of those accused of being 'anti-Semites' is an instructive illustration of the affinity between the different interest groups that use these allegations to protect the Israeli state and the right wing. There is no evidence that Labour is any more anti-Semitic than any other British political party. In 2016, Labour asked human rights lawyer Baroness Shami Chakrabarti to investigate anti-Semitism in the party. While she found that some Labour members had made statements that suggested prejudice against Jews, she began her report with the statement: 'The Labour Party is not overrun by antisemitism ...'[65] A 2020 report by Britain's statutory Equalities and Human Rights Commission (EHRC) that sought to find fault with Labour was repeatedly portrayed in the media as an endorsement of the claim that the party was indeed 'overrun by anti-Semitism' and was 'institutionally racist' towards Jews. But it made no such finding. One journalist described its report as 'deeply flawed, intentionally vague and glaringly inconsistent'.[66] The commission found two cases of unlawful anti-Semitism and 18 'borderline cases' in which 'there was not enough evidence to conclude that the Labour Party was legally responsible for the conduct of the individual'.[67] Even if all the 'borderline cases' were examples of anti-Semitism, a party with over half a million members was host to 20 people who had expressed prejudice against Jews.

No such inquiry was conducted into any other British party. A probe into anti-Semitism in the Conservative Party might uncover a great deal more than 20 cases since disdain for Jews is a very old prejudice in the British upper classes that support the party. In the 1930s, for example, some Conservatives initially greeted Nazism with enthusiasm. The *Daily Mail*, a staunch Conservative newspaper, published an article in 1934 headlined 'Hurrah for the [Nazi] Blackshirts'.[68] A novel, *Seventy-Two Virgins*, by the Conservative former prime minister Boris Johnson features a standard anti-Semitic portrayal, that of a Jewish press baron who fixes elections.[69] John Bercow, a Jewish former speaker of the British parliament, entered the legislature as a Conservative but joined Labour after ending his term. He declared that he had never encountered anti-Jewish racism from Corbyn's Labour Party but had experienced it in the Conservative Party.[70] Yet the campaign to portray Labour as an anti-Semitic party was so successful that a poll found that the British public believed that one-third of Labour Party members faced anti-Semitism complaints, over three hundred times the real total.[71]

Why was Labour falsely portrayed as a party awash with anti-Semites? Partly because support for the Palestinian cause was most likely to be found in Labour and the object of the exercise was to target opposition to the Israeli state. When Labour leader Keir Starmer apologised to a pro-Israeli state Jewish group for the party's alleged anti-Semitism, he did not mention Labour leaders who really *did* dislike Jews. 'One of Labour's founders, Keir Hardie, believed Jewish financial institutions were part of a secret cabal that pushed for the Second Boer War of 1899-1902. Another prominent Labour figure of the era, John Burns, spoke of the omnipresent "financial Jew, operating, directing, inspiring the agonies that have led to this war".[72] But their authentic anti-Semitism was not a cause for apology; Jews who criticised or rejected the Israeli state were. The Israeli-born academic Avi Shlaim remarked, 'Labour does not want anti-Zionist, left-wing Jews like us in the party.'[73]

But it seems unlikely that the British establishment would devote so much effort to making a false charge stick simply because of their support for the Israeli state, solid as it is. Something else was afoot. In another example of the infinite regress, Corbyn was accused of anti-Semitism and expelled from the Parliamentary Labour Party for saying that the problem had been exaggerated, a claim that was consistent with the findings of the hostile EHRC report. Corbyn was Labour's most left-wing leader in decades and was seen by British power holders as a mortal threat to the economic order. 'Combating anti-Semitism' in Labour had become code for 'fighting the left'. It seems likely that some opinion formers who hailed Starmer's campaign against anti-Semitism harboured biases against Jews. But 'combating anti-Semitism' had become code for 'making Britain safe from the left'; attitudes to Jews were incidental.

HATE TRANSFERRED

A further reason for the alliance between the Israeli state and its supporters and right wingers across the globe is that many or most 'traditional' anti-Semites have found a new target on which to concentrate their fear and hate – Muslims.

They had once believed that a sinister conspiracy of Jews was using cunning and money to take over the world and destroy white, Christian society. Now they believe that a sinister conspiracy of Muslims is using religious fundamentalism and terror to achieve the same goal. 'Whereas anti-Semitism emerged in the late 19th century ... Islamophobia is a phenomenon of the current age.'[74] Their antipathy to Jews has not disappeared and, as we will see later, their hostility to Muslims has tended to be accompanied by anti-Jewish racism. But Islamophobia has become the core focus of this form of racism.

The Israeli state's conflict with Palestinians and much of the Arab world, which is wrongly assumed in much of the West to be entirely Muslim, has made it a paragon for anti-Muslim bigots. Asked why he worked closely with Christians who believe that Jews will one day be forced to become Christian or suffer eternal torment, a right-wing rabbi declared: 'From now on, anti-Semitism is Muslim.'[75]

The state of Israel is doubly attractive for ethnic nationalists around the world, even when their anti-Jewish racism is in full view. First, it proclaims itself the state of one ethnic group in a territory where there are others. Similarly, the American white supremacist Richard Spencer proclaimed himself a white Zionist. Just as Zionists wanted a state for Jews only, he wanted one for whites only, even as he repeated the anti-Semitic claim that Jews were 'over-represented' among America's power holders.[76] It will come as no surprise that Spencer is a lifelong anti-Semite.[77] Second, while not all Palestinians are Muslim, ethnic nationalists around the world, including those who govern the Israeli state, assume that they are. Indian prime minister Narendra Modi hopes to turn India into a state for Hindus only, despite a Muslim minority estimated to number between 195 and 200 million.[78] He finds much to like about both aspects. The anti-Muslim Indian right wing has supported Zionism since the 1920s.[79] It has also dabbled in anti-Semitism, as in the case of the extreme Hindu nationalist organisation, the Rashtriya Swayamsevak Sangh (RSS). In February 2021, Modi's government celebrated the birth anniversary of a former RSS head, MS Golwalkar, who had identified Indian Muslims as untrustworthy potential traitors, 'like the Jews in Germany', and had praised the 'race pride' behind the Nazis' anti-Semitic laws. India's Culture Ministry called Golwalkar a 'great thinker' whose ideas 'would continue to inspire and guide future generations'.[80]

In France, it is common for the charge of anti-Semitism to be used to silence Muslims. It is more marked there because France, as a product of its colonial wars, has a very visible Muslim and Arab population whose presence upsets white supremacists. Anti-Semitism accusations are used to express traditional Western prejudices against black people, Arabs and

Muslims (terms which are used interchangeably) and to label them and those who support them. '[Alleged] anti-Semitism is not the description of an actual situation, but *an operation of stigmatization.*' Thus, for Alain Finkielkraut, probably the chief ideologue of the French version of the 'new anti-Semitism', Muslims, Arabs and blacks are not only anti-Semitic; 'it is their fault that republican education is in tatters, that a kind of savagery has established itself on the margins of our big cities, etc.'[81] Those who sympathise with them, who often tend also to be critics of the Israeli state, are labelled anti-Semites in an attempt to silence them.[82]

Needless to say, Zionist right wingers share ethnic nationalists' prejudice against Muslims. That is why Hoenlein and Netanyahu blamed the Grand Mufti of Jerusalem, Haj Amin al-Husseini, for Hitler's death camps. Now that Muslims have replaced Jews as the target of Western prejudice, some Jews can identify with the racist nationalists who had once persecuted them. One way to do this is to shift blame for a very European mass murder to a Muslim in Palestine (who played no role in persuading the Nazis to kill Jews since they had already decided to do this before the one occasion when he met Hitler).[83] It is also why Rafi Eitan, a celebrated military operative of the Israeli state who had planned and executed the capture of the Nazi official Adolf Eichmann, voiced his support for the Alternative for Germany (AfD), a party whose neo-Nazi connections suggested that some of its leaders may see Eichmann as a role model. Eitan did this because 'he felt that it was the only party that understood the dire threat that immigrant Muslims posed to the future of Europe'.[84] The AfD has also received enthusiastic support from a Washington organisation with close ties to the Israeli state, despite the fact that an AfD leader described 8 May, the anniversary of Nazi Germany's surrender to the allies, as 'a day of ... the loss of national autonomy'.[85] Anti-Jewish bigotry is overlooked if it is accompanied by similar prejudices against Muslims.

Bigotry directed at Muslims is often justified by the claim that Islam is a religion, not a race.[86] This implies that the Islamophobe is not prejudiced against a group but against a belief. Beyond the obvious point that generalised hostility towards any group, whether their identity is defined by belief or birth, is bigotry, hostility to Muslims is often also a code for racial prejudice. One sign of the racial bigotry which underpins mainstream Israeli opinion is that, while Palestinians are the primary object of contempt, migrants from Africa have also been subjected to racism, including violent attacks. Black people and Muslims have become fused in the minds of the Israeli right. The migrants were labelled 'infiltrators', a term usually directed at Palestinians. In 2012, the Netanyahu government's interior minister, Eli Yishai, reacted to the attacks on migrants and demands for their expulsion thus: 'Most of those people coming here are Muslims who think the country does not belong to us, the white man.'[87]

Bosnian Muslims, who are white Europeans, were targeted by ethnic nationalists in their home region but are not the butt of anti-Islamic bigotry elsewhere; North African, Pakistani and Arab Muslims are. The chief object of the contempt of mainstream Jewish citizens of the Israeli state is Arabs, whether they are Muslim, Christian or neither. Like many who embrace racial stereotypes, these bigots too are not much interested in differences within the despised group. 'Anti-Muslim' and 'anti-Arab' can be synonyms in their minds. Thus, one leader of a right-wing organisation in the Israeli state joined the far-right Occident movement in France in the 1960s, despite knowing of its anti-Semitism, because it was 'anti-Arab and anti-Communist'.[88] This racial prejudice is shared by ethnonationalists and some centrists in the West who, as Edward Said showed in his celebrated work *Orientalism*, believe Arabs to be inferior to white Westerners.[89]

Crude expressions of racism are now part of the mainstream in the Israeli state. Jews are seen as a 'race' whose 'purity' is under threat. (As we will soon see, viewing Jews as a 'race' is a core anti-Semitic claim.) This is often justified as a concern about assimilation – the fear, which has gripped mainstream Jews ever since other Jews were able to mix freely with non-Jews, that Jews would adopt the culture of the societies in which they lived. Jews are not the only minority in which some members fear assimilation. But when voiced in a country where Jews are the dominant group, it becomes a vehicle for racial bigotry that is expressed, for example, in opposition to the (rare) cases in which Palestinians and Israeli Jews marry. It also has more extreme forms. 'In today's Israel, the most astonishing manifestation of this ideology [of Jewish purity] is the emergence of a school of scientific thought that hopes to make "Jewish genetics" a core justification of Zionism.'[90] To give effect to this 'race science', 'Israel and the United States now have academic institutions committed to the search for the "Jewish gene" … that they hope to uncover'.[91] While these views remain 'marginal', their influence appears to be growing.[92] For some supporters of the Israeli state, the 'race science' that underpinned the Nazi genocide is valid – if it is used by Jews.

This kind of positioning, however, creates a dilemma for advocates of the 'new anti-Semitism'. Their natural ally is the white supremacist right wing, but it is essential to their project to be seen to campaign against a racial prejudice, anti-Semitism. How then might they maintain an ally that is sympathetic to racism in general while they rail against a particular (alleged) racism? The answer, which serves other purposes too, is to insist that anti-Semitism is a racism unlike any other. 'Anti-Semitism is a sui generis hatred, one that is shape-shifting, impervious to logic and eternal.'[93]

But all bigotry is 'shape-shifting' because deeply embedded hatreds can be expressed in various ways, some of which are discerned only by the trained eye and ear; and all bigotries are impervious to logic. Bigotry directed at Jews is no more 'eternal' than that directed at others. But the task of this claim is not to describe reality; it is to justify all Israeli state actions.[94] It asserts that since anti-Semitism is a unique evil, its victims – and the state supposedly established in their name – must be free to discriminate against others if they believe this necessary to combat anti-Semitism. It is politically useful in another way too – if anti-Semitism is not the same as other racisms, it is not inconsistent to denounce anti-Semitism while harbouring deep prejudices against just about everyone else. Claims of anti-Semitism are thus turned from a protest against racism to a blank cheque to harbour hostility against any group – except one. The fact that the one has come to be seen as 'Western' and the others are not is not accidental. A further 'bonus' of this view is that it can silence independent thought because it makes it possible for someone to be labelled anti-Semitic not because they express hostility to Jews but merely because they insist that all racisms are the same.[95]

These factors ensure that the version of 'anti-Semitism' embraced by the Israeli state and governing elites in the global North and parts of the South is now unrecognisable. Opposition to a bigotry that, in the mid-twentieth century, prompted the murder of six million Jews (and millions of Slavs, Romany people and other targets of Nazi hate) has become a weapon in the hands of right wingers who want to bully and silence anti-racists. While prejudice against Jews was deeply embedded in the white European view of the world – and in those countries settled by white Europeans – the label 'anti-Semitism' is now code for opposition to white European dominance. Since more than a few Jews oppose that dominance, it is central to those whose goals are furthered by this newly minted bludgeon that some Jews – those who are left wing or too liberal or opposed to the Israeli state (all of which tend to go together) – be labelled haters of their race and thus of themselves.[96] It is only by separating out the 'bad' Jews from the 'good' that the Israeli state can turn a protest against racism into one of its instruments.

To deepen our understanding of this change, we must understand what anti-Semitism is and how different it is from the version analysed here.

3

What Anti-Semitism Really Is

I n his 2018 book, *The Jewish American Paradox: Embracing Choice in a Changing World*, Robert Mnookin, a long-time leader in American Jewish organisations, writes: 'To me "anti-Semitic" does not mean "critical of Israel" or "opposed to the Zionist project"; it means having prejudice against or hatred of Jews.'[1] As the previous chapter suggests, this is an extremely unusual view among leadership figures in Jewish organisations in the United States (or anywhere else). But it is entirely accurate.

FROM FAITH TO RACE

Prejudice against Jews is very old, though not as old as some historians claim.[2]

Understanding this prejudice is complicated by the fact that Jews are both adherents of a religion and members of an ethnic group. Anti-Jewish prejudice may thus express religious intolerance, ethnic bigotry or both. Originally, it was a prejudice against the Jewish religion – although, as always, history is a little more complicated than it seems. The prime source of the prejudice was European Christianity. In Muslim countries,

Jews were regarded as *dimmi* – they were not treated entirely as equals but were protected and were free to practise their religion.[3] The period of Muslim rule in Spain was a 'golden age' for Jews. One of them, Shmuel ha-Nagid, was appointed the vizier of Granada – effectively prime minister,[4] a role that no Jew was afforded in Christian countries. This did not mean that Jews enjoyed equal rights; the idea that any individual enjoyed rights simply because they were human was yet to take root. But it did mean that Jews were more likely to be tolerated than in Christian Europe.

As the previous chapter suggested, Christian Europe was deeply prejudiced against Muslims and Jews. From the eleventh century, Christian countries embarked on crusades to wrest Jerusalem, in particular, and the 'Holy Land' in general, from Muslim rule. But the hostility to Jews was far more intense than antipathy to Muslims for reasons both religious and mundane; the Crusaders slaughtered Jews on their way through Europe to Jerusalem.[5] The religious antipathy against Jews stemmed from the Christian Bible in which they were portrayed as killers of the Christ. The dominant Christian view of Jews and their religion was supersessionism, the claim that Christians had replaced Jews as the people of God and so God's back had been turned on the Jews. The notion that Jews were demonic enemies of Christianity gave birth to the 'blood libel', the entirely false claim that Jews killed Christian children to use their blood to bake unleavened bread on Passover.[6] The mundane reason for the difference in treatment between Muslims and Jews was that Jews were, unlike Muslims, immediate and visible; they lived in Christian countries (albeit often in segregated ghettos or villages because the law forbade them to live among Christians). A further source of prejudice was that Jews were not allowed to own land and so were forced to turn to occupations such as money lending. This gave birth to the prejudice that Jews were financial exploiters, which was portrayed, in a complex manner, in William Shakespeare's *The Merchant of Venice*.[7]

These prejudices ensured that Jews sometimes lived precarious lives in Europe when, as we will see, feudalism gave way to the centralised national state. They were expelled from countries when the political tide flowed against them, most notoriously from Spain in 1492 after Christianity reclaimed the country from Islam, and were subjected to discrimination. As noted above, they were segregated from the dominant group in society much as black people were separated from white people in apartheid South Africa and some of its neighbours or in the 'Jim Crow' American South. Church doctrine held that contact with Jews was polluting. Not only were they then barred from areas where Christians lived and from their facilities such as bathhouses, Christians were also warned against eating food that a Jew had touched.[8] This view was formally enunciated in a Papal Bull, *Cum Nimis Absurdum,* in 1555. It condemned Jews 'to eternal slavery' because of their 'guilt' and imposed not only segregated living areas but bans which 'Jim Crow' and apartheid were later to emulate. Jews were barred from land ownership, attendance at universities and the like. They were also subjected to laws forcing them to wear distinctive clothing and badges and could not be addressed as 'sir' by Christians.[9]

This discrimination was not couched in racial terms. In principle, Jews were a problem not because they had been born to particular parents but because they practised the wrong religion. It followed that if they converted to Christianity, they would no longer defile society. Jews would be, at times, faced with a choice between death or conversion. But practice did not necessarily conform to theory. In Spain, the Western European country in which Jews converted in large numbers, their embrace of Christianity turned out not to be enough. Jews who would not convert were driven out of Spain in 1492 by the Christian monarch. But those who converted and stayed in the country after the expulsion were not accepted as members of the Christian community for long. In 1546, the Archbishop of Toledo rejected the appointment of a priest to serve at the city's cathedral because he had 'impure blood',[10] presumably because he or his family was originally Jewish. This marked the beginning of the application of the doctrine of *'limpieza de sangre'* or blood purity, which insisted that only 'pure' Christians and their descendants could hold office in the church or state. This ban did not affect only (former) Jews but Muslims too; the number of Muslim converts to Christianity in Spain vastly outnumbered the Jewish *conversos* or converts.

The church initially opposed *limpieza de sangre*. This made sense since its aim was to convert Muslims and Jews and there was no incentive for either to change religions if they were to face discrimination even after becoming Christians. But bigotry within church ranks ensured that its resistance did not last. It was an archbishop who first applied the principle, and secular authorities that imposed bans on converted Muslims and Jews usually responded to pressure from the church or to riots by the faithful. The witch-hunt for those of 'impure blood' was partly 'justified' by the claim that the conversions had not been sincere and that the new recruits had continued to practise their original religions in secret while pretending to be Christian. The church then established the Inquisition, one of whose core tasks was to prosecute and persecute converts who were suspected of practising the religion they had claimed to have left.[11] But it clearly was a racial ban. That the church embraced it, despite the fact that it would deter potential converts, shows that racial bigotry had become deeply intertwined with religious intolerance. The phrase 'religious racism' best sums up the Spanish attitude. It was 'the idea that Spanish hostility to Jews was still fundamentally directed at their religion rather than their ancestry, while confirming that the two cannot be entirely separated'.[12] The fusion of religious and racial prejudice mentioned in chapter 1 is, therefore, not new. Once an 'outsider' group has been demonised, it is hard to give the demons time off for good behaviour – which, in this case, meant conversion. Hostility to Jews and Muslims may have been explained by their religious allegiances but was also motivated by the fact that they were born into communities that the dominant group found distasteful.

Nevertheless, the Spanish case seems to have been unusual. There is no record of restrictions on Jews who converted, whether by force or choice, in other countries. Some converted Jews rose to prominence in Christian societies – Benjamin Disraeli, a nineteenth-century British prime minister, for example. Karl Marx was also a converted Jew although he obviously did not enjoy the same respectability among the establishment. Only Spanish Christians, it appears, were worried about the 'blood' of Jews rather than their beliefs. While hostility to Jews is very old, anti-Semitism, understood as a prejudice against Jews simply because they were born into an ethnic group, is not.

The 'Science' of Hatred

Anti-Semitism or anti-Jewish racism (as opposed to religious prejudice against Jews) emerged in Germany in the late nineteenth century.

It was not by accident that it appeared after the influence of the church on European states had waned, for racial anti-Semitism had nothing further to say about the Jewish religion and was not at all interested in whether Jews converted to Christianity. Jews were a threat because of biology, not spirituality. A scholar of anti-Semitism thus defines it as 'the doctrine that the Jews constituted a separate and dangerous race or people'.[13] If Jews are a race, anyone born Jewish is a problem, irrespective of the religion they practise – or even if they practise none. The term 'racism' was originally coined to describe this kind of prejudice: some European critics of this anti-Jewish prejudice also held deeply bigoted views of black people.[14] Nevertheless, they considered themselves anti-racist since they opposed prejudice against Jews; for them, all Europeans were equal, but not all people were. The critics of this racism insisted that 'there was no such thing as a Jewish race';[15] some, however, presumably remained convinced that there were darker races that were inferior.

The term 'anti-Semitism' is usually associated with the German activist Wilhelm Marr, although it seems likely that he was tapping into prejudices which had been influential among German elites for some time. He used the term proudly. In 1879, he founded the 'Antisemiten Liga', or League of Anti-Semites, after publishing a pamphlet whose German title translates as 'The Victory of Jewishness over Germanness'.[16] Like some other bigots, Marr seemed confused about his attitude to the people who he despised. He married four times, three times to women who were wholly or partly

Jewish – his first two wives were born of two Jewish parents, the third of one.[17] At some stages of his life, he appeared to be quite well disposed to Jews. According to his biographer, Marr renounced anti-Semitism in later life and asked Jews to forgive him for his earlier bigotry.[18] But he never recanted the claims in his pamphlet and so made no sustained attempt to undo the damage he had caused.[19] Peddlers of anti-Jewish hate would continue repeating his central argument for decades; it can still be heard today.

Marr insisted that he had no quarrel with the Jewish religion. Not only did he subtitle his pamphlet 'Viewed from a nonreligious point of view', he also described the allegation that Jews had killed Christ as 'nonsensical' and dismissed the blood libels with similar contempt. The problem with the Jews, he insisted, was 'the loathing Jews demonstrate for real work' and 'their codified enmity against all non-Jews'.[20] Jews, he asserted, were, as a race, interested only in banking, intellectual and cultural pursuits rather than 'real work'.[21] This gave them the power to act on their hostility to all non-Jews and to ensure that they dominated them. According to Marr, the lifting of restrictions on Jews had freed them to take over Germany. The country of his birth was host to a struggle between 'Judaism', the culture of the Jews, and 'Germanism'. There was no prospect of any compromise between the two; they were so at odds that only conflict between them was possible. One would conquer the other and bend it to its will.

In addition to its many falsehoods and its historical blindness, Marr's pamphlet is oddly written. (Needless to say, it did not mention that the law had prevented Jews from engaging in the 'real work' that it extolled.) It does not contain, as we might expect, a call for the devotees of 'Germanism' to rise up to defeat Judaism. In his Preface, Marr declared that 'Resigned pessimism flows from my pen'.[22] The booklet ends with the words 'Finis Germaniae' – it is over for the Germans.[23] As his title suggests, Marr argued that Germanism had lost the war. He therefore did not call on Germans to do anything about their subjection to 'Judaism'. This is further evidence of Marr's confusion since this fatalism meant that he was wasting his time forming a league of anti-Semites; there was nothing it could do.

The bulk of Marr's readers did not share his defeatism; the pamphlet was widely read. 'The brutality of the despair expressed in *The Victory of Judaism over Germanism* turned the book into a best-seller.'[24] And, whatever Marr's intentions may have been, his readers were quick to see the book as a call not to surrender but to racist action. Readers found what Marr had not written: 'The incentive for a war against the Jews.'[25] Most of Marr's stereotypes about Jews – that Jews were rich, powerful, scheming and wanted to control the world – quickly became standard fare among German anti-Semites and staples of Nazi propaganda. But, unlike Marr, the other anti-Jewish racists believed that Jews could and should be stopped and the pamphlet's ideas thus became fodder for the fear-driven hate that culminated in the Nazi genocide.

Since Marr was at such pains to stress that the problem was not the Jewish religion but the Jewish race, Jews became targets no matter what religion they espoused and even if they did not identify with other Jews. The Nazis later victimised people who had long since abandoned Judaism but who had some Jewish ancestry. German anti-Semitism, influenced by Marr, turned a religious prejudice into textbook racism – the labelling, stigmatisation and domination of people simply because they were born of particular antecedents. For Marr and those whom he inspired, there were no 'good Jews', only bad ones.

While Marr was obsessed with Jews alone – he did not mention other groups in his tirade – racial anti-Semitism (rather than hostility to the Jewish religion) was usually part of a package of prejudices. Houston Stewart Chamberlain, who wrote in the late nineteenth and early twentieth centuries, is usually seen as the author of 'scientific racism', the belief that differences between races – and the superiority of one over others – was a product of nature, not a human invention. But he borrowed at least some of his ideas from the French aristocrat Arthur de Gobineau, who claimed that science had established that the world was divided into races and that the white race was superior to all others.

Chamberlain was English but he much preferred Germany. He lived there for many years and married the daughter of Richard Wagner, the anti-Jewish music composer who became a cult figure for German anti-Semites, including Hitler. His music glorified German legend, which he and his admirers saw as an expression of a 'superior' culture. Chamberlain was a consistent racist throughout his life and in 1899 published *Die Grundlagen des neunzehnten Jahrhundert* (Foundations of the Nineteenth Century), in which he spelled out what he claimed was 'scientific' racism. Like Marr, he believed that a war between races was under way. But he went much further than Marr had dared.

On one side, he argued, was not just 'Germanness' but the 'Aryan race' which comprised, essentially, white Europeans. On the other side was not only Jews but black and Asian people as well (and, no doubt, Arabs too had he been asked). Although he did not explicitly describe the Aryans as the 'master race', his inspiration, Gobineau, had.[26] Chamberlain might as well have since he ascribed all positive traits to Aryans and all negative characteristics to Jews.[27] Every war in human history had, he wrote, been 'peculiarly connected with Jewish financial operations' and had started because Jews wanted to rule the world.[28] Unlike his hero Wagner, Chamberlain did not believe that Jews could ever redeem themselves by ceasing to be Jewish; on the contrary, 'the Jew was an alien virus to be purged from the national bloodstream. The more a Jew took on the habits and thoughts of his gentile compatriots, the more he was to be feared'.[29] This was consistent with his 'scientific' racism: if race is an unchangeable biological feature of the human species, people cannot resign from one race to join another. To be born an Aryan was to be saved; to be born a Jew was to be damned.

Unlike Marr, Chamberlain did not limit his 'scientific' hatred to Jews. In one letter that was part of an exchange of letters with the German emperor, Kaiser Wilhelm, he described black people as 'impoverished in intellect and bestially inclined'.[30] In another, he congratulated the Kaiser on the genocide of the Herero people in today's Namibia. A 'war of extermination' was a 'fine example', he said, of how Aryans should deal with black people. (He did not use the phrase 'black people', but preferred a racist label that begins with an 'n'.)[31] China and East Asia were also the homes of threatening races. In one letter he declared, 'The Great Yellow Danger overshadows us white men and threatens destruction.'[32] Chamberlain relegated even the Slavs of Eastern Europe to the status of an inferior race despite the fact that they were white Europeans and were classified as Aryan in his definition of the term. Russia, he wrote, was a nation of 'stupid Slavs'; it had been saved from total ruin only by the fact that its then monarch, Nicholas II, had German blood.[33]

However, some South Asians were apparently exempt from his derision. Chamberlain, like some German nationalists at the time, was fascinated with Hindu myth and legend, but this burst of tolerance was, in Chamberlain's case, the product of a comical misrepresentation. The term 'Aryan' originated in India where people so described had lived for over 2 000 years. Since these Aryans were lighter skinned than other inhabitants of the region, they were described by some European scholars as 'Indo-European'. Chamberlain built on this to claim that they were 'Germanic people', which, of course, made Hindu culture the product of the (white, European) master race.[34] While this may find echoes in the fact that India's incumbent Hindu nationalist government has found common cause with white supremacists in the United States and Europe, it did not exempt Hindus from being relegated to an 'inferior' status by British imperialism, a point we will discuss in a later chapter.

Nor did it exempt Muslims and others who were not considered white from contempt; one scholar of anti-Semitism refers to a 'tradition marking Jews, Arabs and Muslims … as sharing a common "Eastern" heritage and qualities that allegedly made them pernicious moral, theological, and political enemies of Europeans'.[35] Edward Said noted, 'Hostility to Islam in the modern Christian West has historically gone hand in hand with, has stemmed from the same source, has been nourished at the same stream as anti-Semitism.'[36] Elsewhere, he wrote: 'Both Muslims and Jews in the West have been accused of being threats to public values. Similarly, both Jews and Muslims have been caricatured and treated as threats to public safety.'[37]

Like Marr, Gobineau and Chamberlain laid the ground for the Nazi slaughter of Jews and Slavs either by introducing the notion of the 'master race' or by labelling Jews as all-powerful schemers who had corrupted white European civilisation and who had to be stopped before they could take over the world. Their anti-Jewish bigotry was not new, just as their contempt for 'black, brown and yellow people' was a defence of a system of domination that already existed; the Kaiser did not need Chamberlain to tell him to butcher Hereros. The Atlantic slave trade, which made Europe and the United States rich on the labour of black people who were treated as personal property, was justified by claims of racial superiority long before the 'scientific racists' published their prejudices. Some scholars see racism against 'black and brown' people as a product of colonialism,[38] which was also well under way when Chamberlain wrote.

But their bigotry was new in one important sense: it invented racism just as it invented anti-Semitism. It hardened long-standing prejudices against Jews and, indeed, against anyone who was not white and 'Aryan', into an ideology. Contempt and hatred that had been shared by many white Europeans for centuries became the product of a purported 'science' that claimed to explain the world and justified redoubled efforts to ensure that 'Aryans' dominated everyone else by any means necessary. The word 'racism' only entered the English language in the 1930s and was used to describe the Nazis who had embraced the theories of the 'racial scientists'.[39]

As we have noted, to ground prejudice in race is to make it immutable. When the Nazis took over Germany, many of that country's Jews were no longer Jewish in belief, culture or practice. But the Nazis declared that anyone with 'Jewish blood' was Jewish. 'Victor Klemperer, a professor of French literature in Dresden … converted to Protestant Christianity, married a gentile [non-Jew], served in the German army in World War I, and identified fully with German culture. Under Nazi law, however, he counted as a Jew.'[40] The same applied to blacks, Slavs, Chinese people and other East Asians. European colonialism used claims of cultural superiority to dominate but was sometimes willing to try to turn the Africans,

Asians and Arabs who it dominated into Europeans. Chamberlain's preferred treatment was 'extermination' or mass murder. The Nazis were later to apply this 'remedy' to Jews and Slavs and probably spared black and Chinese people only because they were not near enough. (The Nazis' allies, imperial Japan, did invade China, where its soldiers are accused of visiting atrocities on civilians.[41])

Crucially, Jews were not the only targets of this bigotry. Since it was based on the assumption that there was a 'master race' – white, Aryan, European – all other races were to be subjugated or murdered. As the writings of the first authors to proclaim themselves racists show, to hate Jews usually also meant despising black people, Muslims, Arabs and Asians (including Indians, despite Chamberlain's bizarre view that many of them were really Germans). The theorist of black liberation, Frantz Fanon, understood this very well. He recalled his philosophy professor telling him, 'Whenever you hear anyone abuse the Jews, pay attention, because he is talking about you.'[42] So did Said, who, as we have seen briefly, noted that hostility to Muslims and to Jews tended to go together. Alain Badiou and Eric Hazan note: 'In the 1932 edition of the Larousse dictionary, black people were still presented and drawn as midway between ape and man. And in such racial arguments, anti-Semitism played a major role.'[43] It is also important to note that the Nazi genocide employed some of the techniques – such as concentration camps – used in the German colonial attempted genocide of Namibian indigenous people.[44] The racist slaughter of Europeans had been refined in the equally racist mass murder of Africans.

OVERTURNING HISTORY

This account should underline how grotesque a departure from history the current misuses of anti-Semitism are.

The anti-Semitism discussed in this chapter is an extreme white supremacist ideology – which is the way in which the term has been understood ever since it was first used. It is grounded in the claim that white (non-Jewish) Europeans are superior to everyone else and that those who were not lucky enough to be born into this select club are to be dominated, enslaved, killed or all three. While Jews, like everyone else, are not immune from bigotry, anti-Semitism gave them an inherent incentive to oppose legalised racism, if only because they might be its victims. It was entirely predictable that when the National Party, which had preferred the Nazis to the British and had barred Jews from membership, took over South Africa in 1948, many Jews believed that it would pass anti-Jewish laws and attempt to do to them some of what the Nazis had done to European Jews. After all, anti-black bigots were also anti-Semites (and Islamophobes).

As we have seen, anti-Semitism is an attitude that power holders in the West now usually attribute to Muslims, black people and the left. In France, Badiou and Hazan argue, the charge of anti-Semitism is used to mobilise prejudices against people who are not white Europeans, which the writings of the eighteenth-century racists encouraged. It is, more specifically, a means to justify the exclusion of black and Arab French people from mainstream society.

> Sowing distrust and hostility towards young people from the lower classes is of course a very traditional class practice. Today, however, one particular aim is to establish a kind of frontier dividing them from the white, educated petty bourgeoisie … The point is to establish a social segregation, and the accusation of anti-Semitism is again very useful for this.[45]

The irony could not be clearer: anti-Semitism is no longer part of the racist package of those who despise anyone who is not white; it is now attributed to, and weaponised against, precisely those people whom the original anti-Semites hated. Allegations of racism have now become an important weapon in the armoury of racists.

A similar but equally important reversal is the recruitment of some Jews – the 'good ones' who support the Israeli state – to the cause of 'the

West'. A common theme of the anti-Semites discussed here is that Jews were seen – with Muslims – as a threat to white Western Europe and, later, by implication, to the whites from Europe who settled in the United States, Australia, Canada and southern Africa and identified as 'Western'. Now the Israeli state and its supporters are seen not only as allies of the West but as its representatives in the Middle East. Like white South Africa before 1994, the Israeli state is in, but not of, the region in which it finds itself; the claim of its former prime minister, Ehud Barak, that it is a 'villa in the jungle' sums up the prejudice that it is an island of 'First World' Western civilisation in a barbaric neighbourhood.[46] So neatly does it sum up their worldview that apartheid's ideologues no doubt wish they had coined the phrase. This, with the other realities described in chapters 1 and 2, combines to persuade 'Westerners' convinced of the superiority of their way of life (a view which stretches across the political spectrum) that the Israeli state is on the frontline of the fight for 'civilisation'.

One example of this is the constant reference in the West to the Israeli state as 'the only democracy in the Middle East'. The claim is patently false. Democracies do not declare themselves the nation state of one ethnic group in a territory where there is more than one; they do not discriminate against citizens who are not of a particular ethnic group; they do not, as policy, dominate citizens who are not of the dominant ethnic group.[47] The Israeli state and its courts do not even recognise an 'Israeli' nationality; for them, only ethnic labels describe nationhood.[48] All this raises the obvious question: why is the Israeli state regarded as a democracy at all? The answer is that 'democracy' is very often used by Western academics and elites as a code for 'Western' – despite the fact that some non-Western societies are more democratic than those in North America and Western Europe. (The United States considers itself the ultimate democracy despite the fact that elections are not necessarily won by the candidate who wins the most votes and laws in many states effectively deprive many people of the vote.[49]) It is therefore clear that 'the only democracy in the Middle East' really means 'the only Western state in the Middle East'.

In service of this Western agenda of protecting its main Middle East ally, the Israeli state, the term 'anti-Semite' has increasingly become code for 'not Western' or 'not Western in the way we want them to be'. 'Good' Jews believe that the West is best, 'bad' ones cling to the strange belief that race and location are no measure of democracy. 'For those who weaponise anti-Semitism on behalf of white France,' write Badiou and Hazan,

> what matters for them is not the name 'Jew' but 'the fate of the West'. This is the reason they identify 'Jew' with the state of Israel, and so eagerly support this state's war against Palestinians and other Arabs. This also explains why the American far right, traditionally anti-Semitic, has organized an unlikely alliance between Christian ultra-conservatives and formerly 'progressive' Jews who have converted to the new world order.[50]

It is also, they add, why the French right-wing leader Marine Le Pen, whose party was originally notoriously anti-Semitic, has shown 'nothing but kindness to Jews while denouncing "Arab-Moslems" for saying prayers in the streets'.[51] Le Pen's father, Jean-Marie Le Pen, the former leader of her party, was convicted by a French court for 'contesting crimes against humanity' when he declared that the Nazi occupation of France was 'not particularly inhumane'.[52]

Of course, authentic anti-Semitism, the kind that expresses hatred towards Jews, has not disappeared. And contrary to the claims of the Israeli state and its supporters, anti-Jewish racism remains an overwhelmingly right-wing bias. An answer to a question in the German parliament revealed that, in 2020, police recorded over 1 300 anti-Semitic incidents; 1 247, or 93.5 per cent, were the work of right wingers.[53] This authentic anti-Semitism mixes prejudices against Jews with a similar loathing of people who are not Christian or not white. Its most obvious manifestations have been in the United States. In 2017, white supremacists at a rally in Charlottesville, Virginia, chanted 'Jews will not replace us', thus expressing 'centuries-old fears that Jews, in league with peoples of color, are engaged in a nefarious plot to destroy the white Christian civilization'.[54] Alex Linder, a neo-Nazi who operates a racist website, wrote that Jews merely pretend to be white 'in order to shame, discredit, blame, mock, harass and otherwise discomfit and discredit white people and the white race'.[55]

In October 2018, Robert Bowers opened fire on worshippers at a Pittsburgh synagogue, Tree of Life, killing 11 people. Bowers was enraged by the work of the Hebrew Immigrant Aid Society (HIAS), which had started life as an organisation that had assisted Jewish immigrants to the United States but had become a source of support to newcomers of all races and origins. Responding to a National Refugee Sabbath that HIAS had organised, Bowers responded: 'Why hello there HIAS! You like to bring in hostile invaders to dwell among us?' In another internet post he wrote 'Open you [sic] Eyes! It's the filthy EVIL jews Bringing the Filthy EVIL Muslims into the Country!!'[56] Decades of anti-Semites would have recognised the rhetoric immediately: Jews are not only a threat to white Western Europeans, they also work with others who are neither white nor Western to undermine 'Western civilisation'. In both this and the Charlottesville example, replacement theory, which claims that whites are being replaced in their traditional homelands by other, inferior races,[57] became a vehicle to denounce Jews along with Muslims, Arabs and black people – everyone who is not considered white.

Those who trade on the 'new anti-Semitism' may well make it harder to guard against real anti-Jewish bigotry. First, they distract attention from the real problem – the hatred of Jews which prompted Bowers to murder people simply because they were Jews. An American rabbi, Mike Rothbaum, complained: 'Our local schools are plagued by antisemitism. There's a speaker engaged by a local shul [synagogue] ostensibly to discuss antisemitism. 3/4 of the talk is about defending Israel. My students aren't targeted for Zionism. They're targeted for being Jews.'[58] He seemed unaware that, in the view of official US Jewish leadership, his students were entitled to safety only if that assisted the goals of the Israeli state.

Second, their effect could also be 'the accentuation of antisemitic con-spiracy theories and anti-Jewish stereotypes'.[59] Repeatedly levelling the charge of anti-Semitism whenever anyone criticises the Israeli state can blind people to real bigotry directed at Jews. It also becomes a meaningless slogan which induces not alarm or concern but apathy and indifference in those who hear it. Repeated exposure to a word or phrase 'diminishes one's emotional responsiveness to it',[60] particularly if the word is negative, and is meant to warn against a threat. The effect of repeatedly and loudly branding normal political conversation as 'anti-Semitic' may well be to reduce concern for a problem that remains real despite the manner in which it has become distorted. As Israeli human rights lawyer Michael Sfard pointed out: 'If everything is antisemitism, then nothing is.'[61] Or as a non-Jewish writer put it: 'If we truly wish to combat antisemitism, we must first recognize and accept the diversity of the Jewish community and act meticulously to avoid the perilous generalizations and unfounded conflations which have formed the backbone of antisemitic sentiment for decades.'[62]

The prejudices of Bowers and the Charlottesville marchers and the replacement theories that motivate them are much, much older than the verbal gymnastics of the 'new anti-Semitism'. Not long ago, all Jews were, in the view of those who hated them, threats to the West, along with anyone who was not white. Now some Jews are friends of the West and so, in this view, enemies of others who were also once seen as threats. Not only have these Jews been accepted into the West, they have become role models for the same cultural arrogance and bigotry that once demonised them. According to this view, to oppose racism, cultural arrogance and the attitudes that underpinned colonisation is the same as being hostile to Jews. (The fact that the Israeli state is seen to have colonised its terri-tory no doubt strengthens this view.) In this sense, these Jews who are friends with the West, and those who agree with them, have not only come to terms with the anti-Semites, they have become them.

But not all Jews feel this way; many continue to believe that the attitudes that have underpinned claims of Western superiority are bad for humanity and for Jews themselves. These Jews continue to champion equality and non-racialism, in Palestine as well as everywhere else. The Jews who now hold state power and those who support them can deal with this only by expelling the pro-non-racialism Jews from the Jewish body politic over which they hold sway. A Chicago rabbi claimed that Jews who say that there is a contradiction between Zionism and 'progressive values' are 'more dangerous to the Jewish people than the right-wing antisemites who shoot up synagogues'.[63] The 'good Jews' hold power in a state and in Jewish institutions and so they can proclaim themselves the only Jews and label the 'bad Jews' as 'anti-Semites' when they oppose the 'new Jew' who has enthusiastically embraced white dominance.

The 'good Jews' are now the anti-Semites and the 'bad Jews' are the identity they have left behind them.

4

The Israeli State as a 'Cure' for Anti-Racism

The devotees of the 'new anti-Semitism', the previous chapter argued, now stigmatise Jews who embrace attitudes that have been associated with Jewishness for centuries. But why do Jews not leave traditional mainstream understandings of Jewish identity behind?

The Israeli state and the architects of the 'new anti-Semitism' may well agree that the values and worldview of the 'bad Jews' are consistent with a long-standing way of being Jewish, which is not the only expression of Jewish identity but the one that dominated for centuries. But, they would add, this traditional way of being Jewish deserves to be left in the past. The 'bad Jews' have failed to realise that the world has changed, and they remain museum pieces and obstacles to the new 'good Jews' who have created a superior present and a more promising future. They would be bound to say this because it is a central principle underpinning political Zionism and its understanding of Jewish identity.

This belief is based on an interpretation of Jewish history that justifies the creation of a Jewish state but is also, interestingly, adopted by some of the state's critics. According to this view, the Jews had a state 2 000 years ago but lost it in the year 70 CE. Thereafter, Jews were stateless and, therefore, powerless. Because they lacked a state, they had no control over their lives and no way to protect themselves from those who wished them harm. Their plight reached its peak in the mid-twentieth century when Jews could do nothing to stop the Nazis slaughtering six million of their number.

This view was summed up by David Ben-Gurion, the first prime minister of the Israeli state. In 1944, he told a gathering of youth groups in Haifa that Zionism and the state it was fighting for was a unique 'revolution'. 'All other revolts, both past and future, were uprisings against a system, against a political, economic, or social structure. Our revolution is directed not only against a system, but against destiny, against the unique destiny of a unique people.'[1]

For Ben-Gurion and the Zionist movement, Jews were 'a unique people' because they had lacked a state for centuries. That had forced on them a 'unique destiny' – to be persecuted and bullied by the peoples and rulers of the countries in which they had settled. By creating a Jewish state, they argued, Zionism would overthrow that destiny. Once they had a state, Jews would no longer be different; like everyone else, they would enjoy the power to protect themselves and to shape their own destiny. This conjured up a stark contrast: a people without a state was powerless and persecuted; with a state, it was the captain of its own destiny. As the scholar Shaul Magid points out, this view rests on a portrayal of centuries of Jewish history as 'just one bloody antisemitic act after another'. Its message is that 'the diaspora is bad for the Jews, even when it seems good, and the only way to ensure safety is for Jews to have a state of their own. It constituted what one might call a "negation of the diaspora" historiography'.[2]

This 'lachrymose' notion of Jewish history was criticised by the celebrated twentieth-century American Jewish historian Salo Baron,[3] and is the subject of an important book by a contemporary Jewish historian, David Biale, titled *Power and Powerlessness in Jewish History*.[4] Biale's work is path-breaking precisely because it demolishes the stark contrast between a powerless Jewish people *without* a state and a powerful group *with* one. He observes that Ben-Gurion's view was shared, although from a different perspective, by non-Zionists.

Hannah Arendt, the Jewish philosopher who believed that the creation of the Israeli state was a tragic mistake, wrote that Jews were a people 'which began its history with a well-defined concept of history and an almost conscious resolution to achieve a well-circumscribed plan on earth and then, without giving up this concept, avoided all political action for two thousand years'.[5] The anti-Zionist Michael Selzer argued that 'Jewish ethics and purpose derive from the rejection of power' and that Jews sought to 'radicalize the world through Jewish powerlessness and suffering'.[6] So, Arendt and Selzer agree that statelessness made Jews powerless. But they present this as a choice; to opt out of politics, according to Arendt, or, for Selzer, to embrace the suffering that came with powerlessness. Both imply that, in the circumstances in which Jews lived, it was their religion, not the secular government that they did not have, which shaped their values.

Zionism's founders agreed, but from an opposite perspective. For them, clinging to religion as a substitute for political action was precisely what had ensured Jewish suffering. Early Zionists were hostile to the Jewish religion, which they saw as a cause of Jewish misery because it encouraged prayer and religious study instead of the exercise of power.[7] They did, however, want to have their cake and eat it too by insisting that the Bible that they had rejected was also a history book that justified Jewish control of Palestine.[8] The Israeli prime minister Golda Meir epitomised this attitude when she declared: 'I do not believe in God, I believe in the Jewish people.'[9] She and other Zionists would no doubt see Selzer as the epitome of the 'bad Jew' who felt that suffering and powerlessness was a condition that Jews should always endure. The purpose of the Israeli state, they would insist, is to replace Selzer's 'bad Jew' who revels in powerlessness and suffering and to create a 'good Jew' with the will and the power to ensure that Jews suffer no more.

In the opinions of both sides, Jews spent two millennia without power and politics: one side decries this perceived reality, the other exalts it. But this chapter and the next will show that both understandings misread the Jewish past and present. This chapter will discuss the claim that Jews were powerless when they were without a state and were powerful with it, and will show the flaws of this claim. The next chapter will ask whether the 'new Jew' that Israeli statehood claims to have created really is superior to the 'old Jew', and, thus, whether the implied distinction between 'good Jews' (who are what Jews should be now) and 'bad Jews' who cling to a failed past holds water.

BEYOND EITHER-OR: POWER AND POWERLESSNESS

Biale's work shows that the difference between Jewish statelessness and statehood was nowhere near as stark as Ben-Gurion, Arendt and Selzer had believed.

First, it demonstrates that Jewish statehood in both ancient and modern times never meant that Jews wielded total power over their own destiny. It is questionable whether any state at any time in history has ever enjoyed full control over its fate; even the most powerful states sometimes must adjust what they want to do because other states can thwart them. But the Jewish states of ancient times were particularly limited in their choices; they survived only because they enjoyed the protection of larger and more powerful states. The same is true of the Israeli state today. If the powerful state on whose patronage it relies were to decide that it no longer benefited from protecting the Israeli state, the latter might not survive – just as, in ancient times, Jewish states did not. Jewish sovereignty survives only because it is allowed by another state (or other states).

Second, Biale shows that, contrary to the 'lachrymose' view that suggests that Jews were always on the receiving end of power when they did not have a state, Jews have enjoyed significant control over their own affairs and have been political actors in those many centuries. While the idea of the all-powerful Jew scheming behind the scenes even without holding government office is an anti-Semitic prejudice which has always overestimated Jewish power,[10] Jews were not condemned to do what they were told during the long period in which they did not control a state.

The reality, he writes, 'lies somewhere between Jewish fear and anti-Semitic fantasy'.[11] This is true not only in the post-Enlightenment period when Jews enjoyed – and continue to enjoy – civil and political rights in many countries, but also in the feudal period when Jews were supposedly rightless subjects of royalty and nobility.

On the first score, Biale points out that, in antiquity, when a Jewish state (or, at times, two Jewish states) existed, 'The most important political reality of the ancient Middle East was imperialism.'[12] Small nations could achieve control over their own affairs only at times when the imperial powers declined. This was entirely out of their control and meant that, for very long periods, they had little or no sovereignty because they were obliged to do what the imperial state wanted. Most of the time, 'small nations could not aspire to independence and sought instead to maximize their power by striking advantageous alliances with one of the empires'.[13]

By historical accident, the ancient Jewish kingdoms had some bargaining power because they were located on the borders of imperial realms and could therefore defect from one to the other. But this strength was also a weakness. Precisely because no empire could be entirely sure of the Jewish states' loyalty, they were 'subject to constant suspicion of treason and brutal suppressions of real or imagined revolts'.[14] So, even an advantageous location did not offer real power. It offered merely, at best, the opportunity to do something that some countries in the global South were able to do during the Cold War: to play the imperial blocs off against each other while remaining aware that both had the power to destroy your state. It also threatened great danger, given the constant risk that any of the larger powers might see Jews as disloyal and seek to crush their state.

The modern reality is no different, despite Ben-Gurion's implied claim that the Zionist 'revolution' overthrew Jewish powerlessness. Biale notes that the Israeli state has always required a powerful patron. In the 1950s, France played that role, 'but for most of the history of the Jewish state, it is the alliance between Israel and the United States that has ensured survival'.[15] Readers of the daily news headlines know that the United States is a patron of the Israeli state.[16] Biale suggests that it is unlikely that it would be able to survive very long without US support. While it does have a strong and well-armed military, which might seem to offer the prospect of independence, its fighting forces are heavily reliant on US military assistance and it might be unable to fund its very large army without US economic aid. If we add the protection that it is afforded by a US veto at the United Nations (or one from Britain or France if needs be), we can see that the contemporary Israeli state is not nearly as sovereign as it claims to be. A sharp change in US (and Western) foreign policy – which is always theoretically possible, even if current realities suggest otherwise – might strip the state of much of its power and could doom it. 'Israel is at once a world power and a very small power indeed.'[17]

Ironically, one reason for US support is the actions of Jewish pro-Israeli lobby groups that,[18] while much less representative of Jewish opinion than they claim to be, wield influence even though they are, according to this theory, meant to be powerless outside a Jewish state. The supposed source of Jewish safety, the Israeli state, survives partly or largely because citizenship of democracies elsewhere give some Jews the power to support it and to protect what it sees as its interests. This raises the second issue highlighted by Biale's work – that, in the period when they had no state, Jews were not entirely powerless and dependant on the whims of others.

NOT BY STATES ALONE

Jewish sovereignty, such as it was, ended in 70 CE with the destruction of a temple by the Roman empire. This temple, the second in ancient Jewish history, was the centre of Jewish religious observance at a time when religion played a central role in shaping human identity and underpinning secular power. Its destruction ended the Jewish state which centred around it. Much conventional Jewish history sees this as the beginning of the period of powerlessness. It was not. In reality, it was far more a shift in power within the Jewish community.

Legally, once Rome had destroyed the temple, Judaea, as the Jewish state had been known until then, became a province ruled by the Roman Senate. But the Romans 'still needed a strong Jewish government to control the internal affairs of the people.'[19] This required them to recognise the power of Jewish leadership. Had the temple not been destroyed, the obvious candidates for the ruling group would have been the priests who presided over the temple ritual. But their power had centred on the temple. As it happened, a ready substitute was at hand: the rabbis, religious scholars who studied, interpreted and made Jewish law.

Since they were not only a source of religious authority but lawmakers as well, the rabbis perfectly satisfied the requirements and were recognised by the Romans as the source of Jewish authority. The Sanhedrin (or legislative high court), which had presided during the temple period, was revived.[20] Allowing a dominated people to have their own courts was a tactic sometimes used by colonial or occupying powers who wanted the dominated to play a role in maintaining order.[21] While the rabbis were obviously not free to challenge the Roman Empire, they were the day-to-day source of Jewish law. Students of rabbinic ethical texts know how frequently they contain advice or instruction to judges, which would have made little sense if they were not responsible for the routine adjudication of the common law. The rabbis further entrenched their power as a source of law by forbidding Jews to use non-Jewish courts,[22] a prohibition that would remain in force for centuries. (For observant Orthodox Jews, it still does.)

During the medieval period, Jews were, similarly, able to exercise considerable autonomy despite the fact that they lived in countries governed by others. Medieval Jewish political thought assumed a balance in the relationship between Jewish authorities and the authorities among whom they lived. This was encapsulated in the Talmudic term *dina-de-malkhuta-dina* or 'the law of the kingdom is the law'.[23] Rabbinic authorities defined this phrase in the Talmud, the core Jewish legal text, as the right of the non-Jewish sovereign to impose taxes on the people and to pass land ordinances (since the sovereign was assumed to be the owner of the land). 'In all other areas, the Jewish community presumably retained full jurisdiction. This strict limitation on the power of gentile [non-Jewish] rulers had its basis in the actual privileges the Jews enjoyed, and it persisted throughout the Middle Ages.'[24]

This bargain was, therefore, not simply the product of optimistic musings by the rabbis. It described, Biale shows, the way in which power was exercised through the Middle Ages. Jewish authorities recognised reality – that others held power – and so accepted that this had consequences. They were obliged to pay taxes to the sovereign and, presumably, recognised that it was not politic to side with the ruler's foreign enemies. The reference to land ordinances, of course, also recognised the authority of the sovereign. But, for the rest, Jews governed themselves. For Jews, the 'Middle Ages' was the period in which 'Jews had ceased to have a political center in the Land of Israel but still enjoyed political autonomy and a protected or privileged status in the lands of their dispersion'.[25]

Such an arrangement was made possible by the religious understandings of non-Jewish sovereigns and by the corporate nature of medieval power. On the first score, neither Muslim nor Christian teaching treated Jews as religious equals. Religious tolerance was not a value in this period of history (and, of course, is still not a value to many today). Adherents of religions assumed that theirs was the best and they were not inclined to hide this belief. Christian and Muslim doctrine at the time blamed the Jews for not accepting their teachings. (The Jews, of course, also blamed the others for not accepting *their* teachings but they were not in a position to act on this view.) But for different reasons, the doctrines of Muslims and Christians held that Jews were also to be protected. The Jewish political theology that produced *dina-de-malkhuta-dina* dovetailed neatly with the teachings of those who ruled Jews. In all these understandings, Jews were forced to accept the authority of others but, because they were protected, they also enjoyed considerable autonomy. Later, the principle was cited by some Jews who advocated accommodation with ruling powers even when they enjoyed political rights and when such accommodation violated ethical norms; apartheid laws in South Africa were a case in point. But during the Medieval period, this protection also enabled Jews to exercise political agency by making alliances with the reigning powers – in particular, they were able to 'serve the needs of new and rising forces in society' and so to form alliances with new elites.[26]

These alliances often enabled Jews to win privileges that refute the notion that they were subject only to grim repression. There are many examples to illustrate this point. Given the 'new anti-Semitism' writers' lack of enthusiasm for peace, they would, no doubt, be pleasantly surprised that these examples include the right to bear arms. It was because of these privileges that the thirteenth-century rabbi and poet, Meir of Rothenburg, was able to write: 'Jews are not subjugated to their overlords as the Gentiles are … The status of the Jew in this land is that of a free landowner who lost his [sic] land but did not lose his personal liberty.'[27]

Jews also exercised power both as individuals and as a community. On the first score, we have already mentioned Shmuel ha-Nagid who held high political office in Muslim Spain. He was not alone; other Jewish luminaries of the time also held government office during the period of Muslim rule and some Jews wielded influence in government. This period in Jewish history has, however, been romanticised. As noted earlier, the notion of equal rights across religious barriers was unknown at the time and so Jews did not enjoy the same legal status as Muslims. They were also, at times, victims of violent attacks, although these were not initiated by the authorities. But even an author sceptical of the degree of harmony between Jews and Muslims in Spain at that time acknowledges that access to the Arabic language gave Jews 'entrance to the corridors of Muslim power' and that the period of Muslim rule was generally marked by 'Jewish-Muslim coexistence'.[28]

In several Western European states, Jews were not given national government office but were, at least up to the fifteenth century, treated as full citizens who sometimes held municipal office and helped to defend the town from attack. An Italian jurist of the time observed: 'Jews are considered to be of the same people and of the [political] body of the same city, although they may not be considered members of the same spiritual body.'[29] They also exercised collective power. In Eastern Europe, for example, the Jewish authority for Poland and neighbouring areas, called the Council of the Four Lands, not only wielded considerable authority over Jews but also routinely lobbied the Polish parliament – often with great effect. One Jewish historian claimed that the council was so effective that it did not allow any laws unfavourable to Jews to be passed.[30] Even if this is an exaggeration, the council played much the same role as effective lobby groups do in legislative politics today and was, at times, able to influence decisions.

This was possible because of the way in which non-religious power was exercised in that period. Jews enjoyed no individual rights in the Middle Ages, but neither did anyone else; the concept of individual rights emerged in the eighteenth century and was incorporated, at least formally, into law by the French and American revolutions. But groups, including ethnic groups, did enjoy rights. 'It was entirely consistent for medieval political theory to grant discrete corporations, and especially separate ethnic groups, rights of internal self-government.'[31] The power Jewish authorities enjoyed was extensive – 'Their legal jurisdiction often extended far beyond religion and philanthropy to full control over civil and criminal law in cases involving only Jews.'[32] In Western Europe, according to Salo Baron, Jews enjoyed greater communal autonomy than the cities they inhabited.[33]

The medieval order in which this was possible was therefore one in which the power of central authorities – monarchs, usually – was limited by the prerogatives of the groups over which they ruled. It was replaced by the absolutist state in which power was centralised.[34] This spelled the end of the communal power that Jews had enjoyed and ushered in a period in which they were far more likely to be herded into segregated ghettos, expelled from their countries or subjected to legal discrimination and violence. But this may have had far less to do with, as the 'lachrymose' view insisted, eternal hatred of the Jews than it did with the desire of absolutist states to eliminate any communal power that stood in their way. There were certainly some absolutist rulers who were hostile to Jews but 'they were hostile to any power concentrations outside of their immediate grasp'.[35] Absolutism made Jews' lives worse not because their statelessness meant that they were doomed to be subjugated but because it was a political order which was threatened by group power. And it did not show that Jews were doomed to be oppressed by the lack of a state, but that some forms of government discriminated against Jews and some did not.

While absolutism was, in general, very unfavourable to Jews, some absolutist rulers also removed the disabilities to which Jews had been subject. Perhaps the best-known example is Napoleon Bonaparte, who told Jewish leaders that they were to be regarded as full citizens in France but that they would have to renounce their separate communal institutions. This approach was famously summed up in 1789 by Clermont-Tonnerre, a delegate to the Estates General: 'But, they say to me, the Jews have their own judges and laws. I respond that is your fault and you should not allow it. We must refuse everything to the Jews as a nation and accord everything to Jews as individuals.'[36] This has been interpreted, accurately, by some historians as an attempt to deprive Jews of their own institutions. But the goal was not to suppress a particular identity – as the reference to judges shows, it was to suppress separate institutions. This was not, of course, a benign view; it has been used in contemporary France to ban public expression of religion, mainly by Muslims.

Napoleon was no democrat, but the fact that Jews were asked to make this choice after the French Revolution indicated another reason why the claim that Jewish statelessness was a recipe for automatic subjugation misunderstands history: the absolutist state in Western Europe and North America became the democratic state in which Jews, like all others, were granted full citizenship rights. Democratic states were not necessarily free of discrimination against Jews. In France, in the last years of the nineteenth century, the Dreyfus affair,[37] which profoundly influenced some Zionists, suggested that Jews did not always enjoy in practice the rights that they had been granted in theory. Dreyfus was a French army captain wrongly convicted of treason. He was exonerated only after a public campaign on his behalf. His ordeal was widely attributed to the prevalence of anti-Semitism in the French military.[38] In other Western democracies, there was, for example, a limit to the number of Jews admitted to some universities.[39] But no legal restrictions or disabilities were placed on Jews and it was democratic rights which enabled the campaign that corrected the injustice visited on Dreyfus. Despite the prejudices that existed, Jews were neither powerless nor oppressed, a statement that cannot be made about certain other groups, such as black people in the United States. Democracy has protected Jews far more effectively than any ethnic state has. In no democracy were Jews denied full civil rights; it was only when democracy had collapsed, most notoriously in Germany in the 1930s, that Jews faced peril.

The 'destiny' that Ben-Gurion sought to escape was not nearly as oppressive as he – and the Zionist movement – had implied. While Zionism sought to portray the history of Jews as an endless chronicle of powerlessness and prejudice from the fall of the ancient Jewish state to the founding of the modern Israeli state, history was a great deal more complex. And it provided no evidence for the claim that Jews could not exercise power over their lives unless they had a state.

A DISTINCTION, NOT A DIFFERENCE

It is important to clarify what this brief history does and does not show.

It does not show that Jews were, after 70 CE, an empowered people guaranteed a safe existence, or that the slaughters and the legal disabilities stressed by the 'lachrymose' view were unfortunate blips on an otherwise placid screen. The medieval bargain described here was not able to save thousands of Jews from being murdered in the Crusades. The autonomy that Jews had enjoyed in the medieval period was largely obliterated by the absolutist state, whose effects were felt deep into the twentieth century. In the non-democracies of Eastern Europe, where many Jews lived, Jews remained targets of discriminatory law and policy. When the fragile post-World War One German democracy collapsed, Jews were unable to prevent an attempted genocide that killed millions of them.

What it *does* show is that the Zionist assumption which underpins the view of the apostles of the 'new anti-Semitism', that the 'old Jew' without a state was powerless while the 'new Jew' with one is powerful, is false; the distinction between the power which is said to come from controlling a state and the powerlessness of lacking one is a misreading of history. Jews in the two millennia in which they were stateless sometimes exercised real power. On the other hand, and despite appearances to the contrary, the contemporary Israeli state is not as powerful as it believes it is; it survives only at the behest of another state. The nub of the issue is expressed by Biale (who, it must be noted, does not appear to be an anti-Zionist): 'The restrictions imposed on the sovereignty of small states have forced Israel to relate to the non-Jewish powers in ways similar to those adopted by medieval Jews. In order to assure its survival, the state must follow a medieval strategy of alliance with those in power.'[40] So, the state that was meant to rebel against 'destiny' by ensuring a power that statelessness is said to have denied Jews turns out to be subject to precisely the same calculations as the stateless Jews: it must make accommodations with the powerful so that it can retain the right to govern itself. Jewish statehood is thus no greater protection against anti-Semitism than statelessness was. While it is an article of faith among Zionists that the Nazi genocide was possible only because of Jewish statelessness, the millions of Slavs who the Nazis killed were helped not at all by the fact that they did have their own states.[41] The claim that the existence of the Israeli state protects Jews from the violent effects of anti-Jewish racism is a core article of Zionist faith. But there is no reason why an ethnic nationalist Jewish state should be any better at protecting Jews than the functioning democracies where millions of Jews found refuge from the Nazis. A world so hostile to Jews that no state would offer them refuge would presumably not tolerate a Jewish state for long.

Democracy has offered Jews more safety and personal autonomy than an ethnic nationalist state can. In practice, democracies around the globe – from France to India – have not discriminated against Jews. Where there is anti-Jewish racism in these societies, it is not imposed by the law but perpetrated by racist individuals. This is why Jews who were able to escape Nazi rule and move to democratic societies were able to survive and, often, to flourish. The point holds by definition: democracies are democratic only if they respect the rights of all citizens and grant them equal rights regardless of race, ethnicity or faith. As long as a state remains democratic, Jews are safe. Protecting democracy is thus a more credible strategy for Jewish survival than an ethnic state.

The difference between Jewish self-government in the Middle Ages and Jewish statehood in the twentieth and twenty-first centuries is, at most, one of degree. The much-vaunted difference between statehood and statelessness dissolves in the knowledge that the similarity between the two outweighs the differences. If there is little or no difference between the circumstances of the 'new Jew' after 1948 and the 'old Jew' before it, the rationale for discarding the 'old Jew' for the 'new' also dissolves. History reveals that the redefinition of anti-Semitism that stems from exaltation of the 'new Jew' and demonisation of the 'old' is an excuse to justify the power of a governing elite and its patrons.

But there is another way in which the distinction between the 'new' or 'good' Jew and the 'old' or 'bad' Jew is not what the redefiners of anti-Semitism claim. There is an important sense in which the purported attempt to assert 'real' Jewishness – by consigning Jews opposed to racism and violence to the historical scrap heap – is the opposite of what it claims to be. The Israeli state and its 'good Jew' supporters may be an expression not of Jewish selfhood but of precisely the opposite. It is to this argument that we now turn.

5

Zionism as an Escape from Jewishness

A common way in which 'good Jews' place 'bad Jews' beyond the pale is by labelling them 'self-hating'.

The obvious implication is that the 'self-hater' loathes the fact that they were born Jewish and that others see them as Jews. A scholar who acknowledges that the term is used 'to silence and discredit' says that it is aimed at 'those Jews whose overly unfavorable attitudes toward their Jewish heritage or overly favorable attitudes toward non-Jewish culture allegedly threaten the survival or well-being of Judaism and Jewry'.[1] He adds that authors – including the pioneering psychoanalyst Sigmund Freud and the philosophers Hannah Arendt and Jean-Paul Sartre – 'basically agree that self-hating Jews regard negatively all or some aspect of Jewish identity, including their own, in terms acquired from a dominant, non-Jewish, culture in which mistaken and malicious perceptions of Jews and Judaism prevail'.[2] The term is as much an accusation as a description. Mick Finlay, a social psychologist, notes that it 'is often used rhetorically to discount Jews who differ in their lifestyles, interests or political positions from their accusers'.[3]

The 'self-hating' Jew is the 'bad Jew' in purest form: she or he is Jewish in the eyes of others but not themselves. It follows from this that the 'good

Jew' is the genuine article, the 'real Jew', and that the 'bad Jew' is trying to opt out of Jewishness. In this view, the 'self-hating' or 'bad' Jew would be much like the black person discussed by Fanon who feels inferior because they internalise the prejudices of white racism. 'The feeling of inferiority of the colonized is the correlative to the European's feeling of superiority.'[4] Understood in this way, the 'self-hating Jews' respond and act much as people classified as 'coloured' by apartheid who tried to pass for white. They seek to be as much like the dominating group as possible to integrate into the dominant society.

But the term 'self-hating' is currently used not to describe Jews who reject Jewish culture or the Jewish religion; it is used as a stick with which to beat Jews who reject the Israeli state or its actions even if, like Diana Neslen (see chapter 2), they identify very strongly with Jewishness. Jews like her – who are the opposite of those who suffer from an inferiority complex because of the identity into which they are born, but who reject the Israeli state – are 'self-haters' by this new definition. Jews who reject all Jewish religious and cultural practices are not, provided that they support the Israeli state. Similarly, white Afrikaners who rejected apartheid were liable to be labelled 'traitors' to their people, even if they embraced their Afrikaner heritage.

Zionists thus label anti-Zionist Jews as people ashamed of their Jewishness, but regard Zionists as people who eagerly embrace theirs. This is a view often shared by people who are not Jewish. Even if they do not negatively judge anyone who rejects the Israeli state, they may well assume that those who hold this view are 'less Jewish' than those who support it and its actions.

But what if the reverse was true? What if, in reality, the 'good Jews', the aggressive Zionists, were the ones who rejected Jewishness while the 'bad Jews' embraced it? Precisely this argument is made in an important book by Daniel Boyarin, a scholar of the Jewish religion.[5] In a startling but convincing response to the charge of 'self-hatred', he uses the writings of two Zionist intellectuals to demonstrate that it is the Zionists, not their opponents, who are the 'self-haters' who want desperately not to be Jewish.

'LIKE ALL THE NATIONS'

The two thinkers who Boyarin discusses are Sigmund Freud and Theodor Herzl, the founder of political Zionism. Both lived and worked in Vienna at the turn of the twentieth century.

While Freud was an avid Zionist, he played no leadership role in the Zionist movement and so he might, perhaps, be dismissed as a marginal figure whose ideas played no role in influencing others to embrace the idea of a Jewish state. But Boyarin shows that there was a close affinity between the thought of Freud and of Herzl – who was as mainstream to Zionism as it is possible to be. Their view was also shared by other Zionist thinkers.

Boyarin takes the title of his book from Freud's account of an incident in Vienna when he was a child. He recalled walking with his father when he was accosted by anti-Semitic bullies who taunted his Jewishness and, to show who was boss, knocked his hat off his head. Freud Senior picked up the hat and scurried off with his son, avoiding confrontation with the bullies. Freud viewed his father's behaviour as 'unheroic conduct'. As Boyarin notes, the actions of Freud Senior showed, for his son, 'his passivity in the face of the virile Aryan'.[6] He cites a study of Freud's Jewish identity which observed: 'If he had to have a Jewish father, little Sigmund would at least have wanted him to be a man proud of his race, a bold warrior'.[7] The incident played a crucial role in reinforcing Freud's Zionism.

Freud's reaction to this humiliation summed up the concerns of the early Zionists. None of them identified strongly as Jewish – they neither followed the Jewish religion nor did they embrace mainstream European Jewish culture, and they despised those Jews who did. They tried to blend into the dominant culture and felt that they had been rebuffed because of their Jewishness; their ethnic identity was thus a source of embarrassment, not of pride. They were influenced by the Dreyfus case because the central character of that incident had tried to absorb himself into a core institution of non-Jewish France, the army, and had been rejected.

While Freud and Herzl considered themselves Jewish nationalists, neither much liked Jews. Freud's Jewish hero was the Prophet Moses, about whom he wrote an idiosyncratic book, *Moses and Monotheism,*[8] but for a reason that reveals Freud's political and social agenda. In the Hebrew Bible, Moses spent much of his time upbraiding the Jewish people for their unfaithfulness to God. Moses was also brought up by an Egyptian princess. Freud combines these two points to conclude that Moses, too, did not like Jews and that he may well have been an Egyptian. In a 1933 letter, he wrote: 'Our great leader Moses was, after all, a vigorous antisemite, and he makes no secret of this. Perhaps he was an Egyptian.'[9] In *Moses and Monotheism,* he points out, correctly, that Moses was an Egyptian name, then goes on to suggest that any author who knew this 'would have drawn the conclusion, or at least considered the possibility, that the bearer of an Egyptian name was himself an Egyptian'.[10] He develops this point through the book. Given Freud's admiration for the 'great leader' Moses, he obviously has no problem with the prophet's purported anti-Semitism. His insistence that Moses was not Jewish suggests that, to Freud, his 'greatness' was – at least partly – due to his (equally purported) non-Jewish origins.

Herzl shared Freud's prejudice. In 1882, he agreed with the anti-Semite Eugen Dühring that Jews were crooked, lacked moral seriousness and were parasites. 'His only disagreement with Dühring was that while the former considered these to be biological characteristics of the Jews, Herzl considered them entirely the product of the Jewish environment.'[11] For the founder of the 'Jewish national movement', Jews were a grubby and disreputable bunch, degraded by the circumstances in which they lived. That was not the only common ground between early Zionists and anti-Semites. We saw in chapter 3 that the notion that Jews are a 'race' was supported by the pioneers of biological anti-Semitism and rejected by their critics. But 'prominent Zionists such as Max Nordau and Arthur Ruppin ... explicitly conceptualised Jews as a race and presented

Zionism as an exercise in racial purity'. Israel, one critique argues, 'both ethnicizes – and indeed racializes' Jews.[12]

Why did Jews so repulse the early Zionists? As the incident that inspired Boyarin's book title suggests, one source of shame was that they endorsed the anti-Semitic prejudice that Jews were weak and 'womanly', not 'real men'. The primary Jewish role model in the more traditional communities of Eastern Europe was the religious scholar, a role available only to men. While other cultures enabled the domination of men by barring women from the professions or from economic activity, the dominant Jewish culture ensured male dominance by reserving the role of religious scholar for men only. Not only was the scholar a prized marriage partner (marriages were usually arranged and parents did whatever they could to marry their daughters to scholars), but women who were married to scholars were expected to earn the family income so that their husbands were free to study. Viewed from the perspective of secular culture today, this created the impression that Jewish society was startlingly egalitarian since women were free to ply the trades and play the economic roles denied to them by other cultures. But it remained a system of male domination. Boyarin points out that religious study was the most prized and respected activity in Jewish communities and so women were denied the right to do what most mattered to the society in which they lived.[13]

For those among whom they lived, however, this apparent inversion of gender roles ensured that Jewish men were labelled as effeminate 'sissies' who pored over their books while the women engaged in the 'manly' pursuits of doing business for profit. This stereotype said more about the aspirations of Jewish communities than about their lived experience. Only a few men could become scholars; the rest were forced to earn their living as scholars' wives did. Challenging this way of life became a key pre-occupation of early Zionists. They portrayed study of the Hebrew Bible and of the Talmud, the books in which rabbis debate religious law and its meaning, as degraded and degrading since it kept men from being 'real men'. For Herzl, the Talmud was 'the product of an unnatural, imposed isolation from the mainstream of humanity, the pathetic consolation of distressed spirits'.[14] Since the Talmud had stood at the centre of the dominant Jewish culture for a millennium, Herzl's sentiment displayed deep contempt for centuries of mainstream Jewish belief and life.

There were other reasons, which did reflect Jewish lived experience, for which Jews were not considered 'manly' by those around them. The rise of the absolutist state ended the right of Jews to bear arms and, by the time that Zionism arrived, Jews had been barred from armies for centuries. They had also not been permitted, until the Enlightenment, to own land. They had thus been excluded from the 'manly' pursuits of making war and farming. And, as Freud's father's 'unheroic conduct' showed, Jews reacted to being dominated as all dominated people tend to do: they assumed that their dominators were far stronger than they and were willing and able to punish them severely if they challenged their domination. And so they adjusted to their subordination rather than challenge it. If their hats were knocked off their heads by their dominators, they collected them from the ground and went on their way, and so remained alive.[15]

This clearly marked Jewish men as weak and passive in the eyes of those among whom they lived, and in the eyes of the Zionists. One of the most influential early Zionist thinkers, Max Nordau, wanted Zionism to create 'a new muscle Jew' who would fight battles rather than run from them. Even the bodies of most Jews (or, at least, most Jewish men) were to him a sign of deformity and decay.[16] Herzl was a great admirer of duelling, in which men protected their honour by engaging in gun or sword fights. His Zionist state, he wrote, would need duelling because it would then have 'real officers' and it would 'impart a tone of French refinement to good society'.[17] In a play that he wrote, *The New Ghetto*, the Jewish hero – modelled on Herzl himself – faced rejection from a non-Jewish friend who was repulsed by his Jewish family and friends, but the hero won back his friend's respect when he was fatally wounded in a duel.[18] Fanon would have recognised this immediately; the hero (and thus Herzl) was worthy of respect only if he rejected who he was (more accurately, who the dominant culture said he was) and especially if he obliged the dominator by dying in the process.

Zionist dissatisfaction with Jews was not only a Viennese neurosis; it was a mainstream Zionist view regardless of origin. Another example was the Russian-born pioneer of labour Zionism, Aaron David Gordon, whose utopian mysticism suggested very different concerns to Freud's and Herzl's. Yet he found most Jews as disturbing as they did. He regarded rural labour as the key to curing Jews of their attachment to the urban life that had cut them off from the soil.[19] According to Gordon,

> We [Jews] are a parasitic people. We have no roots in the soil, there is no ground beneath our feet. And we are parasites not only in an economic sense, but in spirit, in thought, in poetry, in literature, and in our virtues, our ideals, our higher human aspirations. Every alien movement sweeps us along, every wind in the world carries us. We in ourselves are almost non-existent, so of course we are nothing in the eyes of other people either.[20]

This view that Jews' lack of a connection to the soil diminished their human worth was a common anti-Semitic theme. Stalin's Soviet government, for example, called Jewish intellectuals 'rootless cosmopolitans' to question their loyalty to the Soviet state.[21] Implicit in the insult was the notion that Jews were cut off from the soil (hence 'rootless'), a view with which Gordon would heartily agree.

But there was more to Zionist distaste of most of their fellow Jews than a desire to turn them into soldiers and farmers. They found Jews grubby and degraded and the European culture amidst which they lived noble and refined. (Hence Herzl's desire to encourage duelling as an entrée into 'good society'.)

THE ENEMY WITHIN

Contempt for Jewish experience crystallised into a core Zionist principle: 'negation of the diaspora' (Jews who live outside the Israeli state).

This means far more than encouraging Jews to live in the Israeli state. It frames Jewish life without a state as degraded and shameful and 'excludes almost half of the Jewish people and a myriad of Jewish ideologies that have flourished since the advent of modernity'.[22] It also rejects the dominant form of Jewish life and the Jews who lived it for almost two millennia, and so could be seen as deeply anti-Semitic. It is, therefore, no accident, as the Israeli historian Zeev Sternhell pointed out, that Zionism endorsed most assumptions of European anti-Semitism. For Sternhell, 'negation of the diaspora' and the contempt for Jewish life which it required was not an incidental or marginal feature of Zionist thinking. It was central and inevitable. 'A hatred of the diaspora and a rejection of Jewish life there were a kind of methodological necessity for Zionism … Not only was Jewish history in exile deemed to be unimportant, but the value of living Jews, Jews of flesh and blood, depended entirely on their use as raw material for national revival.'[23]

Real Jews and the lives they lived were not only shameful, they were of no consequence unless they could serve the nationalist project, which meant serving the state after it was established. 'National revival' is assumed to be possible only if Jews cease to be Jewish, at least as most Jews understood being Jewish for almost 20 centuries. There are striking similarities between this view and the idolatry against which the Biblical Hebrew prophets inveighed because it requires people to worship a fetish created by human beings – the nation and the state, in this case – which they then invest with Divine power.[24] Since traditional Jewish belief is founded on a rejection of idolatry, Zionists, in effect, embraced that which Jews were taught to reject.

This disjuncture is not only one between Jewish life before the state was formed and after it; it is also one between Jewish life on the rest of the planet and Zionist concerns, despite the fact that official Jewish leaderships outside the state are always vocal and uncritical supporters of the Israeli state, whatever the communities they claim to represent think. The Israeli activist Jeff Halper quotes polling data to show the disparity between actual Jewish life outside the Israeli state and the assumptions of the state and its supporters. American Jews, by far the largest Jewish community outside the Israeli state and of roughly the same size as the Israeli Jewish population, are, surveys show, 'largely defined by social justice, a commitment to civil and human rights, a general liberalism, which they identify as part of their Jewish heritage. Indeed, Jews are the most liberal American ethnic community, 76% defining themselves as liberal or moderate, only 21% as conservative.'[25] These attitudes contrast sharply with those of the Israeli state's Jewish citizenry.

While Jewish citizens of the Israeli state supported Trump in overwhelming numbers, only one in five American Jewish voters backed him. 'The Democratic Party's model of inclusive citizenship fits American Jewish aspirations to cultivate a cultural and religious minority identity alongside civic participation ... The Republican Party's overwhelmingly white Christian character, on the other hand, is far less accommodating.'[26] As noted earlier, while mainstream Jewish organisations in the US support the Israeli state, Jewish public opinion has become far more critical, with more than a fifth of young American Jews (under the age of forty) rejecting a state for Jews only.[27] Furthermore, about half the members of US organisations that support the Palestinian Boycott, Divestment and Sanctions campaign (BDS) are Jewish.[28] The worldview of the vast majority of American Jews is therefore fundamentally at odds with the values of the Israeli state.

This contradiction between the values of a state that portrays itself as the sole vehicle of Jews and Jewishness and those of a very large part of the Jewish people can be resolved only if two conditions are met. First, the expectation that Jews bury their beliefs when they respond to the Israeli state and, second, the demonisation of those who decline to put their principles on hold. The latter then become the 'bad Jews'. (The contradiction also sharply brings into question Netanyahu's claim, on a visit to France, that he was the 'representative of the entire Jewish people'.[29]) In a sense, then, the difference between 'good' and 'bad' Jews today is not new. Because Zionism has always seen Jews who do not live in or loudly support the Israeli state as unworthy fossils, it has always rested on distinguishing between 'good' and 'bad' Jews.

This contempt for the diaspora also manifested, for many Zionists, as derision directed at the Nazi death camps' victims who, they claimed, had simply submitted to the power of Hitler's state and had been led, meekly, like 'sheep to slaughter'.[30] The claim was both untrue, since there were significant cases of Jewish resistance, and deeply insensitive to the very restricted choices of people subjected to overwhelming military power backed by unrelenting hatred. But it suited the Zionist view of the world because it strengthened the false claim that Jews could protect themselves only if they had a state. It also reinforced the notion of the 'diaspora Jew' as a lesser form of Jew compared to those who relied on states and armies. The word most commonly used to describe Nazi mass murder, the Holocaust, reflects this Zionist bias. In the Hebrew Bible, a holocaust is the burning of an animal sacrificed to God. To describe the slaughter of Europe's Jews as a holocaust, then, portrays it as a (voluntary) sacrifice by the victims, so confirming the false notion that they offered themselves up for slaughter. It is, thus, far more accurate and appropriate to describe that period for what it was – the Nazi genocide.

Despite the Israeli state's dependence on the United States, the view that the millions of Jews living outside the state are of no account except inasmuch as they can serve it (either by supporting it or emigrating to it) remains very much alive. 'For Israeli society, the "diaspora" is a dead place. It is telling that the only state-sanctioned foreign trip for Jewish students in Israel is not to meet fellow Jews in New York or Paris, but to Auschwitz. Israel sees itself as the only viable place for Judaism to exist, and its narrow definition of Judaism as the only one worthy of legitimacy.'[31] By imposing the view that Jewish life can be lived out only through the state, it seeks to alter that identity. The debates over whether Jewishness is about religion or ethnicity are at an end; it is really about fealty to a state.

Since the Israeli state and its allies now define anti-Semitism as antipathy to the state, not to Jews, and since some of their firmest allies are anti-Semites, it follows logically that Jews who fall victim to racial bigotry cannot rely on the Israeli state for support. After all, it did not complain when its ally, Donald Trump (after whom a planned Israeli settlement on land seized from Syria has been named),[32] claimed that there were 'very fine people' among white supremacists who chanted 'Jews will not replace us'.[33] In Hungary, 'Netanyahu told his ambassador not to get involved when the Jews there were enduring an anti-Semitic campaign.'[34] It therefore seems plausible to assume that 'if a wave of anti-Semitism arose tomorrow … and Israel had a close relationship with the regime where that was happening, the Jews there might be abandoned to their fate'.[35] All this is entirely consistent with the attitude that Sternhell analyses. The 'Jewish state' is all-important; Jews exist only to serve it. If they must endure bigotry in its interests, so be it. The self-proclaimed cure for anti-Semitism is now its accomplice.

It is only a short conceptual step from despising 'diaspora Jews' to expressing the same contempt for Jews who live in the Israeli state but who criticise the denial of Palestinian rights – thus identifying themselves as weak, humanist, 'diaspora Jews'. This explains why some Zionists have demonised the human rights movement inside the state in crudely anti-Semitic terms. Tzipi Hotovely, the Israeli state's ambassador to the United Kingdom at the time of writing, made a campaign video for her bid to win primary elections for Netanyahu's Likud Party that depicted her leading 'A war on [the group] Breaking the Silence'. Its members are caricatured lamenting their loss of funding thus: 'Oy vey! My German Euros!'[36] Breaking the Silence is an organisation of Jewish Israelis who served in the state's army and are dedicated to exposing its abuses of Palestinian rights. 'Oy vey' (O woe) is an expression in Yiddish, a language of the Jewish 'diaspora'. It is, presumably, used to portray Breaking the Silence's members as 'diaspora Jews' who should, of course, be negated. The claim that the organisation is motivated not by concern for humanity but by a desire for money repeats a standard anti-Semitic slur – that Jews are motivated by lust for money. The founder of the British Institute for Jewish Policy Research, Antony Lerman, said the video contained 'an anti-Semitic trope'. Dena Shunra, a writer and Hebrew translator, said it was 'the most antiSemitic trope I've seen today, and that's saying something'.[37] Had a non-Jew produced the video, there is no doubt that it would have – correctly – been denounced as crude anti-Semitism.

But Hotovely's video is not the most extreme example of Zionist anti-Semitism. In 2017, Adam Milstein, a businessman and supporter of the Israeli state, depicted the Jewish financier and philanthropist George Soros, a favourite target of the right, as an octopus with his tentacles circling the globe.[38] The claim that Jews use money to advance their quest for world domination is a standard anti-Semitic theme that was central to Nazi ideology. But even this could not compete with the Samaria Residents Council, which receives Israeli government funding and represents settlers in the territories occupied by the Israeli state in 1967; these settlements are widely regarded as a breach of international law.

The council produced an animated video whose main character, presumably meant to represent Jewish critics of the Israeli state's expansion into territory outside its original borders, was an 'ugly, big-nosed' man named only as 'Ze Jew', who 'by turns rubs his hands, passes over a video tape dripping with blood and looks around the room with shifty eyes'. At the end of the clip, he takes his own life.[39] The clip is titled *The Eternal Jew*, which is also the title of one of Nazism's most notorious anti-Semitic propaganda films; it claimed that there was a Jewish-Bolshevik conspiracy to achieve world domination.[40] The title was fitting since the clip's portrayal of a Jewish character echoed in content and form the Nazi depiction of Jews. The only change is that the stereotyped Jew is an enemy not of Aryan civilisation but of the Israeli state's territorial expansion. The *+972 Magazine* Israeli website said it may have been 'the most anti-Semitic Israeli cartoon ever made'.[41] The settlers who made the clip, however, were unrepentant. They accused their critics of being 'upset because they do not like what they look like in the mirror'.[42] The makers of the 1930s original would, no doubt, have said the same.

Similarly, a vice president of the liberal Zionist New Israel Fund, Libby Lenkinski, described how Netanyahu and his allies launched an attack on left-wing NGOs and human rights defenders that used the tactics, imagery, and language from classic European antisemitism, the kind that killed my ancestors. They put up billboards and newspaper ads with New Israel Fund President Naomi Chazan's face featuring an elongated, exaggerated nose and a horn coming out of her forehead. They developed elaborate conspiracy theories about progressive philanthropists like George Soros, and they began to accuse Jewish Israeli human rights defenders like me of being traitors and double-agents. These are classic tropes: dehumanization and demonization of Jews, accusing us of being untrustworthy, disloyal and all-powerful masterminds behind the struggles of other 'others.'[43]

Since the New Israel Fund supports the notion of a Jewish state, the definition of 'bad Jew' has, it seems, been extended to supporters of the state who also want it to respect United Nations resolutions.

ACHIEVING DOMINANCE

Ironically, Boyarin points out, the early Zionist contempt for real, live Jews – which hardened into the 'negation of the diaspora' – was very similar to that of Christian reformers of the time who wanted to cure Jews of their Jewishness so that they could join polite society. As chapter 4 showed, the period after the French Revolution placed Jewish emancipation on the European agenda. Napoleon and Clermont-Tonnerre wanted Jews to give up their separate institutions to become full citizens; liberal Christians wanted them to give up their way of life.

As opposed to racist antisemites who claimed that what was wrong with the Jews was biological and immutable, the 'liberals' held that everything despicable about the Jews in their eyes was a product of the material conditions with which Jews had to live and, especially, the oppression that they had suffered at the hands of Christians. A further cause of the degraded and decadent state of the Jews was their hanging onto a primitive and 'Oriental' way of life.[44]

These liberals may have rejected anti-Semites' claim that Jews were doomed to remain 'uncivilised' but they agreed that this was what Jews were. The solution was for Jews to give up their way of life and become 'civilised'. Boyarin notes a parallel between a book advocating this, liberal historian Christian Wilhelm von Dohm's 1781 text *Concerning the Amelioration of the Civil Status of the Jews*, and Thomas Macaulay's notorious 1835 document 'Minute on Indian Education'. Macaulay, a British politician and colonial administrator in India, argued in his 'Minute' that colonial education should produce people who would be 'Indian in blood and colour, but English in taste, in opinions, in morals and in intellect'.[45]

As we will shortly see, the plan to turn Indians into English people was partially successful. Herzl may not have known about Macaulay's document but he echoed it; hence his agreement with Dühring about the Jews' many negative qualities and his disdain for the core Jewish religious text, the Talmud. The only difference between his and the Christian reformers' views is that they saw political reform and 'education' as the cure while his antidote was a Jewish state. One of Herzl's biographers thus notes: 'In emphasizing Judaism's Oriental character and foreignness to Europe, Herzl was closer to anti-Jewish polemicists.'[46] Given this, it is perhaps no surprise that Herzl was not only a firm admirer of the operas of Wagner but also credited the composer and his work with inspiring his Zionism. Wagner, as we have seen, was an anti-Semite who inspired Chamberlain. Herzl wrote that while he was writing his Zionist tract *The Jewish State*, his only relaxation in the evenings was listening to 'Wagnerian music', especially his opera *Tannhauser,* which, like all Wagner's major works, was based on German legend. 'Only on those evenings, where there was no opera production, did I feel doubts about the correctness of my thoughts.'[47] Wagner's exaltation of Germanic culture was more than a musical preference for Herzl; it was what convinced him that he was right to advocate a Jewish state.

For both Dohm and Herzl, the fundamental problem with Jews was that their lifestyle was not that of white Christian Europeans.[48] If the Jews were to win acceptance, they would need to be like their European neighbours. When Herzl recalled that Wagner's music convinced him of the 'correctness' of his ideas, there is no suggestion that he was so horrified by the composer's anti-Semitism that he concluded that Jews would never fit into European society; his enthusiasm for Wagner's work is clear. His inspiration was his fervent hope that Jews would one day be like the heroes and heroines of Wagner's operas, heroic Aryans. And he was convinced that the Jewish state about which he wrote during the day would enable Jews to achieve the cultural 'heights' scaled by the operas to which he listened at night. The purpose of the state was not to escape German culture – it was to enable Jews to become Germans. 'For Herzl, Jewish distinctiveness and disfigurement were one and the same.'[49]

Freud shared this horror at Jewish difference. So important was this matter that it was at the heart of a dream that Freud discussed in his work and which has been much analysed by Freud scholars. Dreams play a crucial role in Freud's psycho-analytical theory. They may, he believed, be the key to our deepest emotions and thoughts. This, of course, gives his dream added importance. Freud called it 'My Son, the Myops …' and, significantly, he recalls dreaming it on an evening on which he had seen Herzl's *The New Ghetto*,[50] whose key message was that, although physical and legislative walls between Jews and Germans had broken down, spiritual, cultural and social barriers remained.

There are several aspects to the dream but the one that most concerns us here is that it begins in Rome with Freud needing to remove his children to safety. In his discussion of his dream, Freud noted the connection with Herzl's play and adds that the dream was obviously prompted by 'the Jewish problem' and 'concern about the future of one's children, to whom one cannot give a country of their own, concern about educating them in such a way that they can move freely across frontiers'.[51] There is nothing in Herzl's play that complains that Jews were likely to be forced to flee; its message was that they were now physically safe. But frontiers were important to its theme. Jews, it claimed, were unable to move freely across cultural, spiritual and social frontiers into the non-Jewish world. A further aspect of the dream is that Freud recalls being in front of a gateway, 'double doors in the ancient style'. The gates were, he says, those of the Porta Romana in Siena, portals in its medieval walls. But the German word he uses to describe the doors, *Tore*, is, Boyarin observes, 'a typical dream-work pun on the word *Torah*', which means Jewish religious teaching.[52] In Freud's theory, puns may reflect a person's subconscious thoughts.

If we consider all this together, Boyarin argues convincingly, we realise that Jews are, in Freud's subconscious, hemmed in by the gates of their religious teachings and culture (by *Torah*). The freedom to move that he wishes for his children is not a physical freedom; it is, rather, the freedom to move beyond the gates of tradition into the dominant culture. 'The phrase reflects Freud's conflicted desire to educate his children in such a way that the borders between them and the [dominant culture] would be broken down, that they would be able to freely cross that frontier – whether by conversion or, more likely, by assimilation.'[53] For Freud, Zionism is assimilation. It is the process of ceasing to be Jewish (and, thus, hemmed in by *Torah)* without actually converting to Christianity, the dominant religion in German-speaking Europe.

It was assimilation for Herzl too. Before he set his mind on Zionism as his way out of the ghetto, he had advocated mass Jewish conversion to Christianity, a plan that he had wanted to propose to the Pope.[54] His novel *Altneuland* pictures the Jewish state as a Middle Eastern Germany or Austria whose citizens speak not only Hebrew and Yiddish but German too (and, of course, duel). Its citizens are given, as are the German middle and upper classes of Herzl's day, to attending the theatre or opera. Its two lead characters are a Jewish intellectual (Herzl himself) and a Prussian nobleman.[55] Despite some concessions to Jewishness as it was understood in his milieu, Herzl sees the Jewish state essentially as a German state inhabited by Jews.

Of course, the Jewish culture that Freud and Herzl found embarrassing is not the only way in which Jews had chosen to express their Jewishness. Pluralism is ever-present within identity groups since people who wish to belong choose to express this in different ways. So the problem was not that Freud and Herzl rejected 'Jewish culture' – as if this was an unchanging essence. On the contrary, it was that they, and the Zionism that they espoused, adopted an essential and unchanging understanding of European culture and were mortified that Jews were unable to embrace it. They were looking not for new ways to be Jewish, but for ways to be European.

Zionism was not, therefore, a rebellion against Europe's refusal to accept and include Jews. It was an application form for membership to the European club from which Jews were excluded. Its exponents claimed to want to escape European domination but, in reality, they wished to join their dominators. To further illustrate this, we now turn to a seemingly different experience that parallels that of Zionism's founders: Indian reaction to British occupation and colonisation.

6

Mimicking the Oppressor

For Zionism's founders, establishing a Jewish nation state was the way to become European. Ironically, this quest for a state serving one group only in territory inhabited by others has found its parallel in a place far from Europe – India.

PASSING FOR NON-JEWISH?

As chapter 5 shows, Freud, Herzl and their fellow European Zionists initially saw assimilation, blending into European society, as their way out of the new Jewish ghetto.

But as Herzl's play *The New Ghetto* shows, they felt that they were constantly rebuffed. Jacob Samuel, the play's (Herzl-like) main character, is challenged to a duel but initially declines because he is busy with his dying father. He complains to a non-Jewish friend that, if the friend had backed out of a duel in this way, he would have seemed like a 'solid clear-headed chap'. But if Jacob, a Jew, did so, it 'makes [me] a coward'.[1] Like Herzl, Jacob wants to fit in but feels unable to. This view was obviously hardened by the Dreyfus affair. After that case, Herzl, Freud and their fellow travellers did not abandon blending into European society (whether by mass conversion or by other means); rather, they tried to do it in a way that seemed most feasible. Founding a state seemed simpler and a better bet than hoping that European society would admit them. It was this which prompted them to become the first architects of what the Jewish theologian Marc Ellis has called 'Constantinian Judaism' – a religion (or form of ethnic identification) that centres on a state.[2]

Why would a state enable Jews to become like everyone else? As Max Weber famously pointed out, states are not states unless they use force. He believed that states deserved that title only if they could 'uphold a claim to the monopoly of the legitimate use of physical force.'[3] And that is why states have armies and soldiers. They are manly and they enable Jews to become the heroic, duelling and fighting Europeans around them – not effeminate scholars. This entailed not a return to Jewish cultural roots, but the opposite. One consequence of the absence of statehood was that the dominant Jewish culture had developed an ethic which associated violence with non-Jews and so excluded such force from Jewish cultural expression.[4] The Haggadah, the book that Jews recite at their Passover meal, tells of four sons who ask the meaning of the festival. One is wicked, another wise. In the Middle Ages and beyond, the wicked son was usually portrayed in these books as a 'martial figure.'[5] It was only after the advent of Zionism that, in some versions, the wise son began bearing arms.

Zionists also claim that every group has a state. This is untrue. Jews are adherents of a religion or members of an ethnic group or both. Secular states are not meant to be the property of any one religion and many states are multiethnic. In numerous cases, different ethnic groups share the same state. But it has become a mantra of Zionist ideology and defence of the Israeli state that every group has a state and to deny one to Jews would be to discriminate against them. This claim would have been particularly appealing to admirers of German culture in the late nineteenth century when the nation state and nationalism were all the rage among intellectuals. While traditional Judaism had viewed Jews as a 'light to the nations' – people called upon to set a standard in ethical behaviour – a core aspiration of Zionism was that Jews should become 'like all the nations', a desire that is included in the Israeli state's Declaration of Independence.[6] This reflects a desire not to be 'real Jews' but to be 'real non-Jews', not to celebrate a distinctive Jewish culture but to be like everyone else. However, everyone else is not, of course, the same and so it meant being a particular kind of someone else. For Herzl and Freud, it was to be German; for today's Zionists, it is to be right-wing white Europeans.

Mahmood Mamdani notes that, in the West, 'Judaism has been recast and the Jewish people have gone from being a prominent other who lived inside Europe to become an integral part of Europe.'[7] In his view, the 'shift of perspective … that relocated Judaism and Jews to the heart of Western history and Western civilisation signifies no less than a sea change in consciousness'.[8] He dates this change to the period after the Nazi genocide which, he implies, shamed Europe into including Jews rather than 'othering' them. That may well have been true in the couple of decades after World War Two. More recently, and particularly currently, however, the event which enables Jews to win acceptance from a European mainstream that once rejected them happened a few years after the end of the last World War – the creation of the state of Israel in 1948. It is this homage to 'Westernness' that enables European anti-Semites of various stripes to embrace the state, however low their opinion of Jews might be.

In one important sense, Herzl and his fellow Zionists were right: establishing a state in the Middle East has indeed been the Jews' passport to respectability among the European power holders who they had so admired. But this also exposes the state and its impact on Jewish identity for what it is – not a 'national liberation movement' but a ticket to the conservative white European respectability which Zionism's founders craved. For Zionists, the physical move out of Europe was not a departure from Europeanness – it opened a new frontier for it.

It could be argued that the first initiative by a Western power towards the establishment of the Israeli state was an anti-Semitic move. The Balfour Declaration, hallowed by Zionists, was the first signal that the colonial power in historic Palestine, Britain, favoured a Jewish state in the area. Its architect, British foreign secretary Arthur Balfour, was also responsible for the 1905 Aliens Act whose aim was to save Britain from, he said, 'the undoubted evil' of 'an immigration which was largely Jewish'.[9] So, while geopolitics – the desire to extend European influence in the Middle East – played a role in Balfour's declaration, it seems likely that a desire to ensure that Jews could move to some place other than Britain was also a factor. The only Jewish member of the British cabinet at the time, Lord Edwin Montagu, did see the declaration as anti-Semitic. He responded, 'All my life I have been trying to get out of the ghetto. You want to force me back there.'[10]

The Zionist search for Europeanness has come at the expense of the dominant traditional understanding of Jewishness and Jewish culture. Golda Meir's comment that she believed not in God but the people (see chapter 4), is not only an expression of secular non-belief in a Deity but it also treats 'the people' as an object of religious veneration. And since Zionism equates the state with the people, it is fair to assume that she also meant that she bestowed on the state the same religious veneration as practising Jews have traditionally bestowed on the Deity. As noted in chapter 2, traditional Jewish understandings would see such veneration as idolatrous. More recently, at the 2014 national conference of J Street, an American liberal Zionist organisation, 'Rabbi Sharon Kleinbaum said that nowadays, if potential congregants come into almost any non-Orthodox synagogue and say they do not believe in God and do not keep any of the commandments, they would be welcome. But if they say they are not Zionists or do not believe in the state of Israel, they would not be welcome.'[11] Jews' religious beliefs, which have defined most Jews in their own eyes and that of their neighbours for millennia, and for which they were despised by mainstream European society for centuries, are now of little consequence; adherence to the European notion of a nation state is all-important. 'Religion as a life in search of meaning that houses a covenantal promise for a redemptive future, however defined, is overtaken by political power as the religion of the non-believer, with the Six-Day

War as its central miracle.'[12] It is hard to think of a more acute example of self-hatred.

Herzl's and Freud's wish to become European by founding a state only for Jews has been granted. As chapter 3 showed, Jews were never accepted as European by the Europe in which they lived. Nor *are* they European. They originated in the Middle East and are at least as much of the East as of the West. The Israeli state has made some of them European – in their own eyes as well as in Europe's. This has both denied much that was central to the dominant Jewish identity over centuries and broken the link between 'good' Jews and much of the rest of humanity. 'We have been pulled by both a Western Christian establishment and the outstretched arm of the Zionist state into the Eurocentric and exclusionary borders of the human ... It is not the first time in history that Jews have been bestowed with humanization, a dubious gift which divides us from other non-Christians and non-whites.'[13]

Particular victims of this shift are black Jews who, because they do not fit the European self-image of Jewish power holders, are often labelled not entirely Jewish.[14] One of many examples is the Lemba people of southern Africa who not only practise the Jewish religion but whose DNA, researchers found, suggests that their ethnic Jewish pedigree is a great deal more authentic than that of the power holders who refuse to recognise their Jewishness.[15] This marginalisation of black Jews obscures the fact that Jews were 'once majority Black and Brown'.[16] Today, for the Israeli state and the Jewish elites who support them, black and brown Jews are an embarrassment to their quest to become fully European.

'Good Jews' are not an antidote to self-hatred; self-loathing lies at the core of their belief system. Freud's loathing for his Jewishness is as straightforward as Nordau's desire to create a new Jewish body. Boyarin notes that Freud repeatedly refers to the Jewish Passover as 'Easter', the Christian festival celebrated at roughly the same time.[17] Herzl's biographer believes that his emotions were more complex: 'Herzl experienced intense Jewish self-disdain and feelings of inferiority, but he was also animated by feelings of Jewish pride, loyalty, and solidarity. In this sense, the contempt for Jews Herzl was struggling with was, not least, his own.'[18] Herzl's ambivalence about his Jewishness was surely Freud's and Nordau's too. None of them converted to Christianity as more than a few German Jews did at the time. But while they wanted to be Jewish, they also wanted to be so in a way that enabled them to blend into European society. That is why they were 'self-hating'. Had they simply walked away from their Jewishness, they would not have hated themselves since they would presumably have changed who they were. Zionists chose to remain Jewish and, so, to remain self-hating. A Jewish state was meant to enable them to have their cake and to eat it too.

It is not the 'bad Jews' who are self-hating but the 'good' ones. If either can be said to accept the basic premises of anti-Semitism, it is not the Jews who today are branded anti-Semitic, it would be their accusers. But Jewishness is not the only culture in which those who claim to be 'authentic' turn out to be estranged from their tradition. To underline this point, we must move from Freud and Herzl's Vienna to colonial India.

THE COLONY OF THE MIND[19]

Ashis Nandy, a psychologist and social critic, is one of India's most important intellectuals. In *The Intimate Enemy*,[20] a prescient book he wrote four decades ago, he offers a critique of Indian advocates of militant 'decolonisation' that has important implications for today's headlines in India. It also throws light on the division between 'good' and 'bad' Jews.

Nandy builds his critique on a discussion of two contrasting figures – the author Rudyard Kipling, who was perhaps the most fervent praise-singer of the British Raj, and the Indian nationalist and spiritual leader Sri Aurobindo. Kipling was to British colonialism what Chamberlain was to anti-Semitism – an ideologue of domination. Like some other advocates of racial or national power, he did not fully belong to the dominant group whose dominance he justifies. Nandy points out that Kipling was 'not merely born in India; he was brought up in India by Indian servants in an

Indian environment. He thought, felt and dreamt in Hindustani, mainly communicated with Indians, and even looked like an Indian boy'.[21] At a young age, he was sent by his parents to England, where he initially failed to fit in. His response was to prove that he belonged as an Englishman by offering a cultural defence of British colonialism. He did this by 'his tendency to absolutize the relative differences between cultures'.[22]

Kipling insisted that there was a strict and unbridgeable divide between 'British' and 'Indian' culture. It was thus impossible for one to influence the other and they certainly could not blend. While Kipling 'liked to see colonialism as a moral statement on the superiority of some cultures and inferiority of others',[23] he romanticised those Indians who made no attempt to become British and so, in his view, remained true to their identity. His scorn was reserved for the clerks and bureaucrats who adopted English ways in attempts to become part of the dominant group. Their sin, of course, was to believe that, as members of an inferior group, they could join the superior culture. Colonialism depended on violence, which Kipling greatly respected. It was, therefore, perhaps inevitable that he admired but greatly exaggerated the military strain in Indian culture. He thought that 'the ideology of Ksatriyahood' – the warrior caste – 'was true Indianness, apart from being consistent with the world view of colonialism'; he inevitably missed the fact that this ideology had a very limited role in traditional Indian thought.[24] But in this and other respects, a key aspect of his worldview was that the 'good Indian' was not one who wished to become British and to thereby share in the benefits that this might bestow.

Kipling was, therefore, an essentialist. He believed that racial identity was deeply embedded – probably biological – and his most obvious South African counterparts would be the ideologues of apartheid who insisted that not only racial but ethnic difference was innate. Kipling's South African counterpart was Hendrik Verwoerd, the intellectual architect of apartheid, and he would have found a kindred spirit in Daan de Wet Nel, sometime minister of Bantu Administration and Development. De Wet Nel justified apartheid thus: 'The Zulu is proud to be a Zulu and the Xhosa proud to be a Xhosa and the Venda is proud to be a Venda, just as proud as they were a hundred years ago.'[25] These ethnic groups, he added, derived the greatest 'fulfilment' from their identity; they had no need to 'become white' by enjoying the rights that whites enjoyed.

For Nandy, the opposite to – and antidote for – Kipling is not militant Indian nationalists who celebrate Hindutva, Indianness, and who exalt the violence used to enforce it. It is Sri Aurobindo (Aurobindo Ghose). He was raised in the sort of Anglophile Indian home that horrified Kipling; he had even been given the middle name Ackroyd, although he later dropped it. He became a nationalist and a spiritual leader, advocating a traditional form of Indian spirituality. But, Nandy insists, Aurobindo did not fall into Kipling's essentialist trap; rather, he searched for 'a more universal model of emancipation'.[26] 'He never thought the West to be outside the reach of God's grace. Even when he spoke of race and evolution … not once did he use the concepts to divide humankind.'[27] While other Indian nationalists sought the help of Germany and Japan to remove the British, Aurobindo always 'regarded Nazism as a Satanic force … [and] abhorred Japanese militarism'.[28]

Aurobindo, then, 'did not have to disown the West within him to become his version of an Indian'.[29] He recognised that, since all cultures are influenced by other cultures, a human being shaped by only one culture did not exist. Recognising that our culture is influenced by others acknowledges reality; it does not make our culture mean less to us or make us any less 'authentic' members of our own group. Often, 'authentic' expressions of a particular culture are, on closer examination, signs of just how influenced they are by other cultures. Many Jews and non-Jews would regard the black cloaks and hats worn by some Orthodox men as the ultimate in 'real' Jewish dress. That is certainly the claim of the men who dress this way and who insist that Jewish religious law commands them to dress differently to others and to remain distinctive. In reality, this 'real' Jewish dress mimics that of the Polish nobility;[30] they, in turn, dressed this way because they thought they were imitating Iranians.[31]

Colonialism, Nandy argues, rests on essentialism and violence. The claim that others are not as advanced as the coloniser and so must be controlled justifies colonisation. Dominating others is impossible without violence. Therefore, militant, essentialist Indian nationalism, before and after independence, is an expression of colonial thought. The real threat to colonisation and its worldview was not the Indian nationalist movements that colonialism had 'bred and domesticated';[32] it was, rather, the India that refused essentialism. 'It carried intimations of an alternative, cosmopolitan, multicultural living which was ... beyond the dreary middle-class horizons of Kipling and his English contemporaries.'[33] The notion of an 'authentic indigenous identity' is just as essentialist as Kipling's view of culture and is not an alternative to the coloniser; it in fact endorses the colonial worldview. The most profound alternative to colonisation lay beyond its sight. 'The cry of the victims of colonialism was ultimately the cry to be heard in another language – unknown to the colonizer and to the anti-colonial movements.'[34] This 'other language' adopts an instrumental view of colonial culture. It takes that which is of use and discards that which is not. If this means, at times, pretending to admire the coloniser to resist it, that too is valid.

Nandy recalls being told of a group of Aztec priests, around the sixteenth century, who, on being forced by their conquerors to hear a Christian sermon that proclaimed that the Aztec gods were dead, declared that if their gods were no longer living, they would rather die. Their conquerors did as they had asked and killed them. Nandy responds: 'I suspect I know how a group of Brāhman priests would have behaved under the same circumstances. All of them would have embraced Christianity and some of them would have co-authored [praise poetry] to praise the alien rulers and their gods.' In reality, he says, they would have remained devout Hindus and, after a while, 'their Christianity would have looked ... dangerously like a variation on Hinduism'.[35]

He observes, 'The response of the Aztec priests has seemed to the Westernized world the paragon of courage and cultural pride; the hypothetical response of the Brāhman priests hypocritical and cowardly.'[36] All imperialist observers have loved India's 'martial races' – who are seen as authentically Indian – and have felt threatened by Indians who are willing to compromise. Why do they valorise the priests and reject the Brahmans? Because the Aztec priests obliged their conquerors by dying and leaving the scene; the 'cowardly', on the other hand, remain and 'may at some opportune moment assert their presence'.[37]

Nandy argues that submission of this sort is deeply embedded in Indian culture.[38] It is derived not from some contemporary Western source but from 'non-modern' India which 'rejects most versions of Indian nationalism as bound irrevocably to the West'.[39] The 'cowardly' response threatens the coloniser because it expresses the autonomous understanding of the colonised, not that which is imposed by the coloniser.

The 'cowardice' is not, Nandy suggests, simply a survival strategy in the face of superior power. If this was all that the Brahmans were doing, they would not be defeating colonisation, they would be submitting to it. Rather, they were challenging colonialism – in a manner that was unavailable to the militant decolonisers. Their challenge was their refusal to buy into the myth of the 'noble savage', which insists that colonised people are at their most authentic when they live out the cultural stereotypes of the coloniser by dying 'nobly' at its hand. Instead, they rebel by subverting colonisation rather than by allowing it to kill them.

Indians who responded in this way were drawing on cultural wellsprings unknown to the British, so they could relate to colonial power on their own terms. In that sense, they, and not those determined to live out an Indianness framed by the coloniser, were the authentic decolonisers. 'What looks like Westernization is often only a means of domesticating the West, sometimes by reducing the West to the comic and the trivial.'[40] Indians who adopted this strategy believed that it was 'better to be a comical dissenter than to be a powerful, serious but acceptable opponent. Better to be a hated enemy, declared unworthy of any respect whatsoever, than to be a proper opponent'.[41] The coloniser could dominate but could not decide for the colonised how to respond.

Colonialism, Nandy argues, tried to 'erect an Indian self-image which, in its opposition to the West, would remain in essence a Western construction'.[42] The authentic rebellion against such a construction was the mimicking of Kipling by 'set[ting] up the East and the West as permanent and natural antipodes'.[43] The Indian 'has no reason to see himself as a counterplayer or an antithesis of the Western man [sic]. The imposed burden to be perfectly non-Western only constricts his … cultural self, just as the older burden of being perfectly Western once narrowed – and still sometimes narrows – his choices in the matter of his and his society's future … It in fact binds him even more irrevocably to the West'.[44] Colonialism's modus operandi is that it limits and restricts. Those who claimed to be 'purely non-Western' limited and restricted themselves by shutting out influences that might enrich them culturally. In doing so, they did the work of the colonial project for it.

Who are those Indians who insist on mimicking the West by proclaiming themselves 'pure Indians'? Nandy mentions 'a subgroup of Kipling's Indian brain-children [who] have set up the martial India as the genuine India which would one day defeat the West at its own game. They … are quite willing to alter the whole of Indian culture to bring that victory a little closer, like the American army officer in Vietnam who once destroyed a village to save it from its enemies'.[45] Hindutva – 'Indianness' or 'Hinduness' – is one example of this kind of response. This is the core principle of the currently dominant strand of nationalism in India and of its current governing party, the Bharatiya Janata Party (BJP). This despite the fact that 'Hinduness' was unknown in India until colonialism invented it because it needed a way of making sense of diverse indigenous cultural and religious expression. 'To use the term Hindu to self-define' is, therefore, to embrace a colonial creation and 'to assert aggressively one's Hinduism is to very nearly deny one's Hinduness'.[46] Nandy's point, that the loudest devotees of decolonisation are products of that which they decry, was perfectly captured by Rabindranath Tagore's fictional masterpiece *Gora*, in which the eponymous character is a militant Hindu essentialist blissfully unaware that he is actually English and had been adopted and brought up as Indian by his Indian foster parents.[47]

Nandy's book was first published more than three decades before current Indian prime minister Narendra Modi and his BJP became India's government. But their rule has confirmed Nandy's diagnosis. As the party of Hindutva, the BJP has proclaimed itself the vehicle of the 'real India', an essentialised idea of Indianness which, like colonialism, uses force to dominate. It divides India into those whose origins enable them to wield power and those – primarily, but not only, Muslims – who must be forced into powerlessness. It seems entirely oblivious to the fact that the 'Hinduness' it is imposing on the rest of India, including on hundreds of millions of people who are Hindu, was invented by British administrators who had been unable to cope with the complexity of India's indigenous faiths. It is no accident that Modi and his party eagerly embrace the Israeli state. The idea of a state for one group only in a place where there are several is extremely appealing to colonialism's 'authentically Indian' offspring. This is particularly so since Palestinians, the group which is excluded from power and the rights and entitlements that go with it, happen to be mainly Muslim. But that is not the only link between the Indian nationalism that Nandy criticises and the Zionism of the Israeli state.

From Gora to the Ghetto

Despite some inevitable differences in detail, the synchronicity between the dynamics described by Boyarin and Nandy is uncanny.

In both contexts – Indians and Jews – a dominated people needs to find ways of responding to its domination – colonisation of its land in Nandy's case, exclusion from rights and the life which they offer in Boyarin's. In both, a nationalism emerges that presents itself not only as the cure for domination but as the expression of 'the true essence' of the people. Both can represent the 'real' nature of their own group not only by dominating others (mainly Muslims in one case, Palestinians in the other) but also by excluding members of their own group. 'Indianness' for the nationalists criticised by Nandy can be asserted only by denying some Indians the right to be Indian. 'Jewishness' for Zionists now requires that their Jewish opponents and critics must be labelled anti-Semites and, thus, enemies of the people to which they belong.

There are also strong parallels between the European Jewish response to exclusion that Boyarin celebrates and the non-nationalist but still anti-colonialist Indian culture that Nandy embraces. Freud's father scurrying away with his hat and Nandy's imaginary Brahmans loudly embracing Christianity as they quietly turn it into a version of Indian religion would have recognised and understood each other. This despite the fact that they are not identical – one is dominated by exclusion, the other by inclusion. The Jewish culture that Freud's father represents and the Indian culture of Aurobindo and many others were both premised on rejecting the dominator rather than using force to resist. In both cases, the result, intentional or not, is a set of values and understandings that reject domination regardless of who the dominated happen to be. This is very different from the view of Zionists and Hindutva adherents that domination is desirable as long as their group dominates.

As a consequence of the situation in which they found themselves – deprived of a role in the states and societies in which they lived – Jewish cultural elites before Zionism developed a view of the world in which violence and domination were dismissed as *goyim naches*, the pleasures of the non-Jews.[48] Their equivalents in India maintained an anti-essentialist view and a rejection of violence that undercut the worldview of the coloniser. Both were stigmatised – or simply ignored – by the nationalist elites that proclaimed themselves the 'real' Indians or 'real' Jews but who were modelling their values and priorities entirely on those who had dominated them.

It comes as no surprise that, in a very new twist, the proponents of Hindutva have trained their sights on 'self-hating' Hindus who they compare, explicitly, to 'self-hating' Jews. These 'self-haters' are, we are told, found 'in your homes, amongst friends and relatives, on TV channels, in

Bollywood, pretty much every conceivable place'.[49] The internal enemy, then, is everywhere. 'And yet, all this while they claim to be Hindus and maintain that they are trying to reform the religion and make it relevant to the modern time. The reality is that they are working as agents of Mullahs and Missionaries, seeking to lead gullible Sheep to a religious conversion.'[50] The cause of this denunciation was an article in the *New York Times* by the novelist Pankaj Mishra, who is a tireless critic not of India and Indians but of the Hindutva of the BJP and of its capacity to divide Indians into the 'good' and the 'bad'.[51]

We end this discussion by returning to Fanon and his diagnosis of black internalisation of racist prejudices. While 'self-hatred' sounds like a contradiction in terms, it is, sadly, very common among people who have been dominated and demeaned. As Fanon and others, such as Steve Biko,[52] were to show, dominated groups bear mental as well as physical scars. Since their lived experience and everything that they hear from their dominators tells them that they are inferior, they come to believe this themselves. So, in a sense, do the dominated people discussed by James Scott;[53] they conclude that the power of the dominator is too strong and that they cannot openly resist. So they subvert and dissemble but do not rebel.

In the cultural weaponry of Zionism and Hindutva, the 'self-hating' or 'bad' Jews and Hindus are those who are said to have absorbed the sense of inferiority and are therefore alienated from their group. But, in different ways, Boyarin and Nandy show that the reverse is true. The culture that dismisses violence as *Goyim Naches* or the Indian response which refuses the violence and essentialism of the coloniser are not surrenders to domination. They are its antithesis because they reject not only the physical and material power of the dominator but also the fundamentals of its worldview. They show too that it is, in fact, the 'good' Hindus and Jews who have absorbed the inferiority complex by becoming what they claim to reject: Kipling's 'Indian brain-children' or the duelling martial men of Freud and Herzl's Vienna. It is they who are the 'self-haters' because it is they who have rejected crucial aspects of their heritage in their desire to become their dominators.

It is hardly surprising, then, that both the Israeli state and Modi's India are today key cogs in a right-wing international alliance of the like-minded. They celebrate ethnic essentialism and have no problem with violence as long as it is used by the 'right' people against the 'wrong' ones. Not that long ago, global racism was a white, non-Jewish phenomenon. This is not to say that only whites and non-Jews are capable of bigotry but to point out that they alone had the power to force theirs on others. Today, it has acquired both Jewish and Indian adherents, both of whom are unaware that they have been admitted to the club only because they are no longer Indian or Jewish in the eyes of those who once despised them because they have rejected the values that were associated with being Jewish or Indian. Their rejection of these values includes their attempts to expel from the fold anyone in their own group who embraces these values.

The 'good' Indians and Jews, it turns out, are a great deal less Indian and Jewish than the 'bad' ones. 'Self-hatred' is indeed rampant in both groups. But it infects those who use the term as a weapon, not those against whom they use it.

7

Two Religions and the Nightmare the West Created

As the introduction to this book noted, its title is inspired by a work that seems to cover very different ground but, on close inspection, throws important light on the discussion of Jewish identity in these pages: Mahmood Mamdani's *Good Muslim, Bad Muslim.*

Mamdani's book was written in the shadow of the events of 11 September 2001, or, more accurately, following the Western reaction to them, the consequences of which are still very much with us. The 2001 attack on the World Trade Centre hardened already strong hostility to Muslims in the West – strengthening the stereotype, mentioned in chapter 2, that they are inherently violent and fanatical. These prejudices seemed, to some degree, to be leavened by the view, publicly expressed by authority figures in the United States and Western Europe, that only some Muslims were threats to peace and security. They distinguished between 'good Muslims' who were law-abiding domestic and international citizens and 'bad Muslims' who were violent religious fundamentalists hostile to the West. Great energy and effort have been spent in Western countries on 'deradicalisation', 'preventing violent extremism (PVE)' and 'countering violent extremism (CVE)' programmes that have sought to prevent 'good' Muslims from becoming 'bad' ones (and, sometimes, converting 'bad' ones into 'good' ones).[1]

This distinction, Mamdani's book seeks to show, ignores a key reality – that while the 'bad Muslims' were not inventions of Western powers, particularly the United States, they were, nevertheless, their creations in that they would never have acquired their impact without active US assistance. The United States enabled them when it was fighting the Cold War against Soviet communism and it saw 'fundamentalist' Muslims as allies against the Soviets – particularly in Afghanistan where militant Islamist groups played a central role in defeating the Soviet occupation. It was the US's own protégés who were later to turn on it and to attack its people and its installations. Given this, the existence of 'bad Muslims' says less about the Islamic faith and the people who adhere to it than it does about the way that power is wielded in the world and the new forms of colonial strategy and ideology.

VIOLENCE TWO WAYS

Before discussing Mamdani's central argument, it is important to mention a section of the book that sets the framework for it and is directly relevant to our topic.

Mamdani observes: 'By the beginning of the twentieth century, it was a European habit to distinguish between civilized wars and colonial wars.' The former were governed by the 'laws of war' and the latter by the 'laws of nature'.[2] Wars between 'people like us' were fought within rules that were meant to limit their barbarity, but wars against people who were not full members of 'Western civilisation' were not bound by any rules at all. World War One was brutal and bloody, but European civilians were not attacked and armies treated prisoners of war relatively well. None of these rules applied to the colonised. Mamdani traces the beginnings of the massacres of colonised people to the first years of the nineteenth century, when first Australians were slaughtered by colonists in Tasmania.[3] As noted earlier, the genocide of the Herero and Nama peoples of Namibia (then German South West Africa)[4] was a precursor to the Nazi genocide.

Mamdani sees a link between the violence of the coloniser and the slaughter of Jews and Slavs by the Nazis. The racial theories of Chamberlain and others – who claimed the superiority of the Aryan race – meant that Jews and Slavs, who were both regarded as not Aryan, could be placed beyond the pale of civilisation and were thus candidates for the 'laws of nature', not of war. In World War Two, the Nazis 'observed the laws of war against the Western powers but not against Russia',[5] and not against Jewish civilians and resistance fighters. British, American and French prisoners of war were treated according to the rules of the Third Geneva Convention,[6] but Russians were not.

A bizarre feature of this distinction between the 'civilised' and those ripe for the slaughter was that the Nazis' Jewish prisoners of war serving in the Western armies (estimated at around 60 000) were not slaughtered, but Russian soldiers were. This does not mean that Jewish and non-Jewish prisoners were treated entirely equally; Jewish prisoners were usually separated from others and there is some evidence that they were treated more harshly. But the vast majority survived the war and there is no evidence that any were killed because they were Jewish.[7] Scholars have made various attempts to explain this, but perhaps the most plausible explanation is one that none of them offers – that serving in a Western European or American army meant that Jews, in the eyes of their Nazi captors, had attained at least a sufficient degree of 'Europeanness' to save them from death. Serving in the Russian military conferred no such 'honorary Aryan' status because Soviet Russia was considered a mortal enemy of the Aryan race – a 'non-Western' presence in Europe.[8]

Nazi extermination camps, where gas chambers were used as instruments of slaughter, were all situated in occupied Poland, not in Germany. There were concentration camps in Germany, but these were forced labour camps, not death camps. An obvious explanation for this seemingly odd fact is that the Nazis worried that Germans might learn what was happening in death camps and might not share their government's view that wholesale slaughter was acceptable. This was similar to the tactics of the architects of apartheid who ensured that brutality directed at black people was usually imposed in areas away from the gaze of white people. But it seems unlikely that this explanation would hold. Apartheid showed that human rights abuses do not need to be moved to another country to hide them from the sight of the dominant group. Rather, it seems likely that the reason was that which Mamdani's analysis suggests: by siting the camps to the east of Germany, the Nazis were, in effect, removing them from Western Europe where such barbarism was not considered acceptable. The east of Europe became, in a sense, a colony inhabited by people who were not considered Aryan and therefore not fully European. They were thus subject only to the 'laws of nature'.

It was noted earlier that Nazi anti-Jewish bigotry was originally labelled racism while bigotry against people who were not white Europeans was not. The context of the situation of the camps helps to explain that. Bigotry was acceptable only if it was directed at people who were not European. Mamdani cites *The History of Bombing*, the work of Swedish author Sven Lindqvist. He observes that the Nazi genocide was 'born at the meeting point of two traditions that marked modern Western civilization: "the anti-Semitic tradition and the tradition of genocide of colonized peoples"'.[9] The first was (mainly) the prejudice of the right, the second produced the less obvious but still real prejudices which justified colonisation and continue to underpin mainstream European attitudes. Mamdani notes, 'The fate of the Jewish people was that they were to be exterminated as a whole. In that, they were unique – but *only in Europe*.'[10] This point, he adds, was not lost on intellectuals from colonised countries, such as the Martinican thinker Aimé Césaire who wrote that the European bourgeoisie could not forgive Hitler for 'the fact that he applied to Europe colonialist procedures which until then had been reserved exclusively for the Arabs of Algeria, the "coolies" of India, and the "niggers" of Africa'.[11] In the same vein, Fanon wrote: 'Not long ago Nazism transformed the whole of Europe into a veritable colony.'[12]

This, of course, explains why a Europe that was justifiably appalled at the Nazi genocide had no great qualms about the wholesale slaughter of Congolese or about the Herero genocide. It might be argued that the reason was not bigotry but distance; events in Africa were simply not noticed in Europe because they happened far away, and few people were aware of them. But Mamdani's view that race prejudice was at work is supported by the fact that these attitudes persist today, when communications technologies ensure that the Western mainstream knows what is wrought on people in far-off places. A clear example is the attitudes prompted by the Russian invasion of Ukraine.

As numerous critiques have shown, European politicians and journalists drew repeated attention to the fact that the Ukrainians were white Europeans or 'people like us' – and therefore 'civilised' – in contrast to Iraqis, Yemenis, Syrians, Afghanis, Africans and, until not that long ago, Jews.[13] A former Ukrainian deputy prosecutor general lamented the fact that people with 'blue eyes and blonde hair' were victims of violence.[14] While this could be dismissed as the view of a bigoted few, the fact that Europe and the United States acted with a level of anger never directed at the Israeli state's bombing of Palestinians, Saudi bombing of Yemen or Russian bombing of Muslim Chechnya and Syria suggests that Mamdani's hypothesis explains this reaction too. That the United States led the charge, despite its own incursions into Iraq, Afghanistan and other countries, could be explained as plain hypocrisy but could also fit in with Mamdani's thesis. The Russians had broken the rules of 'civilised war' by treating white European Ukrainians in a manner that should be reserved for colonised subjects (even if the colonisation is now less direct than it had been in the last century). Had they restricted themselves, like the West, to visiting misery only on people who were not European, such as the Syrians who they had earlier bombed, they would have acted well within 'civilised' bounds.

But it seems not always possible to restrict barbarism to the colonies. Mamdani shows how European behaviour in Namibia set the stage for the Nazi genocide in Europe. It was in Namibia in the first years of the twentieth century that Eugen Fischer, a German geneticist, conducted 'racial experiments' on Herero people who were, as Jews would later be, interned in concentration camps. Fischer claimed to have shown that people born of mixed Herero and German parentage were 'physically and mentally inferior to their German parents'.[15] Adolf Hitler read Fischer's book that made this claim, *The Principle of Human Heredity and Race Hygiene*, and later appointed him rector of the university of Berlin, where he taught medicine. One of Fischer's students was Josef Mengele, who conducted experiments in Auschwitz on Jewish human beings and who also selected victims for the gas chambers.[16]

Nazism was, seen through this lens, what Fanon's remark suggested it was: a form of colonial rule extended into Europe. It took the 'anti-Semitic tradition' to its logical conclusion by relegating Jews to the status of Africans whose slaughter Chamberlain celebrated in his letters to the Kaiser. We can see current attempts to align Jews with white supremacy and ethnic nationalism as attempts to escape this history and to position 'good', Zionist Jews as the white Europeans that Nazism insisted they were not. This gives added significance to the fact that the first American writings claiming a 'new anti-Semitism' devoted much effort to blaming black people for anti-Semitism, thus signalling that Jews shared the prejudices of the white European mainstream and so should never have been treated as the Congolese and Hereros had been.

The current alliance between the Israeli state and other ethnic nationalists is a further example of the attempt to become European – as discussed in previous chapters. Viewed in this way, today's right-wing Zionism is not, as it is sometimes portrayed, a departure from the movement's supposed humanist past. There is a direct line from Herzl, whose Zionism was inspired by the music of a virulent anti-Semite, to the Israeli state and its supporters who find sustenance in the prejudices of Donald Trump and Viktor Orban. Much the same impulse surely drives British Jews who today unite with those who had once excluded them from their clubs and, more recently, stereotyped them in novels. These stereotypes are used to denounce left wingers who the right has always associated with Jewishness.[17] Mamdani uses the term 'conscripts of Western power' to describe those who were once oppressed by the West but are now allied to it.[18] But today's 'good Jews' are not conscripts; they are volunteers.

His argument also sheds new light on the visits of right-wing anti-Semites to the Yad Vashem memorial to Nazi victims discussed in chapter 1, a practice aptly described by the Israeli journalist Noa Landau as 'Shoah-washing' ('shoah' is a Hebrew word used to describe the Nazi genocide).[19] The Israeli anti-Zionist activist Orly Noy notes:

> If Zionism previously justified its crimes against the Palestinian people in the name of the Holocaust, today it uses the Holocaust as a tool to justify antisemitism itself in exchange for political profit. More than that: it allows an antisemite to define what antisemitism is. This is the bitter truth we face today – for the official State of Israel, the concept of the Holocaust and antisemitism are purely political means, and as such can be manipulated, distorted, and deceived, just like any other political tool.[20]

It was noted earlier that Nazi crimes are used by the Israeli state to justify violence against Palestinians. But viewed through Mamdani's distinction, and the core role that Nazi mass murder plays in Zionism's justifications, the Israeli state's use of the Nazi genocide may also be seen as a continuing attempt to remind ethnic nationalists that by forming an ethnic nationalist state, Jews should be treated as the Nazis would not treat them – as fellow Europeans, rather than as 'darker people' who are deserving targets of racism. Noy's reference to allowing anti-Semites to define anti-Semitism may also shed light on why today's anti-Semites are happy to accept the invitation to mourn a slaughter that they usually excuse. An obvious explanation is that their admiration for the Israeli state makes a little hypocrisy necessary. If their favourite ethnic nationalist state wants heads of government who feel that the Nazi genocide has received an unfair bad press to shed a ritualised tear for its victims, that is a small price to pay. But they may also be signalling that the establishment of an ethnic nationalist state, which itself colonises the 'darker races', entitles 'good Jews' to the European status that the Nazis had denied them. This, of course, does not mean that 'bad Jews' – those who are not fervent ethnic nationalists – deserve the same consideration.

The distinction between European and colonial wars may also shed more light on why 'good Jews', those who support the Israeli state, are so firmly supported by Western centrists and liberals. If Jews are, as the opponents of Nazi racism insisted, European, then the Israeli state can be seen as another colonial enterprise, which, in the view of some of its opponents, is exactly what it is.[21] And so its response to Palestinians is, in the eyes of its European allies, governed by the 'laws of nature', not by the 'laws of war'. To brutalise Ukrainians is to violate the 'laws of war' and is unacceptable to Europe and its heirs. To brutalise Palestinians is to follow the 'laws of nature'. The Israeli state may do as it pleases to Palestinians without violating the code of those to whom 'Europeanness' or 'whiteness' is a valued identity – many of whom are liberals or centrists.

The distinction between European and colonial wars, then, throws important light on the new way in which Jews are viewed both by white supremacists and by mainstream Europe. The distinction between 'good' and 'bad' Muslims also illumines aspects of that between 'good' and 'bad' Jews.

A CULTURAL CREATION

It was then president of the US, George W. Bush, who first distinguished between 'good' and 'bad' Muslims after the September 2001 attacks on that country. The 'bad' ones, according to him, made war on the West; the 'good' ones did not.

But, Mamdani points out, to qualify as 'good', Muslims had to do more than refrain from acts of violence. They were required to show that they were 'good' by fighting those who were 'bad'. He notes, 'The president seemed to assure Americans that "good Muslims" were anxious to clear their names and consciences of this horrible crime and would undoubt-edly support "us" in a war against "them". … All Muslims were now under obligation to prove their credentials by joining in a war against "bad Muslims". This demand that 'good' Muslims demonstrate their goodness meant that 'unless proved to be "good", every Muslim was presumed to be "bad".[22] What appears to be an attempt to avoid stigmatising all Muslims is, in reality, a labelling of all except those who go out of their way to show that they are not what the West assumes them to be.

The intellectual origin of this view can be found in, among other sources, the writings of Bernard Lewis, a scholar whose racial and cultural biases made him a target of Edward Said's celebrated book *Orientalism*. But he has been regarded by the Western establishment as an impeccable source of knowledge of Muslims and Arabs and was, therefore, influen-tial in official policy discussions. In his 1990 essay 'The Roots of Muslim Rage', Lewis acknowledged that religious fundamentalism is not the only Muslim tradition and that other traditions also exist.[23] He urged Western powers not to engage in a religious war against Islam but rather to rely on the 'good' Muslims to defeat the 'bad' ones. This may have sounded like a warning against cultural imposition, but Mamdani points out that it meant that the West should rely on a Muslim civil war in which the 'good' Muslims would defeat the 'bad'.[24] While Lewis argued that the West could do nothing to influence this, by predicting a war between Muslims (governed by the 'laws of nature'?) he was, in effect, remaking Muslims in the West's image by insisting that only one type of Islamic identity, that which won the West's approval, was acceptable. And it is hard to see why Western governments that accepted his analysis should adopt the neu-trality Lewis proposed rather than trying to ensure that those Muslims who they approved would win the battle.

Lewis' view seems to avoid what Mamdani calls 'Culture Talk', which 'assumes that every culture has a tangible essence that defines it' and 'then explains politics as a consequence of that essence'.[25] Applied to Muslims, Culture Talk claims that violence is inherently Islamic. This way of thinking is identical, albeit in a different context, to Kipling's essentialist view, analysed by Nandy in chapter 6, but without any pretence that the culture which is being stereotyped has any merit.

Mamdani suggests that it was another Western scholar who influenced US policy towards Muslims after September 2001: Samuel Huntington. He attracted attention by arguing that the Cold War would be replaced by a 'clash of civilisations' between, in effect, the West and Islam.[26] This is an extreme form of essentialism since it reduces hundreds of millions of people, with different perspectives and values, to members of a 'civilisation' with a single view of the world. There are eerie parallels between it and Marr's or Chamberlain's idea of a clash between 'Aryan' or 'German' racial culture and the rest (more specifically, the Jews). If Huntington did not explicitly say that one side would have to win and the other lose, he certainly implied it. The concrete consequence of his claim was that the West should definitely not stand by and let Muslims fight it out; it should eliminate the 'bad' Muslims before they eliminated it. Mamdani uses the example of the Iraq war to show what this meant in practice.[27] But in that case, the Western powers had to invent a reality by portraying Sadam Hussein, a secular nationalist who had no truck with fundamentalists, as an ally of 'violent Islamism'. A more exact fit was Afghanistan, where the West spent two decades trying to prop up 'good Muslims' in their battle with 'bad' ones.

But, as Said's critique showed, Lewis was no less essentialist than Huntington. His sweeping claims about 'Islamic culture' included such gems as: 'The Western doctrine of the right to resist bad government is alien to Islamic thought.'[28] The claim is not even an oversimplification; it is patently false.[29] Lewis' claim that Islamism is an expression of centuries-old Islamic culture ignores the fact that it is a creation of twentieth-century thinkers. In his book *What Went Wrong? Western Impact and Middle Eastern Response,* Lewis begins with what Mamdani calls a 'reductive' discussion of 1 300 years of Muslim history, which appears to consist only of 'conquest' by Muslims and 'reconquest' by Christians.[30] Lewis also writes of a clash between Islamic and 'Judeo-Christian civilisations',[31] a theme echoed by Huntington. The notion that

Jews and Christians share a common culture that is opposed to Islam is, as we saw in chapter 2, consistent with current prejudices and popular among white supremacists. But it is also easily shown to be false. It was noted in chapter 3 that the Crusaders, who were largely responsible for the Christian 'reconquests' (which, of course, Muslims might see as conquests), began by slaughtering Jews on their way to remove the Muslims from 'the Holy Land'. Lewis also seems unaware – or obfuscates the fact – that Jews had been considered threats to 'Christian culture' for long periods in European history.

Mamdani thus notes: 'The notion of a Judeo-Christian civilization crystallized as a post-Holocaust antidote to anti-Semitism.'[32] Understood in this way, the term was an attempt to erase the toxic notion that Jews were implacable enemies of 'Christian civilisation'. But, like Huntington's book, it was also meant to justify a battle between 'us' and 'them', except that 'good Jews' had been allowed to join 'us'. This is, no doubt, why the phrase 'Judeo-Christian civilisation' has become a favourite of the white nationalists with whom the Israeli state is allied.[33] It enables them to distinguish between those who are European (or Western) and those who are not. 'Judeo-Christian' is, in essence, a euphemism for whiteness.

All of this flows from Lewis' invention of a 'Judeo-Christian' identity which seems far more suited to a fight with Muslims than to a position which leaves Muslims to fight each other. Why did he advocate leaving the fight to 'good' Muslims? Surely because he believed that Islamic culture (or his caricature of it) was inferior to (his) 'Judeo-Christian' alternative, the product of a teleological view of history in which events lead in a particular, desired direction – in this case, the defeat of the 'bad' by the 'good'. Lewis' prejudices against 'Islamic culture' mean that, despite the talk of differing traditions, what was particularly 'good' about 'good' Muslims was that they were turning their back on the beliefs that he had stereotyped. Muslims can be left alone to battle it out because the 'good' Muslims are superior and are therefore sure to win. And they are superior because they have abandoned 'Islamic culture' and no longer fit his definition of a Muslim.

So, while the distinction between 'good' and 'bad' Muslims appears, at first glance, to argue against the bigotry that lumps together everyone of a particular faith, it is as much a justification for imposing white, European values on others as Huntington's implied call to 'Western civilisation' to do battle against its foes. This is not changed by the fact that it places in the frontline Muslims who, in its view, have chosen to reject their tradition.

MANUFACTURING THE ENEMY

The great irony about 'Culture Talk' and its claim that Muslim beliefs are threats to peace and democracy is that, as Mamdani's book shows, it was the US which created – or at least empowered – 'bad Muslims'.

It did this during the Cold War, more specifically in the war against the Soviet occupation of Afghanistan. The Soviets were resisted by a range of groups holding differing views but since Muslim fundamentalists were implacably hostile to communists, the US saw them as a key proxy. This approach was entirely consistent with the difference between European wars and colonial wars and explains why Mamdani points out this distinction. The Soviets might have been Europeans, but they were not Western Europeans and they were seen as bearers of an ideology that threatened the West's survival. That was why the right-wing Zionists mentioned in chapter 2 sided with anti-Semites who were also 'anti-Arab and anti-Communist'. While the Americans were obviously not Nazis, they viewed the Soviets in much the same way as Nazis had – as enemies of Western civilisation. They thus regarded the Soviets much as they do today's 'bad Muslims'. Add to this that the war in Afghanistan was waged in a colonial setting and it becomes predictable that it should be governed by the 'laws of nature'.

Mamdani does not claim that the United States invented Islamism; it existed before US strategists decided to make use of it. He argues, rather, that there were two forms of political Islam, one 'progressive' and the other 'reactionary'. The latter is 'state-centred' since it seeks state power to implement its programme, and fundamentalist in the sense that it rejects the reinterpretation of Islamic law in the light of current events and understandings. It also justifies using violence to protect Islam.[34] But the fact that people harbour certain beliefs does not automatically mean that they will act on them. Mamdani questions 'the widely held presumption – even among critics of Culture Talk – that extremist religious tendencies can be equated with political terrorism'.[35] He adds: 'The question we face today is not just why a radical state-centered train of thought emerged in political Islam but how this thought was able to leap from the word to the deed.'[36]

The answer, he argues, does not lie in the claim that violence is embedded in 'Muslim culture' but in stressing 'the *political* encounter that … is central to understanding political terrorism'.[37] That encounter, the key to understanding political violence by Islamists, is the Cold War. Mamdani's characterisation of political Islam oversimplifies the phenomenon to make his point. There are numerous exceptions to his characterisation. One example is the Tunisian Islamist Rachid Ghannouchi and his political party Ennahda, which would be regarded as state-centric since it had sought, and then wielded, state power. But its members are democrats, and far closer to the 'progressive' than the 'reactionary' camp.[38] But, in general, the evidence strongly supports Mamdani's view that it was the US that strengthened fundamentalist Islamists and enabled them to put their convictions into practice.

While the US repeatedly denounces terrorism, Mamdani observes that it 'embraced terror as it prepared to wage the Cold War to a finish'.[39] In the 1980s, the Reagan administration declared that its strategy against communism was not containment, preventing its extending its influence to the West, but 'rollback' – to defeat it or at least to reclaim from the Soviet bloc what the West had believed to be its rightful domain.[40] In the mid-1980s, the United States engaged in a series of 'low intensity conflicts' in which it supported guerrillas in Nicaragua, Angola and Afghanistan. In each case, this was 'justified' by the Cold War against the Soviet Union. In Afghanistan, the US supported the mujahideen who fought against the Soviet occupation of that country. Reagan described both the Nicaraguan contras and the Afghan mujahideen as 'the moral equivalents of [the US's] founding fathers'.[41]

It was in Afghanistan, which Mamdani calls the 'high point in the Cold War' and the 'bloodiest regional conflict in the world' at the time,[42] that the weaponising of the 'reactionary' strain of political Islam became a key feature of US strategy. The US mustered huge resources to 'hand the Soviet Union its own Vietnam' and was willing, in Reagan's words, to use 'all means necessary' to defeat the Soviet occupiers. The US sought to bolster the mujahideen's resistance by recruiting 'the most radically anti-Communist Islamists to counter Soviet forces'. This search did not restrict itself to Afghanistan; Islamists were recruited from all over the world, including from within the US and Britain.[43]

The US did not, Mamdani reports, see militant Islamists as one among many allies worthy of support in Afghanistan; they were its pre-ferred partners. One organisation resisting the Russian occupation was considered 'insufficiently Islamic' to receive aid. The CIA, America's intelligence agency, 'backed not just Islamist ideologues but extremists over moderates'.[44] An important feature of this venture was to turn many madrassahs, Islamic religious schools, into 'politico-military training schools'. 'The point was to integrate guerrilla training with the teachings of Islam and thus create "Islamic guerrillas".'[45] Many students in these schools 'had been taught literacy in primers that stated that the Urdu letter *tay* stood for *tope* (cannon), *kaaf* for *Kalashnikov*, *khay* for *khoon* (blood), and *jeem* for *jihad*'.[46]

There is huge irony in this tactic. It created, at the initiative of the US, precisely the armed Islam that later became a source of fear in the West and that stoked the stigmatisation of Muslims. In its desire to defeat communism in Afghanistan, the CIA gave fundamentalist Islamists the means to put ideology into action by arming them and offering them support. 'The CIA was key to the forging of the link between Islam and terror in central Asia and to giving radical Islamists international reach and ambition.'[47] A *Los Angeles Times* investigation found that almost all the key leaders of major terrorist attacks against the West were veterans of the Afghan war,[48] which means that they were products of the American programme to promote violent Islamism and to train its adherents. But consumers of news who were repeatedly regaled with stories of 'militant clerics' who had turned Islam from a religion into a weapon of war were never told that they were products of an American military strategy. And, according to Mamdani, despite America's enthusiasm for a 'war on drugs', the US-sponsored Muslim holy war relied on the drug trade for much of its financing. As American politicians indignantly denounced the use of addictive drugs, US security operatives and Afghan mujahideen were using the drug trade as a key income source.[49]

VARIATIONS ON A THEME

Mamdani provides a compelling account of the manner in which 'bad Muslims' turn out to be products of the West, which later declares their badness. How does this account throw light on our theme of a reinvented Jewishness that uses manufactured claims of anti-Semitism to silence other Jews?

The link between Mamdani's critique and those of Boyarin and Nandy discussed in chapter 6 is that all, in very different contexts, are critiques of essentialism. Boyarin shows that both Zionism and current notions of Jewish manhood are not eternal or immutable features of Jewish belief and culture; on the contrary, he argues, they were invented by European intellectuals. What passes today for eternal and essential Jewishness in the imagination of politicians and political entrepreneurs is very new and at variance with tradition. What is 'new' about the 'new anti-Semitism' is not what is happening in the heads of those it labels hostile to Jews but in those of the accusers who have legitimised a new view by insisting that it is old. Nandy shows that Hindutva is a new response to colonisation and that older Indian views of the world are marked precisely by their lack of essentialism and by their openness to cultural blending and borrowing. Mamdani argues that what 'Culture Talk' brands as 'Islamist fundamentalism' is a product of the twentieth century, not ancient history. It is an innovation in Muslim thought, not the centuries-old 'culture' that Lewis invented.[50] It is also a product of political events initiated by non-Muslims who then obliterated their own roles by blaming Muslims. This was similar to colonial rulers in Africa who denied its indigenous people education and then penalised them for being 'uneducated'. What is presented in media and public discussion as the essence of a faith or culture is a fairly recent invention which is rejected by many or most of its adherents.

The other common theme, albeit one made more explicit in Mamdani's and Boyarin's work than Nandy's, is the role of politics. We have seen Mamdani's explicit concern to show that what 'Culture Talk' seeks to explain was created by politics, not culture. Boyarin discusses the way in which the desire to pursue a political project, the creation of a state, prompted a shift in Jewish identity that was then misrepresented as an expression of culture or religion. Zionists rejected the Hebrew Bible as a religious text but turned to it repeatedly to justify their claims to land and territory.[51] And Hindutva is far more a political than a cultural or religious ideology. In all three cases, politics remoulds or invents an identity, even while the politicians or ideologues who do this insist that they are discovering the essence of a religion or culture.

While Mamdani's focus is to show the complicity of the United States in creating the political terrorism on which it would later wage war, there is also a parallel between Zionists, proponents of Hindutva and Muslim fundamentalism. All three are an ostensible rebellion against the power of the West that, in reality, became Western. The Zionist 'liberation' from Europe was a way of fitting in with Europe's political goals. (Europe is understood here not only as a geographic entity but as a worldview and a range of political objectives that are shared by the United States and other countries in which Europeans settled.) Hindutva adopted the views and values of British colonialism. The violent Muslim fundamentalism that the West fears which seems the polar opposite of the West, is in its political origins (rather than its religious outlook) the product not only of the West but of its most militantly colonial strain – the fighting of foreign wars using the 'laws of nature' rather than the 'laws of war'. In all three cases, the militant alternative to the West is its own creation.

On the surface, Mamdani's book is a critique of the West – primarily the United States – while Boyarin's and Nandy's are critiques of the responses to the West by groups that it had rejected or colonised. But this distinction is a matter of detail, not substance. All three are powerful critiques of the way in which an essentialised misuse of culture or religion can not only cause great damage but can also mould what appears to be an attempt to return to the authentic 'essence' of a faith or value system into a new way of becoming the West from which they claim to be breaking. Zionism, Hindutva and those Islamists who have used terror have all perpetrated this misuse.

This is only one of the lessons of this discussion that sheds light on race and identity everywhere. The remainder of the book will discuss these lessons.

8

Colonising Anti-Racism

The new abuses of anti-Semitism shed important light on racial dynamics in much of the world. In South Africa, despite claims on both the left and the right that race is a fiction manipulated by economic power holders or attention-seeking activists (depending on your side of the ideological divide), it continues to be the society's chief fault line and the core factor in most of its conflicts. The manipulation of anti-Semitism in the service of an ethnic nationalist state that defines itself in racist terms has important lessons for the state of race in the world in general, and in South Africa in particular.

THE ART OF VICTIM BLAMING

The most important focus of our analysis has been the way in which allegations of racism have been used, ironically, to protect racism. Here the Israeli state and its admirers have no monopoly – on the contrary, they reflect a wider trend.

The white supremacy of the late nineteenth century – of which the anti-Semitism of Chamberlain discussed in chapter 3 was a prime example – was explicit in its insistence that discriminating against human beings who were not white and Christian was justified. Colonialism shared this assumption. Kipling was not an eccentric exception. The notion that a 'superior' group of people, defined by their race, deserves to control others, and that this would 'civilise' the latter societies,[1] was a mainstream view in Europe and among those, originally from Europe, who colonised the Americas, Asia, Africa and Australia.

Not all colonisers shared Kipling's view that the colonised could and should not be recruited into the coloniser's 'way of life'. The idea that, as the political philosopher Rick Turner noted, '"western civilisation" is … superior to other forms, but … that blacks can, through education, attain the level of western civilisation'[2] was a very strong theme in colonial thought. One of many examples of this attitude was the franchise rule of the British-run South African territories before 1910. Black people were allowed to vote if they had acquired a sufficient degree of 'Westernness', which was expressed as property ownership or formal education.[3] But this was only another way of asserting white superiority; black people, according to this view, could become white if they tried hard enough. It was assumed that blacks should want this because to be white was to be better. (In theory, apartheid was less of a white supremacist doctrine than this form of 'liberalism' because apartheid claimed to hold all ethnic cultures to be equal. The claim was false but it showed more of a bad conscience about white supremacy than its supposedly less racist alternative.)

Inevitably, then, arguments against racism stressed the evidence that there was no difference in capacity or morality between races (or cultures or religions). They posited that the distinction was between those who believed that being born into a particular group of people somehow made some humans superior or more worthwhile than others, and those who could show these claims to be false. But this began to change around a half century ago. The shift was limited at first but, over the past decade, it has gathered momentum in the United States, Western Europe and South Africa.

The first sign of a change emerged in the United States in the 1970s when whites began to launch legal challenges to affirmative action laws.

The laws being targeted had sought to overturn the effects of centuries of racial domination by requiring schools and universities, businesses and the professions to provide opportunities for people who had been victims of racism, gender prejudice or other forms of bias. A white applicant for a place at a medical school claimed that he had been rejected because affirmative action had been used to give his place to a black person. He therefore claimed that he had been discriminated against on grounds of his race.[4] This soon became a trend. White men who, because they had previously dominated, were not eligible for affirmative action insisted that they were victims of discrimination. It could be argued – and often has been – that this view was inherently racist because it assumed that any black person who was chosen over a white person must be the beneficiary of favouritism since whites are inherently superior to blacks. But the argument which has been advanced in support of this view is fundamentally different to earlier justifications of white male supremacy.

The critics of affirmative action insist that they are the 'real' opponents of prejudice because it is *they* who believe in 'merit'. Measures that give preference to black people, women or any other dominated group are forms of discrimination because the measures allocate opportunities on grounds other than ability. The concern to protect the dominance of white people – and of white men in particular – remains the same but the vehicle has shifted; the earlier explicit claim that they were superior to other people has been replaced by the charge that they are 'victims of discrimination' because their assumed merit is not recognised.

Of course, the case would not need to be made if there were no programmes or policies that forced white men to accept that they would need to compete for opportunities more fiercely than in the past. Affirmative action programmes do not generally exclude dominant groups from appointment, and many continue to receive places at educational institutions or jobs where they apply. But because there is a preference, there are fewer places available for them and so they have to compete more vigorously to receive those that are available. The use of the language of 'merit' or 'non-discrimination' to pursue the interests of dominant groups is therefore a reaction to a threat to their dominance. More generally, the claim that dominant groups are victims of discrimination emerges when their domination is – or is perceived to be – in peril. As a result, 'groups who have traditionally been the objects of racial subjugation and violence are set up as today's "real racists".'[5]

This explains why the 'merit' argument has become so strong a theme among those who want to preserve their dominance over others. Inspired, no doubt, by the affirmative action example, they now take refuge not in spurious claims of superiority but in constant claims that it is *they* who are victims of bias. The new claims are, of course, equally baseless. Lentin observes that 'not racism' – the practice of labelling as racist anyone who challenges continued racism – 'entails the constant redefinition of racism to suit white agendas.'[6] It is important to clarify what 'white agendas' means here. If we see race, as Lentin argues we should, as 'racialized power', criticisms of 'white agendas' do not express a prejudice against whites.[7] They are, rather, a response to vehicles of power that enable some to dominate others. To analyse how power operates in a way that privilege whites is to describe the workings of a system, not to impugn the morality of white people. This logic has not, however, prevented the defenders of domination from using the argument not only to claim privileges but to defend their right to express their prejudices. As racism has become more subtle, so one of its defences has become the claim that white people are victimised if attention is drawn to their dominance. 'Decolonial and political antiracists are denounced as racist for referring to race,'[8] and whites are deemed to be under threat because their claimed right to dominate is challenged.

In 2021, conservative commentators in the United States claimed that there was a concerted attempt to 'take down white culture'. A rightwing television pundit appeared on air with a graphic in the background reading 'Anti-White Mania'; a Christian evangelist television personality complained that 'people of colour' have the 'whip handle' and were in a position to 'instruct their white neighbors how to behave.'[9]

There are strong parallels between some of these complaints and those by white southerners after their defeat in the nineteenth-century

American civil war; then too, white domination seemed under threat. The slave-owning states had been defeated and, for a brief time, the victorious North tried to encourage a degree of racial equality in southern states. Then, as now, a sense of victimhood was created by the fear that discrimination would end. In the nineteenth century, complaints that whites were under siege were wrapped in overtly white supremacist language. One newspaper complained in 1875 that efforts to achieve more equality were a 'scheme of upturning society and placing the bottom on top: an effort to legislate the African into an Anglo-Saxon'.[10] This was the language of racial dominance. The natural order is one in which whites dominate; the 'Anglo-Saxon' was born to rule over the always-inferior 'African'. An editorial in another newspaper a few years earlier articulated this clearly. It complained that racial equality was an 'inversion of … just and lawful relations'. What was needed, it asserted, was a future in which 'the white race would spring back to its position of natural supremacy, while the black race would fall back to its position of natural subordinacy'.[11]

The 2021 complainants do not explicitly say that whites are superior. Instead, they insist that their culture, their ways of living – even their physical beings – are under threat by moves towards greater equality. The unstated implication is that they see the need to dominate black people as central to their being.

A cause of this recent panic is said to be a four-decades-old field of scholarship, Critical Race Theory (CRT), which is an attempt by black scholars to examine racism in the United States as a product of the law and society's institutions, and not as the prejudices of individual white people.[12] Despite having remained in the classroom until recently, CRT has become the target of a loud right-wing campaign. Right-wing candidates running for public office do so on a pledge to remove it from classrooms by banning books and dismissing teachers who do not conform.[13] In Britain, a similar response greeted demands by black people for fairer treatment. There, the term 'woke' is used to serve the same purpose as attacks on 'Critical Race Theory'. 'Woke' has been used by some black anti-racism activists to denote someone sensitive to racial injustice,[14] but has never achieved anything like the prominence in thought among anti-racists as it has among those who use it to conjure up fear of a savage band of zealots determined to vilify whites and all their works. 'Wokerati' ('woke' people) are said to employ a tool called 'cancel culture' to ensure that 'decent citizens' who do not sign on to the latest left fetish are said to be 'cancelled' and so denied the right to speak.[15] In reality, those who claim to be 'cancelled' enjoy far more opportunities to be heard than those whom they accuse. It is not uncommon for people who enjoy unlimited access to the media to claim that they are being silenced by 'cancel culture'.

The parallels with the theme of this book should be clear. Critical Race Theory is an attempt to challenge racial dominance, but it is labelled an attempt to perpetuate racism by forcing whites to the margins. The term 'woke' was a call to awareness of racial injustice. It too is now denounced as an attempt to make life unpleasant for white people by, for example, demanding the removal of statues commemorating slave traders or overtly racist politicians.[16] This is said to be an attempt to obliterate history and memory, a charge that conveniently ignores the fact that there are ways of remembering slavery and racial exploitation that do not entail maintaining memorials to those who were responsible for them.

Architects of the 'culture wars' that target campaigners for racial equality seem unaware of what their complaint says of their prejudices. If enslaving human beings or reducing them to an inferior status because they were born into a particular race or religion is a core ingredient of the dominant culture, that culture is a danger to humanity. This dominant belief system is no more central to 'white culture' than gang violence is intrinsic to 'black culture'. Some white people are addicted to dominating black people, others are not. And so, to belabour the point, rejecting that culture is not a rejection of white people. But, like the proponents of the 'new anti-Semitism' idea, the proclaimers of white victimhood are concerned not with accuracy but with using invented claims of racism to ensure that the dominant group remains in charge.

A parallel phenomenon is the tendency of right wingers who had previously rejected democracy and freedoms to invoke both in defence of white privilege. Former US president Donald Trump, after losing an election because black voters had supported his rival, did not denounce democracy; rather, he invented false claims that it had been denied. His supporters passed laws to deny black people the vote, but insisted they were defending democracy by acting against 'voter fraud'. Demagogues in Hungary and Poland insist that elected governments act 'for the people' even though they ride roughshod over freedoms. Brexiteers in Britain tried to silence anyone who disagreed with them, claiming that anti-Brexiteers were ignoring the will of the people.

The appeal to free speech is also a new favourite of those who believe they are better than others. 'Thinkers' beloved on the right never tire of claiming that their free speech has been undermined because they are denied the right to insist that women are inferior to men, heterosexuals are superior beings and whites are right to dominate others. They insist that 'wokeness' and 'cancel culture' deny them their right to speak (which means, in effect, their right to express their prejudices).[17] The freedoms that were once used to challenge their dominance – such as the right to speak one's mind and to choose who governs – have been distorted and are now used to defend the right of the dominant to continue to dominate. There is no difference in substance between this new defence of racial dominance and the one it has replaced. An 'anti-white mania' is, in reality, a critique of whites' right to wield power over others. 'Telling white neighbours how to behave' sounds like an authoritarian attempt to police lifestyles but is, in reality, code for telling bigots not to insult others. The assumption that whites are born to be in charge has not changed; only the tactics that are used to ensure dominance have.

Why have they changed? Because the overt racism that they would have espoused decades ago has been discredited. The horrors of the Nazi genocide, the American civil rights movement's rebellion against racial laws, and the formal decolonisation of Africa and Asia have made it far less acceptable to talk about race as Chamberlain had done, or as mainstream politicians in the West once had. Racism and other ideologies of dominance are no longer respectable in polite society but the prejudices that inspired them are very much alive. How then may the dominant express what they feel without appearing to repeat unacceptable prejudices? By portraying the dominance of a group as its 'way of life', and by depicting any challenge to it and its prejudices as an attack on the group. It regards its leading and controlling role in society not as a power relationship but as its innate essence. By painting its position of power as its natural state, it expresses its anxiety over the possibility that it might lose its dominance.[18]

Labelling campaigners against Israeli state racism as 'anti-Semites' is therefore part of a wider attempt by the defenders of dominant groups to portray anti-racists who challenge them as racists, a ploy that mobilises the language of rights and equality to deny both.

APARTHEID IS DEAD, WHITENESS LIVES

Given this context, it would be surprising if this means of justifying white supremacy was not a feature of South African social reality.

Apartheid is, of course, dead. But whiteness is alive and well. 'Whiteness' here does not refer to the state of being white or of being part of a particular racial group; rather, it refers to the representations of being white, which project white people as superior to others.[19] The power relations that sustained apartheid survive in modified form.[20] Whites are now a minority in politics but remain dominant in business, the professions and many of the society's institutions. A deeply rooted fear that is embedded in the psyche of many white people is that black people will one day rise up and take everything they own.[21] The tendency to regard threats to continued white dominance as attacks on white people and all their works is, therefore, just about inevitable.

The claim that white people are under attack in post-1994 South Africa is commonplace.[22] It is also, at times, a claim made by the other racial minorities whose members are said to be denied jobs and other entitlements because black people are favoured. In its most extreme form, this prompted claims by the white right wing that a 'white geno-cide' had gripped the country.[23] This despite the fact that the number of black people who die in criminal violence far outweighs the number of white victims,[24] and that white incomes and access to services far outstrip those of black people. The problem is not that whites are being victimised because they are white, but that the dominance that they had enjoyed until 1994 is perceived to be under threat.

Since sport is a core South African preoccupation, the claim is fre-quently made that white people are being denied their 'rightful' place in national teams, particularly in the sports that are favoured by most white people: cricket and rugby. This complaint is particularly indicative of our theme because it insists that 'merit selection' is required, not racial preference.[25] This apparent non-racialism does not withstand serious scrutiny since closer examination shows that white players are automat-ically assumed to possess merit and their black counterparts are always assumed to lack it. The demand for 'merit' is a thinly disguised demand that only (or mostly) whites should be chosen. A return to the days of minority rule, when only whites were eligible for selection to national teams, is portrayed as a rejection of race and an assertion of merit. Rigid racism is presented as a rejection of racism, just as endorsement of the Israeli state's dominance of Palestinians is presented as the 'non-racial' option that rejects anti-Semitism.

In South Africa, an important proponent of this approach is the Democratic Alliance (DA), the official opposition in the national parlia-ment. It is a non-racial party and it has had a black leader. But that leader's refusal to see the world entirely through the eyes of white suburbanites irked the party's core leaders, who are white and had hoped that the party could accommodate black leaders who would think, speak and act as most white people do. Inevitably, this failed and the black leaders who did emerge expressed their own perspectives. So the white power holders lost interest in being led by a black person;[26] the elevation of black people to leadership was labelled 'an experiment that went wrong' by former DA leader Tony Leon.[27] This is a similar view to that of the Israeli parliamentarian who told a conservative Palestinian party which was part of the governing coalition that 'the experiment with you has failed'.[28] This was after the Palestinian had voted against a government attempt to give Israeli Jews settled in the Occupied Palestinian Territory certain rights that are denied Palestinians. White leaders of the DA are prone to paint black critics of white dominance as 'racist', which, loosely translated, means insufficiently sympathetic to what they see as white interests. Affirmative action remains a favourite target, as it is for many white people,[29] despite the fact that labour market data show that, almost three decades after the achievement of political democracy, whites occupy most of the senior positions in business and the professions,[30] and white unemployment figures are very low.

These dynamics were highly visible when, during the 2021 local election campaign, the DA erected posters in the Phoenix township in Durban reading 'the ANC calls you Racists, We Call you Heroes'. The posters were roundly condemned because they tried to exploit racial violence, which claimed over 30 lives in July 2021, between residents of the Phoenix township, who are mostly of Indian origin, and neighbouring Inanda, which is home mainly to black people.[31] The clashes were a product of the complex racial dynamics of the area that ensure that, despite long periods of racial harmony, tensions rise to the surface at times of stress. These are often fuelled by memories of racial clashes in 1949 that claimed 142 lives.[32] Like many other conflicts, who you believe is guilty or innocent depends on which side of the fence you sit. What should not be in dispute is that racial tensions were central to events in the area although, as often happens in South Africa, this was denied by some of the protagonists. The novelist and journalist Fred Khumalo pointed out: 'Clearly, race has a lot to do with what happened in Phoenix – even though many would like to pretend otherwise.'[33]

What is also not in dispute is that, regardless of what actually happened and the emotions or perspectives of the protagonists, participants in the South African debate projected their own perspectives onto the conflict, as they always do. For many whites and members of other minority racial groups, the inhabitants of Phoenix had been householders defending themselves from a violent mob; for many black people, they were racists who had assumed that black people had been a threat to them even if they were not. Those who supported the Phoenix residents insisted that race was not at issue; law-abiding people were protecting themselves. Hence Khumalo's comment. For those who did not support Phoenix, the claim to be defending person and property was an excuse for racially based hostility. (To agree with Khumalo that race was at issue is not to side against the people of Phoenix; it is simply to make the point that whatever the motives at play, race was central to the conflict. This observation is true of almost all South African conflicts.)

The DA's poster was widely condemned as an attempt to fuel the fire. It also demonstrated the degree to which the Phoenix conflict had become no longer about anything that had actually happened – and still less about the thoughts, feelings and actions of anyone who had played a role – but about South Africa's racial divisions. The claim that 'the ANC', South Africa's governing party, had branded the entire Phoenix community as racist was, to put it mildly, a stretch. The minister of police, Bheki Cele, had said that he had agreed with 'the community' that racism had played a role in the conflict; but he later said that he refused 'to take the situation here as a racial situation'. Given his earlier comments, this presumably meant that he thought that race had played a role but not one that was defining. Whatever his intent, it is a huge leap from these comments to the claim that the governing party had branded an entire community as racist. But, despite this, the fact that the claim was made was entirely predictable. For the mainstream in the racial minorities, 'the ANC' is less a political party and more a symbol of black demands for change – despite the fact that it is far less zealous in pursuing those demands than the label suggests.[34] Whether or not it actually does so, 'the ANC' is assumed to dismiss all members of racial minorities as racists.

The reason for the DA labelling the people of Phoenix as 'heroes' – rather than, say, people who have been wrongly accused of racism – is also unrelated to actual events. It assumes, regardless of the evidence, that they are defenders of an order that is under threat from the 'mobs' who demand racial change. Like the American right wingers discussed earlier, the minorities for whom the DA wants to speak see allegations of persistent racism not as a valid comment on the state of society but as a ploy to take from minorities that which they have. It is not about seeking equality, they say, but about imposing the will of one group on another. There is little difference between this view and that of American right wingers who see demands for racial equality as a means of destroying white people and their culture. An additional, and implied, DA theme is that the residents of Phoenix are 'heroes' because they are assumed to be property owners whose property is threatened. This concern for the property owner appears to express a 'race-free' interest in defending one economic class against another. But in South Africa, where race is still a prime determinant of access to property, it is a further example of 'whiteness' in non-racial guise.

Given this, it should be no surprise that DA leader John Steenhuisen reacted to criticism of the poster by claiming that the ANC was the 'real racist' because it had 'stigmatised' the Phoenix community. Nor was it surprising that the DA's former deputy chief whip in parliament, Mike Waters, was enraged when his party, at the prompting of some of its senior black members, apologised for the posters and took them down. Waters was so angered that he resigned as the DA's campaign manager in the Ekurhuleni metropolitan area. His resignation letter claimed that, despite the party's retreat, he would stay in the DA 'as long as I and other muscular liberals can raise our voices about the sanctimonious wokerati'.[35] Since he attached this label to anyone who felt that causing more divisions in an area wracked by violence was inappropriate, it applied in this case not only to the usual 'radical' suspects but also to commentators who usually support his party and to its mayoral candidate in Johannesburg.

The rejection of majority rule and racial equality in post-1994 South Africa is no longer phrased in the language of white supremacy; not even the white right publicly claims that blacks are inferior to whites and should be ruled by them. On the contrary, both majority rule and racial equality are portrayed, as they currently are by the American right, as racist because they discriminate against whites. Rather than being the assertion of white supremacy, opposition to it miraculously becomes non-racism. Implicit in this claim, as noted earlier, is the unspoken assumption that whites are indeed superior to blacks because, if they do not occupy top jobs or the best university places or a slot in national sports teams, 'merit' is being ignored and black people are the undeserved beneficiaries of racial preference. The core goal of this rejection of race as a social category is to preserve white dominance without overt claims of white supremacy. Kipling's aim – white control of everyone else – is now pursued not in his language, which insisted on the importance of race, but in the guise of non-racialism.

Similarly, the claim of a 'new anti-Semitism' tries to preserve domin-ance – of the Israeli state over Palestinians. It, too, relies on a bogus anti-racism that insists that anyone who queries the state's right to control is expressing hatred of Jews. In its hands, professions of non-racism, once a rebellion against racial dominance, have become weapons in the armoury of an ethnic nationalist claim. It has deprived Palestinians not only of their land but also of their witness to the racism that shapes their lives. In both South Africa and historic Palestine, the biggest threat to non-racism today is a fake anti-racism that manages to clothe itself in the garments of the real thing. Only a working knowledge of the context within which it is used can enable us to tell the copy from the genuine article.

SELF-HATE AND POWER

Using the 'self-hatred' label is another aspect of the defence of racism by accusing its opponents of being racist – though with much wider applica-tion. The notion that people who have been victims of racial, religious or cultural stigmatisation might react with 'self-hatred' is not a fabrication invented by those who use this weapon; 'self-hatred' is a reality, but it is not the reality that the ideologues of Hindutva and Zionism claim it to be.

An important feature of racism, as writers such as Fanon and Biko have shown, is its effect on the self-esteem and worldview of its victims. People who are repeatedly told by power holders that they are inferior may be inclined to believe this. The value system and biases of the dominant group become so all-consuming that they begin to shape the way in which the dominated see themselves – particularly when their daily experience is one in which everyone who occupies a dominating position is unlike them and everyone who is dominated is like them.

There is an important difference between this internalisation of the dominator's biases and the attitudes that, in the work of James Scott, persuade the dominated that they can never openly challenge their dominator and so must undermine it in other ways. Those who respond in the way that Scott illustrates know that their dominators are not superior to them. They recognise, however, that the dominators have more power and can therefore exact a heavy price for open challenges to their control. The 'mental colonisation' of which Biko and Fanon wrote convinces the colonised or dominated that their dominators really *are* superior. And so they make no attempt to subvert or frustrate the dominant power because they have come to accept that it is a product of the natural order.

When they employ the 'self-hate' label against those who differ with them, both Zionism and Hindutva refer to a real way in which dominated people respond to domination. However, as chapter 6 showed, both ideologies distort these responses in order to defend domination. In the process, they depict as 'self-hatred' attitudes which are its polar opposite. The 'self-hating' Jews with whom Boyarin identifies continue, he points out, a long Jewish cultural tradition in which the use of violence was seen as alien and the refusal to contest for power as admirable. And Nandy's work suggests that 'self-hating' Hindus are those who remain faithful to their tradition, not to the impositions of the coloniser. Both scholars show that, in their contexts, it is, in fact, those who point the accusing finger of 'self-hatred' who express a deep loathing for what they are and a desire to be someone else.

This, too, has important contemporary relevance in South Africa and elsewhere. In the South African case, it could be argued that core aspects of the post-apartheid agenda are, in reality, expressions of a self-hatred, which is often expressed in terms that seem to express pride. The presidency of Thabo Mbeki was shaped by an understandable goal whose pursuit had perverse consequences. Its aim was to prove the falsity of the white bigotry – still a reality in much of the West – that assumes that black people are inherently incompetent. Refuting this was important but Mbeki believed that it could be done only by showing white people that black people were good at that which whites were assumed to value. And that, in turn, meant paying inordinate respect to what were considered to be white values.[36]

Whites were, for example, assumed to value technical efficiency above all else – certainly above approaches that stressed compromise and a willingness to accommodate all views, both of which have strong roots in the traditions of many black South Africans.[37] The attempt was not made to convince whites that, in a deeply divided society with a past marked by racial domination, approaches to government that stress inclusiveness and compromise were more likely to produce lasting solutions. Instead, the stress on technical efficiency was preferred because it was assumed to be what white people, at home and abroad, expected. The methodology, therefore, was to reduce government to a technical exercise in which those who presume to know what must be done would impose it on everyone else (and would become dismayed when they met resistance).

Following current Western orthodoxy, South Africa's elites – across the spectrum – therefore insist that the goal of government is 'service delivery',[38] which is primarily a technical or managerial pursuit. But this approach is likely to leave citizens dissatisfied because it reduces them to being passive recipients of the products of the technical decisions of officials and politicians. In one illustrative case, in the Diepsloot informal settlement in Johannesburg, the 'service delivery' agenda dictated that residents' homes be moved because their location was said to hamper the provision of what was technically required.[39] 'Service delivery' was what people were trying to escape, not what they wanted. Embedded in the notion of 'service delivery' is the assumption that governments in South Africa (and elsewhere in the global South) should concentrate on trying to become an idealised model of an 'efficient' government in the North. The effect is to ensure that citizens are not served by governments that meet their needs. The desire to be someone else has perverse consequences for those it is meant to benefit.

Similarly, the South African public debate about what democracy should achieve has for years been filtered through the notion, popularised by US scholars, of 'democratic consolidation'. Stripped of its outer layer, this is essentially the idea that new democracies across the world are somehow defective until they become clones of a very idealised portrayal of those in the North. This distorts the prime goal of democracy, which is to ensure that citizens have a say in the running of government, whether or not it resembles what the elite believes New York to be. A perceptive analysis by a celebrated Latin American scholar points to the extent to which this influential notion of democracy is driven by a desire to be like Western Europe and North America.

> Democracy, even if – or perhaps precisely because – it had so many different meanings attached to it, was the central mobilizing demand that had to be achieved and preserved forever. Somehow, it was felt, this democracy would soon come to resemble the sort ... found in admired countries of the Northwest – admired for their long-enduring regimes and for their wealth, and because both things seemed to go together ... The Northwest was seen as the endpoint of a trajectory that would be largely traversed by getting rid of the authoritarian rulers.[40]

It was an abiding concern of South African governments for at least a decade after 1994 to demonstrate that they are 'world class'. This term is never defined because it never needs definition: 'world class' has always been another way of saying 'like the global North'. And, again, it skews priorities. Instead of concentrating on what is most likely to serve the needs of the society, policies and programmes focus on what might convince the presumed arbiters of 'world class' that a country on the southern tip of Africa is capable of behaving as they believe that the places in which they live do.[41]

Self-hatred has more insidious effects. One example was the South African government's response to the HIV/AIDS pandemic. It consisted largely of an attempt to deny that the virus existed and a refusal to provide the medication needed to treat it.[42] While many theories were offered to explain this (in)action by the government, the most credible saw it as an attempt to refute racism. The HIV discourse was a fertile source of racial bigotry, which falsely claimed that the virus spread particularly rapidly in Africa because of the sexual behaviour of its residents. For Mbeki, who was the country's president at the time, this made the virus a potent symbol of black presumed inferiority – a point he made in a parliamentary debate on AIDS. He complained that 'bigots' regarded black people as 'sub-human disease-carriers'.[43] According to Mbeki, to acknowledge the virus and seek to treat it was to give credence to a racial stereotype. Thus, his government devoted its energy to denying the virus's existence rather than treating it.

Central to self-hatred is that it does not refute or ignore bigotry and stereotypes; it internalises them. Instead of refuting the northern prejudice by pointing out that there was no connection between race and susceptibility to HIV, and then proceeding to extend treatment to people who had been infected, the power of the racial stereotype was accepted. To recognise that many people were infected was thus seen to be an acknowledgement that Africans had indeed behaved in ways that made them ill. The stereotype could be rejected only by denying that many people had been infected and needed help. There was only one difference between this thought process and that of a Herzl or a Freud who concluded that anti-Semites were correct and that Jews had to do what they could to become non-Jews. In Mbeki's case, there was no easy remedy since there was no cure for HIV and AIDS, but only a treatment. There was, therefore, no way that Africans could become what non-Africans were assumed to have wanted them to be. The only remedy was to deny the reality of the problem which triggered the label.

These examples show that self-hatred is indeed a reality. But the self-haters are not those who believe in an inclusiveness that reaches out to others. Rather, it is those who, as in these examples, internalise the 'inferiority' of their ways of seeing and being and so seek to be what they are not. This form of self-hatred can also, as it did with Freud and Herzl, produce a view of the world that appears to be a radical assertion of who they are but is, in reality, an expression of a desire to integrate into the dominant culture.

In post-1994 South Africa, demands for black economic inclusion, an essential goal, are often a quest for integration into existing institutions and organisations. There is a certain irony attached to the demand for incorporation when it is accompanied by militant rhetoric. In that case, what is being demanded is the power to be someone else, not the power to be oneself. The objective is not to ensure that business and professional life is reshaped to reflect the realities and perspectives of the dominated, but to ensure that they can share in what the dominators created. That system, then, will continue operating in the way it had always done. For Herzl and Freud, forming a state was the key to becoming members of the dominant group; for some South Africans today, it may be acquiring a stake in a company established by the dominant group.

The use of ostensible non-racism to silence anti-racism, and the distortion of 'self-hatred' are not the only implications of the 'new anti-Semitism'. It raises other issues of much broader importance. These are the focus of the concluding chapter.

CONCLUSION: THE 'NEW ANTI-SEMITISM' AND POLITICS TODAY

As the previous chapter showed, a key feature of this analysis has been a critique of racial essentialism, the idea that racial or ethnic groups have an 'essence' to which all members of the group do or should conform.

FREEZING DIFFERENCE: THE PROBLEM OF 'ESSENCES'

We have seen that this essentialism can be used to stigmatise or to impose conformity within a group. As chapter 3 showed, Marr, Chamberlain and other anti-Semites regarded Jews as inherently evil or as threats. In their view this evil or threatening nature is a product of birth, just as a 'black, brown or yellow skin' is a permanent marker of inferiority purely as an accident of parentage. For the ideologues of the Israeli state and their allies – as well as many of today's anti-Semites, of course – a particular brand of ethnic nationalism is 'authentically' Jewish and all other expressions of Jewishness are, at best, cheap imitations, or, at worst, frauds which pretend to be Jewish but are not.

The theorist and philosopher Judith Butler, in her attempt to develop a feminist alternative to essentialism, notes that it enables 'the regulation of attributes along culturally established lines of coherence'.[1] Essentialisms are 'hostile to hybridity in that they promote policing the boundaries of identity and acts of exclusion and domination sanctioned by an appeal to an essential core of an individual'.[2] Essentialism ignores or suppresses differences within identity groups and cultures and vastly exaggerates differences between them. It also denies the reality that all cultures are influenced by others and that the loudest advocates of cultural authenticity often promote practices that are borrowed.

One of the ironies that essentialism produces is that, while it sees all members of a group as one, it creates differences within the group because its adherents use it as a weapon to police the boundaries of what is acceptable within the group. Smearing Jewish opponents of the Israeli state as inauthentic Jews is a frequent tactic. Rudyard Kipling did not regard Indians who valued British education, culture and customs as really Indian; his Indian acolytes today use the ideology of Hindutva to stigmatise 'self-hating' Hindus. His fellow colonial ideologues who encouraged the colonised to become like the coloniser were not breaking with essentialism. Rather, they embraced it in a different form since they insisted that there was something called 'native culture' and something else called 'British culture', and that the latter was superior to the former. The fact that they believed that it was possible to move from one to another did not alter their view that these were entirely separate and that theirs was the better culture. They did not want the colonised to blend their culture with that of the coloniser; they wanted the colonised to abandon that into which they were born and embrace another.

Nandy shows that essentialism is not the monopoly of the coloniser or of the white supremacist; it is also embraced by some among the colonised and the racially dominated who insist that they advocate a militant alternative. His argument is not only a critique of colonial thinking but also challenges the notion that decolonisation should be understood as the replacement of colonial assumptions by an 'authentic' indigenous understanding free of 'Western' influence. This, he argues, would repeat precisely the essentialism that underpinned colonial thinking. As noted earlier, the notion of a 'pure' European, African or Asian culture is a fantasy. To distinguish between people who are 'African (or Asian or European) enough' to qualify for their identity and those who are not is to repeat colonialism's refusal to acknowledge differences within cultures. The alternative to colonial thought patterns is not an essentialism of the dominated but the 'hybridity' and syncretism that Nandy advocates.

This point is directly relevant to South Africa. Here the survival of patterns of white supremacy after the end of apartheid has prompted demands for 'decolonisation', which may be understood as calls for the demise of white supremacist views and values.

South African Essences

It could convincingly be argued that essentialism once dominated in South Africa but no longer does.

Essentialism seems far more akin to the colonisation imposed by Afrikaner nationalism through apartheid than the current version against which advocates of decolonisation are rebelling. Apartheid was founded on an essentialism that falsely claimed that it was giving expression to the diversity of cultures. Chapter 6 noted De Wet Nel's justification for dividing black people into ethnicities because these expressed their 'authentic' identity. This 'diffuse language of cultural essentialism' was pivotal to apartheid ideology because it enabled it to avoid the 'crude scientific racism drawn from the vocabulary of social Darwinism' while still justifying racial domination.[3]

Apartheid ideology did not want to rely on Chamberlain-like notions of Aryan supremacy. Although those were its inspiration, the Nazi death camps and the formal decolonisation of Africa in the 1960s had made that view no longer respectable. Instead, it was claimed that races and ethnic groups possessed a distinctive culture that would be fatally diluted if mixed with others. This was provided as a rationale for strict racial separation. Apartheid ideologues also constructed a rigid and static notion of ethnic identity, extolling those among the colonised who, in their view, fitted the stereotype. The idea that there is a single, essential, African culture with which all Africans (or all who share a common language) identify differs from this thinking only in the sense that it suited apartheid's architects to stress various black ethnicities. They hoped that this would justify their divide-and-rule strategy and would dilute the reality that whites were a small minority. On this basis, some apartheid ideologues insisted that the system could not be considered minority rule since, if you divided black South Africans into 11 ethnic groups, no group was in the majority and South Africa was a country of minorities.[4] Apartheid's creators and apologists were comfortable with the idea that those who they dominated possessed an essentialised culture that had nothing in common with that of white people (whose culture was, of course, also essentialised).

But apartheid is no longer the dominant form of South African colonialism; that form was defeated in 1994. It has been replaced, in large measure, by a revival of the pre-1948 form of cultural domination. Before the victory of Afrikaner nationalism in 1948, South Africa was a British dominion. Its prime minister, Jan Smuts, was a loyal servant of the empire who served in the British war cabinet in both World Wars.[5] The dominant cultural framework was thus British. After apartheid's end, the dominant culture reverted to that which had reigned before 1948. Now the dominance would more accurately be described as Western, rather than exclusively British. American influence plays an important role, as does the fact that Britain is no longer seen as the centre of the universe – a view held by many white English speakers – because it has been joined by the United States and by all of Western Europe. When student protests in 2015 became the catalyst for calls to decolonise the academy, they were aimed at the statue not of an apartheid-era government figure, but of Cecil John Rhodes, the key figure in Britain's colonisation of southern Africa.[6] The view that Richard Turner had attributed to white liberals has become the framework through which the country's dominant culture views the world.

This form of mental and cultural colonisation seems to be the polar opposite of Kipling's essentialism. It does not romanticise African culture to justify the domination of African people but, as much by what it does not say as by what it does, it brands African cultures inferior and assumes that black people attain 'civilised' status only by accepting 'Western' norms and assumptions. It assumes that political and social thought is the work of Westerners and so marginalises African ideas and values. One source of conflict on university campuses is a complaint by black students that the curricula in the humanities exclude thinkers who do not share the outlook of Western thought and topics that would throw light on the experience of people who are heirs to other traditions.[7] One possible response is to advocate a clean break with Western culture and to unconditionally embrace an African alternative. But, as Nandy suggests for the Indian context, this break is not a departure at all since the new cultural supremacy is as wedded to the idea that there are separate cultures that cannot blend as the old one was.

This becomes clear if we grasp what the current form of domination is seeking to do. In contrast to Kipling's essentialism and apartheid ideology, today's colonised education does not triumphantly declare the superiority of the 'West' and the inferiority of Africa. It simply excludes Africa except for that version of its realities and experiences that are seen from Western eyes. Black political thinkers are not denigrated; they are ignored. Western frameworks are not exalted; there is no need, since they are the only ones that shape what is said and written.

South African media, while proudly proclaiming its cultural and political neutrality, assiduously presents the perspectives of a suburbia that mirrors the attitudes and experiences of southern California.[8] While diversity and debate are in theory permitted, there is little room for pluralism or hybridity within the dominant culture. Mmusi Maimane, the DA's sole black leader (from 2015 to 2019), ran afoul of the policers of suburban orthodoxy when he had the temerity to refer to 'white privilege' and 'black poverty' at a Freedom Day rally,[9] a remark that may well have cost him the party leadership. Like the Muslims who must show that they are 'good' if they do not want to be labelled 'bad', the culturally colonised are never integrated into the 'superior' culture that they are implicitly exhorted to join until and unless they show extraordinary commitment to its worldview.

The persistent racial domination assumes that a particular way of viewing the world is the only way and withholds acknowledgement of alternatives and of those who adhere to them. It is as keen as Kipling and apartheid have been to set boundaries; the difference is in the methods it employs. Its understanding of what is permitted is as rigid as apartheid's – it too has little room for the blending of cultures. It neither professes nor feigns admiration for indigenous cultures. It is as committed to imposing a template upon them as the overt essentialists are, and as intolerant of admitting even aspects of these cultures into the closely guarded borders of 'Western culture'.

For some, the alternative to this cultural imposition is to replace the dominant Western culture with an essentialised African rival. But this liberates no one; it simply replaces one template with another. The term 'Western culture', used routinely by most participants in the debate, is itself an imposition because it assumes that, in Western Europe and North America, there is only one way of thinking and seeing. In reality, there are many. Similarly, there is no single 'African culture'. There are many African cultures and to impose one cultural understanding on Africans as if it is the only one is itself a form of colonisation.[10] In Africa, as in 'the West', culture is inevitably contested. Claims by the powerful that particular practices are culturally required may be challenged by alternative understandings of what a particular culture expects.[11]

India is no different. Nandy argues that an authentic anti-colonial position would need to recognise that 'culturally, it is a choice neither between the East and the West nor between the North and the South. It is a choice – and a battle … *within* India and *within* the West'.[12] To be Indian – or African or European – is not to endorse a particular view of the world since, within each, rivals contend and no one view can claim to be more 'real' an expression of the culture than any other. Not only is ideological pluralism a constant feature of cultures, it is essential for their survival and growth. 'A plurality of ideologies can always be accommodated within a single lifestyle. Fittingly so; a living culture has to live and it has an obligation to itself, not to its analysts. Even less does it have any obligation to conform to a model.'[13]

This essentialism also refuses to acknowledge that cultures are influenced by other cultures. It thus imposes on (African) doubters and dissenters only one way of thinking and being. This single way does not reject the dominant colonial culture but replaces it with a home-grown variant that is every bit as inclined to impose on Africans that which alienates some. Since this sets up artificial barriers between cultures, it also becomes, like colonisation, a way in which some exert power over others. The core feature of both Kipling's essentialism and the colonial culture that currently dominates South Africa is not that they are Western; it is that they are imposed and that they exclude. To stigmatise Africans who do not think and behave in the required 'anti-colonial' manner is to remove them from sight, speech and thought just as colonial ideologies do.

The cure for one form of imposition of thought and behaviour cannot be a new form of imposition and exclusion. It must, rather, be a view that includes and opens cultural and intellectual horizons to all influences. To avoid the inevitable misunderstanding that occurs when people take strong positions, it should be said that this is not an argument against resisting intellectual and cultural decolonisation. On the contrary, it argues that colonisation's grip on our thinking may well be even more insidious than we imagine because many of the loudest contemporary complaints against it may be deeply influenced by the colonial view of the world. It is, if anything, an argument for a more thorough decolonisation than those currently on offer. It insists that African ways of thinking are a crucial element of an alternative. But, if other influences are ignored or vilified, the result will be as inauthentic as Kipling's or apartheid's fraudulent vision of the 'real' African, or cultural equivalents of the Jewish zealot's Polish coat that claims to signal an authentic Jewishness but is actually a symbol of the dominated absorbing the dominating culture. If we consider that the most 'Jewish-looking' Jews dress like Poles who wanted to be Persians, then we will be very wary of an 'authentic' culture that hides its influences.

Colonialism, like any other form of cultural domination, does not allow other ways of thinking and, in Kipling's version at least, brands those among the dominated who have a different view of belonging as 'self-hating' traitors to their culture. The cure for this form of bullying cannot be to continue to impose thought and behaviour on people and to exclude those who do not conform. The problem with the dominant form of South African colonisation is that it values only the West and denies other ways of seeing and doing, accusing them of importing 'inferior' strands into the 'only and true' culture. The rejected 'other ways' include those within the West who challenge the dominant view. The constant claim of those who protect cultural domination in South Africa is that the alternative 'lowers standards'. This claim suggests that the culture and values that underpinned white supremacy are a 'standard' to which all others must aspire. Besides imposing mental and emotional burdens on the colonised, it silences their voices not only because it finds value in the norms and ideas of the West (or of any place else outside Africa) but because, beneath a veneer of tolerance, it insists that there is only one way of thinking about and seeing the world. To colonise is to close down and to suppress, whatever the identity of the coloniser and the colonised might be.

Some seemingly radical 'alternatives' to this imposition actually continue the practice. As Nandy shows in India, the claim that we can be truly opposed to colonisation only if we reject all Western thought and deny all difference between us does not decolonise. It retains the barriers between 'the West' and the rest while ostensibly choosing to be on the 'right side' of a ghetto that remains firmly in the heart and mind of the rebel. The truly radical alternative insists on not being part of any ghetto at all. It seeks to open minds to all that is African (and Asian and European and Latin American) and to remain open to the full range of human ways of believing and doing. Thus, one African advocate of intellectual decolonisation observes: 'Western modes and forms of knowledge are important, but they are not the only valid or viable kinds; other forms of modern knowledge and thought, just as advanced and even groundbreaking, are available in cultures and civilisations the world over.'[14]

Just as the Jewish and Hindu peddlers of cultural conformity turn out to be imitators of those who they claim to reject, so too does any exponent of any culture who denies the differences within it or the degree to which that which is claimed to be peculiar to it alone is the product of an inevitable borrowing from others. The anti-Zionist Jew and the Hindu who reaches out to Indian Muslims and Christians are at least as Jewish and Indian as those who try to turn their version of the culture into a weapon. The same can be said of Africans – or Europeans or Asians – who believe that they can be proud and authentic members of their groups while valuing the influences of others.

STATE AND IDENTITY

The use of fake claims of anti-Semitism to demonise Jews who insist on clinging to a more traditional view of Jewish identity is a creation of the Israeli state. This raises the important issue of the relationship between states and ethnic, racial or other identities.

It was noted in chapter 6 that it is a favourite Zionist argument that a state for one ethnic group on territory that houses several groups is justified because 'every other nation has a state', and so Jews should have one too.[15] This often-used rhetoric has become a stock response to criticism. (Of course, this argument is not used as frequently as the allegation that the critic is an anti-Semite.) Whether Jews are a nation – rather than a religious or an ethnic group – is not at all self-evident. Shlomo Sand's important work argues that Jewish 'nationhood' is an invention of Zionist ideologues who turned a religion and an ethnic group into a 'nation'.[16] A celebrated and oft-quoted study of nationalism argues that all nations are 'imagined communities' and not the organic products of nature as nationalists assert.[17] The claim that Jews are a nation is very new in the span of Jewish history; it is not the product of some centuries-old tradition but of the European cultural climate in the eighteenth century in which 'nations' were seen as natural foundations of human society and the state was regarded as a vehicle for the expression of nationhood.[18] The 'nation state' that is said to embody this 'reality' is also a recent invention in human history and it is this European idea that inspired Zionism.

Current definitions of 'nation' stress common ancestry as well as 'common myths and historical memories'. Members of a nation, we are told, share 'beliefs in a common ancestry and a common genealogy'. But these definitions could equally well describe ethnic groups.[19] Using this definition, many 'nations' (or ethnic groups) do not have states while many states are not political vehicles for nations. India alone is home to at least 50 ethnic groups;[20] China has 56 officially recognised groups.[21] 'Western' states are home to multiple groups that believe they have a 'common ancestry' that is not shared by other citizens. In Africa, no state is inhabited by only one ethnic group. Botswana, which is often cited as an example of a country with only one ethnicity, is in fact home to 12.[22] Given these realities, no 'nations' have states in the way that the European nationalists who inspired Zionism believed they should.

The Zionist claim that all nations have states is a product of confusing citizenship and nationality, which is ironic since, as noted earlier, the Israeli state recognises the difference by issuing documents that reflect the nationality, not the citizenship, of its citizens. In keeping with the nineteenth-century European thinking that inspired it, the Israeli state privileges nationality over citizenship. The German, Indian and Ghanaian states, to take a few random examples, 'belong' to their citizens but not (at least formally) to any one 'nation' or ethnic group. So the Israeli claim serves only to highlight the core Zionist aim: to create a state that is the property of only one ethnic group. This is not an international norm; it is an exception and thus gives Jews in the Israeli state a status that is an outlier across the globe. An obvious consequence of the claim that the state belongs to a particular group is that others who live within it are denied their rights. Within the dominant group in the Israeli state and its allies 'you find a level of disdain for human rights when they involve an undesirable minority – immigrant, religious, ethnic, or national – and the public's total support for deliberately ignoring the rights of other people'.[23]

Zionists are not alone in wanting a state for one nation only. This idea is still very much alive in the rhetoric and, at times, the policies and laws that some dominant ethnic groups demand in some states. We have already seen how Hindutva in India seeks to create a state for one group of Indians only. Similar motivations lie behind the Burmese assault on the Rohingya,[24] and the Chinese bullying of the Uighur minority.[25] The Trump slogan 'Make America Great Again' has been interpreted, accurately, by critics to mean 'Make America White Again'.[26] The American right is, generally, driven by a desire to return to a past in which only whites were considered 'real Americans' even though other ethnic groups also inhabited the United States. In France, the claim of a common 'Republicanism' is used to deny rights to minorities on the grounds that they are violating an essence of French nationhood by being what they wish to be.[27] Britain's exit from the European Union was, for some of its architects, a vindication of 'Britishness',[28] which, they believed, was threatened by both the European Union and immigration.

In all these cases, the invention of the nation is a reaction precisely to the fact that this idea of nationhood does not describe social reality. The American right, for example, is preoccupied with reviving a state run by whites precisely because white domination is under threat by demographic changes that will make whites a minority by 2045.[29] While the dominant groups in France or Hungary – or elsewhere where nationhood is used to impose one identity on all – are not about to be outnumbered, changing demographics and cultural norms do instil in dominant groups a fear that 'the nation', which here means the rule of their group over others, is in danger of being drowned by a multi-identity reality.

A state that represents one ethnicity (or 'nationality') can be democratic only if its residents belong only to one group. But this applies to very few countries (South Korea and the Democratic People's Republic of Korea [North Korea] are two possible examples).[30] In most cases, an insistence that a state represents only one group would automatically deny rights to a significant section of the state's population. If, as Zionism claims, a 'Jewish state' is a goal for which Jews have yearned over the centuries, then Jewish culture would be inherently undemocratic. But it isn't. In the Pentateuch, the first five books of the Hebrew Bible, which is the founding document of mainstream Jewish belief and culture, the injunction to extend equality to the 'stranger who dwells among you' is mentioned 36 times, more than any other command.[31] While Zionism has been happy to embrace the Hebrew Bible when it serves its interests, its devotees ignore this command, which, translated into modern circumstances, insists that respect for diversity within any political community and equal treatment to anyone who differs is a non-negotiable principle.

The realities discussed here show that common cultures and traditions – whether we call them ethnicity, nationality or peoplehood – can be expressed in monopolistic control of a state only at the expense of others. But it shows too that one effect of reliance on a state may be to divide and distort the identity of the dominating group. Before the creation of the Israeli state, Jews, like other groups, were not free from divisions. Beside differences in religious practice between competing strains of Jewish belief, some of the cultural prejudices of which Jews were victims were also directed by some Jews at others. We have already noted prejudices against black Jews,[32] and scholars have discussed the ways in which some themes of colonial ideology have been used by Western European Jews to stigmatise their East European counterparts.[33] But, in these cases, the antagonists usually acknowledge, however grudgingly, the Jewishness of those with whom they differ. The creation of the Israeli state has increasingly prompted Zionists to redefine Jewish identity as loyalty to the state. Initially, the state was meant to offer an expression of that identity (at the expense of others on its territory); in time, it has become the identity. To be Jewish, in this view, is no longer to be excluded; it is to exclude. And among those whom it excludes are Jews who refuse to fuse their identity with that of the state.

There would be no need to enforce these boundaries between dominant groups and the 'other' if they were not threatened. It is precisely because of challenges to the notion that a state can represent one identity without discarding democracy and that any identity is expressed only through a state that there is a need to defend it. This is the case in India, the United States, France, Britain or on Palestinian lands. In these countries, a backlash is triggered because the conceit that insists that the state belongs to only one group is under threat. As the diversity of these countries becomes ever clearer and the groups that the conceit concealed from view become visible and audible, the need to defend the myth of a nation state in which only white people are considered authentic members becomes urgent.

The changes within Jewish identity discussed here may be part of a significant shift in many societies across the globe which may be realigning the notion of what it is to be a citizen of a state on the one hand, and a member of a community on the other. We are witnessing, across the world, a rise in bigotry, xenophobia and plain, old-fashioned racism. This is because the unspoken assumptions that always excluded everyone but the dominant group – which in Europe, of course, is always white – are being challenged. As disturbing as the resistance to this change currently is, the fact that a reaction is needed at all is a source of hope for those who believe that human beings really are equal and that political institutions should offer equal rights to everyone regardless of birth or belief.

Balad/Tajamoa, a party representing Palestinian citizens of the Israeli state and which contests Israeli elections, adopted the slogan 'a state for all its citizens' to describe what it wishes the Israeli state to become.[34] While the slogan is obviously inspired by and tailored to Palestinian realities, it could well serve as a rallying cry for the change that the current statist reaction is trying to prevent; a change to a situation where to be American, Indian, Chinese or French means offering loyalty not to a particular group but to a common notion of citizenship in which a core role of the state is to protect and provide avenues for multiple identities. In such a case, loyalty to a state or political community becomes loyalty not to a common history but to values and rules, chief among them the equal treatment of and respect for all. In this view, the 'authentic' form of citizenship is hyphenated, a combination of what makes us distinct and what holds us together.[35]

South Africa is as in need of this message as any other state – perhaps even more. Before democracy was achieved, the question of whether people hailed from South Africa was seen as irrelevant; the society's fault line was race, not birthplace. But in the 1990s, as a majority-ruled state became a reality, hostility to people from elsewhere in Africa became one too.[36] Today, it is ubiquitous. The phrase 'porous borders' is a favourite in the national debate. It makes sense only if we assume that a barrier is required to ensure that those who 'own' the state are not disturbed by those who do not. At the grassroots, the message of the elites – that the people who do not 'own' the state are a menace – provides an explanation for poverty and inequality and, at times, a reason for violence (which is then deplored by the elites whose prejudices made it possible). If the reigning message was that the state 'belongs to all who live in it'[37] (as claimed by the Freedom Charter, which was adopted on 26 June 1955 and framed a strain of anti-apartheid politics) rather than all those whose parents happen to have been born in it, South Africa would be less violent and more prosperous, since it would benefit from the contributions of all who live within its borders.

Hostility to people who were born outside South Africa is often defended in terms that are very familiar to the anti-immigrant lobbies of North America and Western Europe. First, critics of this prejudice are routinely stigmatised as racist if they are not black, or 'self-hating' if they are, because antipathy to people from elsewhere is assumed to be an 'authentic' expression of African identity.[38] Second, critics of the regnant prejudice are branded as elitists who enjoy the luxury of moralising because they do not experience what the poor or the marginalised do.[39] This is a standard defence of bigotry everywhere. It portrays human rights as an effete luxury that 'the people' cannot afford, despite the fact that it is always elites who spread the bigotry and that its victims are almost invariably people who live in poverty. The claim that support for immigrants' rights is a white fetish ignores the fact that the victims of anti-foreigner violence are mostly black.[40]

There are echoes here of a familiar theme in the ideology of the Israeli state – the claim that in a world divided neatly into 'them' and 'us', human rights inevitably prevent 'us' from using the violence required to protect our own.[41] But the claim that support for immigrant rights is racist or 'unAfrican' is especially irrational in the South African context where the victims of bigotry are almost always African and black. The South African version of anti-immigrant hostility is a particularly stark example of the dangers of turning the state into a vehicle for identity – at the cost of anyone who happens not to be a citizen. The definition of an ethnic group or nation offered elsewhere is now attached, spuriously, to a state. There are also strains of Nandy here since the state that is fetishised in this way was created not by Africans but by their colonisers; South Africa was born in 1910 out of an agreement between four white-run colonies. Its borders and identity are a white, colonial creation. Using them as vehicles of hostility to other Africans echoes the anti-colonial rhetoric that is used to adopt the coloniser's worldview, which is a characteristic of Hindutva.

The key point here is that the focus of identity should become the state rather than shared history and culture – which are said to be the features of ethnicity or nation. For today's Zionist, 'real Jews' are not those who adhere to the religion or culture of the group, they are those who are loyal to a state. For today's South Africans bent on repelling the migrant 'threat', the identity that matters is not black or African – despite the racial rhetoric that is employed, it is citizenship of a particular state. In this case, it is a state defined and established by governments of another continent who used the states they had created to dominate the Africans they had colonised. The state prompts the same conflict and denial of rights that militant forms of ethnic or national identity do, but in a far more artificial wrapping in which the only commonality between members of the community is a status conferred on them by a colonially created administrative unit with an army and police force.

Reverence for a state – which is always portrayed as a 'nation state' even if it is not – that governs a variety of identities but is said to belong to only one is not restricted to Zionism. It is common and includes the constant efforts of dominant groups to repel immigrants to their states, which has become one of the most serious forms of exclusion and discrimination in the world today. It is no surprise that the Israeli state is so admired by those who use the state as a discriminatory fetish; it is perhaps the starkest example today of a state founded on the principle of exclusion and domination. And so it serves as an inspiration and role model to those throughout the world who see the state as the property of a single group.

Democratic citizenship – based on the assumption that the state is the property of all its citizens and that it should function to protect the rights of and respond to the wills of all – is an ideal rather than a reality. But while there are few, if any, societies in which all are accorded equal respect, the principle that all should at least enjoy formal rights (which they can, in principle, use to fight for substantive recognition) is entrenched in the rules of most democracies. The rise of the right has threatened this notion and the Israeli state is a fulcrum for those who seek to turn the inheritance of all into the monopoly of some. The attempt to divide Jews into the 'good' who are loyal to the state and the 'bad' who are not has much wider application. For democrats everywhere, it underlines the need to resist this fusing of statehood and identity and to insist that the notion that states belong to all who live in them is a fundamental democratic principle.

CONCLUSION: MISTAKEN IDENTITY

The story of how loyalty to an ethnic nationalist state distorted Jewish identity and how it now uses spurious anti-racism to defend racial dominance has lessons that stretch far beyond the Jewish people, the Zionist state, and the Palestinians who the state continues to dominate.

It warns also of attempts in various countries to justify ethnic or national chauvinism and to defend racial domination by painting the dominator as the victim and the dominated as the perpetrator. It alerts us to the dangers of essentialism which straitjackets human groups by ignoring their rich diversity, and to the degree to which purported rebellions against domination may simply repeat its assumptions. It also points to what may happen when states are turned from administrative units into objects of worship.

The Israeli state and its supporters often seek to deflect criticism of its rights violations by claiming that it is treated differently to other states and so ought to be left alone. Its critics point out that pressure on it to change is essential precisely because it does receive special treatment. No other state would be able to perpetrate serial rights abuses and still enjoy the uncritical support of all the Western powers. There may well be another sense in which the Israeli state is special: it has become a talisman for the new racism, some of whose features have been discussed in this chapter.

Gobineau, Chamberlain and the other peddlers of anti-Jewish racism discussed in chapter 3 would find it very difficult to make sense of today's world. Now, those who claim to speak for Jews have become a role model for those – mostly non-Jewish – who seek to maintain Western dominance of the dominated who demand equality. Those nineteenth-century anti-Semites would battle to comprehend how the anti-Semitism that reduced Jews, and anyone else who was not of white European descent, to outsiders at best, mortal threats at worst, has now become a false label that is slapped on all who resist their racist ideas.

Would they, like many of those who keep their ideas alive today, have been gratified that those who presume to speak for Jews have become Aryans? Or would they have been dismayed that they had been admitted to a club that, in their view, should never have allowed them to become members? Whatever their answer, Gobineau, Chamberlain and others of their ilk would survey a world in which the 'good' Jews who identify with a state in the Middle East have become no different from the rest of the West that once rejected Jews. Those 'good Jews' now also qualify for an exemption from the rules that, as Mamdani shows, is awarded to all who represent the West in its battle to dominate the rest. They would no doubt be comforted by the thought that the 'bad Jews', with the rest of the human race, remain threats to Western domination.

In this changed world, the state of Israel's ruling elites are indeed like all other elites who seek new ways of turning the language of the dominated into that of the dominator. But their state is special too because the damage it seeks to do to Jewish identity is a clear and stark example of the new obstacles that confront the search for a world free of racial, ethnic and cultural domination.

NOTES

INTRODUCTION The Tenacity of Race Bias

1   W. E. B. Du Bois, *The Souls of Black Folk* (New Haven and London: Yale University Press, 2015), 12.
2   Du Bois, *The Souls of Black Folk*, 12.
3   Adam Hochschild, *King Leopold's Ghost: A Story of Greed, Terror and Heroism in Colonial Africa* (Boston and New York: Houghton Mifflin Harcourt, 1999).
4   Simha Goldin, *Apostasy and Jewish Identity in High Middle Ages Northern Europe: 'Are You Still My Brother?'* (Manchester: Manchester University Press, 2014), 52ff.
5   Leonard Greenspoon, 'Who Is a Jew? Reflections on History, Religion, and Culture', *Studies in Jewish Civilization* 5 (2014), https://docs.lib.purdue.edu/sjc/5.
6   Avi Shlaim, 'On British Colonialism, Antisemitism, and Palestinian Rights', *Middle East Eye*, 1 March 2021, https://www.middleeasteye.net/big-story/uk-palestine-israel-policy-balfour-johnson-anitsemitism-colonialism.
7   Robert Bernasconi, 'Racism', in *Key Concepts in the Study of Anti-Semitism*, eds. Sol Goldberg, Scott Ury and Kalman Weiser (Cham: Palgrave Macmillan, 2021), 253.
8   Glynis Cousin and Robert Fine, 'A Common Cause: Reconnecting the Study of Racism and Antisemitism', *European Societies* 14, no. 2 (2012), 166–185; Conference on Racism and Anti-Semitism, Hannah Arendt Center Annual Fall Conference, Bard College, Annandale-on-Hudson, New York, October 2019, https://hac.bard.edu/conference2019.
9   Noel Ignatiev, *How the Irish Became White* (London and New York: Routledge, 1995); Brent Staples, 'How Italians Became "White"', *New York Times*, 12 October 2019, https://www.nytimes.com/interactive/2019/10/12/opinion/columbus-day-italian-american-racism.html.
10 Karen Brodkin, *How Jews Became White Folks and What That Says about Race in America* (New Brunswick, NJ, and London: Rutgers University Press, 2000).
11 Patrick Gathara, 'Covering Ukraine: A Mean Streak of Racist Exceptionalism', *Al Jazeera,* 1 March 2022, https://www.aljazeera.com/opinions/2022/3/1/covering-ukraine-a-mean-streak-of-racist-exceptionalism.

12 For a discussion of this view in the South African context, see Steven Friedman, *Class, Race and Power: Harold Wolpe and the Radical Critique of Apartheid* (Scottsville: University of KwaZulu-Natal Press, 2015).

13 Sven Beckert and Seth Rockman, eds. *Slavery's Capitalism: A New History of American Economic Development* (Philadelphia: University of Pennsylvania Press, 2016).

14 Ashutosh Varshney, *Battles Half Won: India's Improbable Democracy* (New Delhi: Penguin Viking, 2013), 264.

15 Anthea Jeffery, 'The State of Race Relations in SA 2019 – IRR', *Politics Web*, 13 June 2019, https://www.politicsweb.co.za/documents/the-state-of-race-relations-in-sa-2019--irr.

16 Gray, Aysa, 'The Bias of "Professionalism" Standards', *Stanford Social Innovation Review*, 4 June 2019, https://ssir.org/articles/entry/the_bias_of_professionalism_standards.

17 Megan Gannon, 'Race Is a Social Construct, Scientists Argue', *Scientific American*, 5 February 2016, https://www.scientificamerican.com/article/race-is-a-social-construct-scientists-argue.

18 Stuart Hall, *The Fateful Triangle: Race, Ethnicity, Nation* (Cambridge, MA: Harvard University Press, 2017), 33.

19 Alana Lentin, *Why Race Still Matters* (Cambridge: Polity Press, 2020), 13. It should be noted that Lentin's book contains a chapter entitled 'Good Jew/Bad Jew'. I became aware of her book only after choosing the title of this one.

20 Lentin, *Why Race Still Matters*, 32.

21 Lentin, *Why Race Still Matters*, 35.

22 Marius Roodt, 'Mboweni Plays the Race Card to South Africa's Detriment', *Daily Friend*, 13 February 2021, https://dailyfriend.co.za/2021/02/13/mboweni-plays-the-race-card-to-south-africas-detriment.

23 Nesrine Malik, 'Sometimes It's Hard to Remember What Life as a Muslim Was Like before 9/11', *The Guardian*, 13 September 2021, https://www.theguardian.com/commentisfree/2021/sep/13/life-as-a-muslim-before-911-islam.

24 Shlaim, 'On British Colonialism'.

25 Mahmood Mamdani, *Good Muslim, Bad Muslim: America, the Cold War and the Roots of Terror* (Johannesburg: Jacana, 2005).

CHAPTER 1 Turning Anti-Semitism on its Head

1 Media also depicted a demonstrator wearing a shirt bearing the letters 6MWE, an abbreviation for 6 Million Wasn't Enough, a reference to the murder of six million Jews by the Nazis. But media reports claimed that the picture was taken at a pro-Trump rally a few days before. Ben Sales, 'Right Anti-Semite, Wrong Trump Protest: Tweets of Racist T-Shirt May Help Bigots', *Times of Israel*, 12 January 2021, https://www.timesofisrael.com/right-anti-semite-wrong-trump-protest-tweets-of-racist-t-shirt-may-help-bigots.

2 Zionism is the ideology which advocates a Jewish state. Christian Zionists share this belief – often more assertively than Jewish Zionists. Stephen R. Sizer, 'Christian Zionism: Justifying Apartheid in the Name of God', *Churchman* 115, no. 2 (2001), 147–171.

3 Ben Lorber, 'How the Israeli Flag Became a Symbol for White Nationalists', *+972 Magazine*, 22 January 2021, https://www.972mag.com/israeli-flag-white-nationalism-symbol.

4 Philip Weiss, 'Capitol Riot Provides Shock to Netanyahu, Friedman … and American Exceptionalism', *Mondoweiss*, 8 January 2021, https://mondoweiss.net/2021/01/capitol-riot-provides-shock-to-netanyahu-friedman-and-american-exceptionalism.

5 Shira Hanau, 'Orthodox Jewish Trump Supporters Decry Violence but Not the Movement That Fueled the Mob', *Jewish Telegraphic Agency*, 6 January 2021, https://www.jta.org/2021/01/06/politics/orthodox-jewish-trump-supporters-decry-violence-but-not-the-movement-that-fueled-the-mob.

6 Knesset, 'Full Text of Basic Law: Israel as the Nation State of the Jewish People', 19 July 2018, https://main.knesset.gov.il/EN/News/PressReleases/Pages/Pr13978_pg.aspx.

7 Bess Levin, 'Trump Goes Full Anti-Semite, Unloads on American Jews in Wildly Bigoted Rant', *Vanity Fair*, 17 December 2021, https://www.vanityfair.com/news/2021/12/donald-trump-anti-semitism-jews-israel.

8 JTA/TOI Staff, 'Trump Praises Israel as "Your Country" to American Jews', *Times of Israel*, 8 December 2018, https://www.timesofisrael.com/trump-praises-israel-as-your-country-to-american-jews.

9 Yair Wallach, 'The Global Right Is a Threat to US Jews – but a Natural Home for Israelis', *+972 Magazine*, 16 November 2020, https://www.972mag.com/israel-us-jewish-divide.

10 Patrick Kingsley, 'A Friend to Israel, and to Bigots: Viktor Orban's "Double Game" on Anti-Semitism', *New York Times*, 14 May 2019, https://www.nytimes.com/2019/05/14/world/europe/orban-hungary-antisemitism.html.

11 Sylvain Cypel, *The State of Israel vs. the Jews*, trans. William Rodarmor (New York: Other Press, 2021), 192.

12 Cypel, *The State of Israel vs. the Jews*, 194.

13 James Carroll, *Constantine's Sword: The Church and the Jews* (Boston and New York: Houghton Mifflin, 2002); Malcolm Hay, *The Roots of Christian Anti-Semitism* (New York: Freedom Library Press, 1981).

14 Robert Leonhard, *Visions of Apocalypse: What Jews, Christians and Muslims Believe about the End Times, and How Those Beliefs Affect Our World* (Laurel, MD: The Johns Hopkins University, 2010), 94, accessed 31 March 2023, https://docslib.org/doc/3974389/visions-of-apocalypse-what-jews-christians-and-muslims-believe.

15 Julian Sayarer, 'The Antisemitic Face of Israel's Evangelical Allies', *Jacobin*, 20 February 2022, https://www.jacobinmag.com/2022/02/israeli-us-evangelical-alliance-zionism-antisemitism.

16 John Brown, 'Rights Groups Demand Israel Stop Arming Neo-Nazis in Ukraine', *Haaretz*, 9 July 2018, https://www.haaretz.com/israel-news/rights-groups-demand-israel-stop-arming-neo-nazis-in-the-ukraine-1.6248727.

17 Orly Noy, 'For the Jewish State, the Holocaust Is a Tool to Be Manipulated', *+972 Magazine*, 20 November 2020, https://www.972mag.com/holocaust-antisemitism-israel-tool.

18 These examples are all drawn from: Cypel, *The State of Israel vs. the Jews*, 175–202.

19 Richard Sanders, '"The Wrong Sort of Jew": How Labour Pursued Complaints Against Elderly Jewish Opponents of Israel', *Middle East Eye*, 24 September 2020,

https://www.middleeasteye.net/big-story/labour-antisemitism-jewish-opponents-israel-targeted.

20 David Hearst and Peter Oborne, 'UK's Labour Accused of "Purging Jews" from Party over Antisemitism Claims', *Middle East Eye*, 12 August 2021, https://www.middleeasteye.net/news/uk-labour-antisemitism-accused-purging-jews-over-claims.

21 Skwawkbox (SW), 'Attacks on Corbyn for Spending Passover with the "Wrong" Jews – and What They Might Mean', *Skwawkbox*, 3 April 2018, https://skwawkbox.org/2018/04/03/attacks-on-corbyn-for-spending-passover-with-the-wrong-jews-and-what-they-might-mean.

22 Andrew Pierce, 'They Raised a Beetroot in the Air and Shouted F*** Capitalism: Minute by Minute, Andrew Pierce Reconstructs Jeremy Corbyn's Four-Hour Meeting with Hate-Filled Group That Mocks Judaism', *Daily Mail*, 3 April 2018, https://www.dailymail.co.uk/news/article-5575579/They-raised-beetroot-air-shouted-f-capitalism.html.

23 Arnold Foster and Benjamin R. Epstein, *The New Anti-Semitism* (New York: McGraw Hill, 1974).

24 Alain Badiou, Eric Hazan and Ivan Segré, *Reflections on Anti-Semitism*, trans. David Fernbach (London and New York: Verso, 2013); Foster and Epstein, *The New Anti-Semitism*.

25 Nathan Perlmutter and Ruth Ann Perlmutter, *The Real Anti-Semitism in America* (New York: Arbor House, 1982), 116.

26 According to Labour Party Member of Parliament Siobhain McDonagh, 'to be anti-capitalism is to be anti-Semitic'. Middle East Monitor, 'Corbyn Critic Claims Anti-Capitalism Is Also Anti-Semitism', *MEMO*, 4 March 2019, https://www.middleeastmonitor.com/20190304-corbyn-critic-claims-anti-capitalism-is-also-anti-semitism/.

27 Ceren Sagir, 'Labour Criticised After Motion of No Confidence in Starmer Branded Anti-Semitic', *Morning Star*, 13 March 2021, https://morningstaronline.co.uk/article/b/labour-criticised-after-motion-no-confidence-starmer-branded-anti-semitic.

28 Andrew Feinstein, 'Zille Is Wrong – There Is No Anti-Semitism in Reclaim the City's Opposition to the Tafelberg Sale', *Daily Maverick*, 8 May 2017, https://www.dailymaverick.co.za/article/2017-05-08-op-ed-zille-is-wrong-there-is-no-anti-semitism-in-reclaim-the-citys-opposition-to-the-tafelberg-sale.

29 Amos Goldberg, 'Anti-Zionism and Antisemitism: How Right and Left Conflate Issues to Deny Palestinian Rights', *Middle East Eye*, 28 April 2022, https://www.middleeasteye.net/opinion/israel-broad-coalition-conflates-anti-zionism-antisemitism.

30 Goldberg, 'Anti-Zionism and Antisemitism'.

31 Robert S. Wistrich, *Antisemitism: The Longest Hatred* (New York: Pantheon Press, 1991).

32 Antony Lerman, *Whatever Happened to Anti-Semitism? Redefinition and the Myth of the 'Collective Jew'* (London: Pluto Press, 2022), 90.

33 Lerman, *Whatever Happened to Anti-Semitism?*, 75.

34 Theodor Herzl, *Old New Land* (Altneuland), trans. Lotta Levensohn (New York: Markus Wiener; New York: Herzl Press, 1987), 68.

35 Norman G. Finkelstein, *Beyond Chutzpah: On the Misuse of Anti-Semitism and the Abuse of History* (Berkeley and Los Angeles, CA: University of California Press, 2005), 64.

36 Goldberg, 'Anti-Zionism and Antisemitism'.

37 Gershom Gorenberg (@GershomG), Twitter, 2 February 2022, 3:59 pm, https://twitter.com/GershomG/status/1488874681423863810.

38 Gideon Levy, 'On This Holocaust Remembrance Day, Let Us Forget', *Haaretz*, 2 May 2019, https://www.haaretz.com/opinion/.premium-let-us-forget-1.7189738.

39 Cypel, *The State of Israel vs. the Jews*, 180.

40 Gabriel Schoenfeld, *The Return of Anti-Semitism* (San Francisco, CA: Encounter Books, 2004), 148.

41 Many examples are provided in Finkelstein, *Beyond Chutzpah*, 37ff.

42 Phyllis Chesler, *The New Anti-Semitism: The Current Crisis and What We Must Do about It* (San Francisco, CA: Jossey-Bass, 2003), 178.

43 Mari Cohen, 'Deborah Lipstadt vs. "The Oldest Hatred"', *Jewish Currents*, 8 February 2022, https://jewishcurrents.org/deborah-lipstadt-vs-the-oldest-hatred.

44 Alana Lentin, *Why Race Still Matters* (Cambridge: Polity Press, 2020), 134.

45 Cohen, 'Deborah Lipstadt'.

46 Yakov Hirsch, '"Never Again" Journalists Rosenberg, Stephens and Weiss Should Not Speak for the Jews on Colleyville and Antisemitism', *Mondoweiss*, 27 January 2022, https://mondoweiss.net/2022/01/never-again-journalists-rosenberg-stephens-and-weiss-should-not-speak-for-the-jews-on-colleyville-and-antisemitism.

47 Irit Keynan, 'Transforming Victimhood: From Competitive Victimhood to Sharing Superordinate Identity', in *Victimhood Discourse in Contemporary Israel*, ed. Ilan Peleg (Lanham: Lexington Books, 2019), 137–152, cited by Yakov Hirsch, 'Bari Weiss Wants to Speak for the Jews', *Mondoweiss*, 27 November 2020, https://mondoweiss.net/2020/11/bari-weiss-wants-to-speak-for-the-jews.

48 Dani Dayan (@AmbDaniDayan), Twitter, 20 November 2020, 5:35 pm, https://twitter.com/AmbDaniDayan/status/1329810703608320002.

49 Lewis Carroll, *Through the Looking-Glass and What Alice Found There* (Digital Scanning Inc, 2007), 73.

50 Shaul Magid, 'Savoring the Haterade: Why Jews Love Dara Horn's "People Love Dead Jews"', *Religion Dispatches*, 20 October 2021, https://religiondispatches.org/savoring-the-haterade-why-jews-love-dara-horns-people-love-dead-jews.

51 For examples and a discussion, see Finkelstein, *Beyond Chutzpah*, 32ff.

52 Perlmutter and Perlmutter, *The Real Anti-Semitism in America*, 155.

CHAPTER 2 Making 'Good Jews' White and European

1 Mari Cohen, 'Deborah Lipstadt vs. "The Oldest Hatred"', *Jewish Currents*, 8 February 2022, https://jewishcurrents.org/deborah-lipstadt-vs-the-oldest-hatred.

2 Anees Rao, 'I Don't Want to Belong to Any Club That Will Accept Me as a Member', *Medium*, 19 September 2016, https://medium.com/@aneesrao/i-dont-want-to-belong-to-any-club-that-will-accept-me-as-a-member-1210a65e49e9.

3 Zubayr Alikhan, 'Israel's Erroneous Slurs Harm Jews and Threaten the Legitimate Battle Against Antisemitism', *Palestine Chronicle*, 12 February 2022, https://www.palestinechronicle.com/israels-erroneous-slurs-harm-jews-and-threaten-the-legitimate-battle-against-antisemitism/.

4 David Cronin, 'EU Snubs Jews Who Criticize Israel', *Electronic Intifada*, 21 January 2021, https://electronicintifada.net/blogs/david-cronin/eu-snubs-jews-who-criticize-israel.

5   International Holocaust Remembrance Alliance (IHRA), 'About Us', https://www. holocaustremembrance.com/about-us.

6   Robert A. H. Cohen, 'We Need to Decolonise Our Understanding of Antisemitism', *Patheos*, 6 March 2021, https://www.patheos.com/blogs/writingfromtheedge/2021/03/ we-need-to-decolonise-our-understanding-of-antisemitism.

7   IHRA, 'What Is Antisemitism?', https://www.holocaustremembrance.com/resources/ working-definitions-charters/working-definition-antisemitism.

8   Open Letter, 'Statement on the IHRA Definition and the Question of Palestine', *Mondoweiss*, 1 December 2020, https://mondoweiss.net/2020/12/statement-on-the-ihra-definition-and-the-question-of-palestine. A 'binational state' would be one in which power would be shared between Jews and Palestinians.

9   Knesset, 'Full Text of Basic Law: Israel as the Nation State of the Jewish People', 19 July 2018, https://main.knesset.gov.il/EN/News/PressReleases/Pages/Pr13978_pg.aspx.

10   Jamie Stern-Weiner, 'The Politics of a Definition: How the IHRA Working Definition of Antisemitism Is Being Misrepresented' (Free Speech on Israel, April 2021), https://s3.documentcloud.org/documents/20689366/stern-weiner-j-fsoi-the-politics-of-a-definition.pdf.

11   Antony Lerman, *Whatever Happened to Anti-Semitism? Redefinition and the Myth of the 'Collective Jew'* (London: Pluto Press, 2022).

12   Shlomo Sand, *The Invention of the Jewish People* (London and New York: Verso, 2009).

13   Karen Armstrong, *The Lost Art of Scripture: Rescuing the Sacred Texts* (London: The Bodley Head, 2019).

14   Aviezer Ravitzky, *Messianism, Zionism, and Jewish Religious Radicalism* (Chicago and London: University of Chicago Press, 1996), 40–78.

15   Shaul Magid, *Piety and Rebellion: Essays in Hasidism* (Brighton, MA: Academic Studies Press, 2019), 481.

16   Shaul Magid, 'Christian Supersessionism, Zionism, and the Contemporary Scene: A Critical Reading of Peter Ochs's Reading of John Howard Yoder', *Journal of Religious Ethics* 45, no. 1 (March 2017), 127. In Rabbinic teaching, the building of a golden calf by the Israelites was an apostasy so great that it has scarred the Jewish psyche and Jewish life ever since.

17   Ben Lorber, 'Jewish Alternatives to Zionism: A Partial History', Jewish Voice for Peace, 11 January 2019, https://www.jewishvoiceforpeace.org/2019/01/a-partial-history-of-jewish-alternatives/.

18   T. Dunbar Moodie, *The Rise of Afrikanerdom: Power, Apartheid, and the Afrikaner Civil Religion* (Berkeley, CA: University of California Press, 1975).

19   Marisa Fick and Lawrence Schlemmer, 'Government Policy: Change or Stasis 1976–1982', *Indicator South Africa* 1, no. 1 (1 January 1983), 8, accessed 4 April 2023, https://journals.co.za/doi/epdf/10.10520/AJA0259188X_580.

20   William Booth, 'The Israeli General Who Compared the Jewish State to Nazi-Era Germany', *Washington Post*, 8 May 2016, https://www.washingtonpost.com/news/ worldviews/wp/2016/05/08/the-israeli-general-who-compared-the-jewish-state-to-nazi-era-germany.

21   Sol Goldberg, 'Jewish Self-Hatred', in *Key Concepts in the Study of Anti-Semitism*, eds. Sol Goldberg, Scott Ury and Kalman Weiser (Cham: Palgrave Macmillan, 2021), 270.

22   Cronin, 'EU Snubs Jews'.

23   Libby Lenkinski, 'How Trump and Netanyahu Made American Antisemitism Come Alive', *+972 Magazine*, 18 November 2020, https://www.972mag.com/how-trump-and-netanyahu-made-american-antisemitism-come-alive.

24   Simon Wiesenthal Center, 'Understand Simon Wiesenthal Center's Mission', accessed 8 June 2023, https://www.wiesenthal.com/about/about-the-simon-wiesenthal-center.

25   Emad Moussa, 'Israel's Antisemitism Accusations Become More Meaningless Than Ever in Row over Amnesty Apartheid Report', *Mondoweiss,* 1 February 2022, https://mondoweiss.net/2022/02/israels-antisemitism-accusations-become-more-meaningless-than-ever-in-row-over-amnesty-apartheid-report.

26   Cohen, 'We Need to Decolonise'.

27   Omri Nahmias, '10 US States Adopt IHRA Definition of Antisemitism on Holocaust Remembrance Day', *Jerusalem Post,* 27 January 2022, https://www.jpost.com/diaspora/antisemitism/article-694812; Gareth Narunsky and Zeddy Lawrence, 'NSW Adopts IHRA Definition', *Australian Jewish News,* 16 December 2021, https://www.australianjewishnews.com/nsw-adopts-ihra-definition; Chris Parr, 'Eighteen Universities Yet to Adopt IHRA Antisemitism Definition', *Research Professional News,* 11 November 2021, https://www.researchprofessionalnews.com/rr-news-uk-universities-2021-11-eighteen-universities-yet-to-adopt-ihra-antisemitism-definition.

28   Ramona Wadi, 'Defeating the IHRA Witch Hunt: An Interview with Palestinian Activist and Scholar Shahd Abusalama', *Mondoweiss,* 7 February 2022, https://mondoweiss.net/2022/02/defeating-the-ihra-witch-hunt-an-interview-with-palestinian-activist-and-scholar-shahd-abusalama.

29   Palestinian BDS National Committee, 'Israel's Legal Warfare on BDS Fosters Repression and McCarthyism across the World', BDS Movement, 17 March 2016, https://bdsmovement.net/news/israel%E2%80%99s-legal-warfare-bds-fosters-repression-and-mccarthyism-across-world.

30   Glenn Greenwald and Andrew Fishman, 'Greatest Threat to Free Speech in the West: Criminalizing Activism Against Israeli Occupation', *The Intercept,* 16 February 2016, https://theintercept.com/2016/02/16/greatest-threat-to-free-speech-in-the-west-criminalizing-activism-against-israeli-occupation.

31   Hebh Jamal, 'Germany Puts Artists, Academics in Its Anti-Palestinian Crosshairs', *+972 Magazine*, 3 July 2022, https://www.972mag.com/germany-artists-academics-palestinian-antisemitism.

32   Greenwald and Fishman, 'Greatest Threat to Free Speech'.

33   Andrea Morris, 'Texas Becomes 4th US State Taking Action Against Ben & Jerry's Unilever over Israel Move', *CBN News,* 1 October 2021, https://www1.cbn.com/cbnnews/israel/2021/september/texas-becomes-4th-us-state-taking-action-against-ben-and-jerrys-unilever-over-israel-move.

34   Middle East Monitor, 'Labour Drops Case Against "Anti-Zionist" Jewish Woman for Alleged Anti-Semitism', *MEMO,* 8 February 2022, https://www.middleeastmonitor.com/20220208-labour-drops-case-against-anti-zionist-jewish-woman-for-alleged-anti-semitism.

35   Dan Sabbagh, 'Labour Adopts IHRA Antisemitism Definition in Full', *The Guardian,* 4 September 2018, https://www.theguardian.com/politics/2018/sep/04/labour-adopts-ihra-antisemitism-definition-in-full. The date of its adoption is of some interest – see note 64.

36 Middle East Monitor, 'Labour Drops Case'.

37 Asa Winstanley, 'David Miller's Sacking Is Just the Start', *Middle East Monitor*, 12 October 2021, https://www.middleeastmonitor.com/20211012-david-millers-sacking-is-just-the-start.

38 Kenneth Stern, 'I Drafted the Definition of Antisemitism. Rightwing Jews Are Weaponizing It', *The Guardian*, 13 December 2019, https://www.theguardian.com/commentisfree/2019/dec/13/antisemitism-executive-order-trump-chilling-effect.

39 Avi Shlaim, 'On British Colonialism, Antisemitism, and Palestinian Rights', *Middle East Eye*, 1 March 2021, https://www.middleeasteye.net/big-story/uk-palestine-israel-policy-balfour-johnson-anitsemitism-colonialism.

40 Shlaim, 'On British Colonialism'.

41 David Feldman, 'The Government Should Not Impose a Faulty Definition of Antisemitism on Universities', *The Guardian*, 2 December 2020, https://www.theguardian.com/commentisfree/2020/dec/02/the-government-should-not-impose-a-faulty-definition-of-antisemitism-on-universities.

42 Shlaim, 'On British Colonialism'.

43 Phyllis Chesler, *The New Anti-Semitism: The Current Crisis and What We Must Do about It* (San Francisco, CA: Jossey-Bass, 2003), 97.

44 Richard J. Evans, *The Coming of the Third Reich* (New York: Penguin Books, 2005), 496.

45 Walter Laqueur, *A History of Zionism: From the French Revolution to the Establishment of the State of Israel* (New York: Schocken, 2003), 210–274.

46 See, for example, a much-quoted letter written by the first Israeli prime minister and an avowed 'socialist', David Ben-Gurion, to his son Amos in 1937. In it, he explains that the Zionist movement was agreeing to the internationally recognised partition of Palestine only as a stratagem until it was strong enough to take control of the land which the agreement had allocated to Arabs. 'Ben-Gurion: Letter to His Son, October 5, 1937', trans. Institute of Palestine Studies, Jewish Voice for Peace, 6 April 2013, https://jewishvoiceforpeace.org/2013/04/the-ben-gurion-letter.

47 Yair Wallach, 'The Global Right Is a Threat to US Jews – but a Natural Home for Israelis', *+972 Magazine*, 16 November 2020, https://www.972mag.com/israel-usjewish-divide.

48 Sylvain Cypel, *The State of Israel vs. the Jews*, trans. William Rodarmor (New York: Other Press, 2021), 82.

49 Jerusalem Post Staff, 'After Chairman Controversy, Eitam Skipped over for Yad Vashem Role', *Jerusalem Post*, 24 December 2020, https://www.jpost.com/israel-news/after-chairman-controversy-eitam-skipped-over-for-yad-vashem-role-653132.

50 Norman G. Finkelstein, *Beyond Chutzpah: On the Misuse of Anti-Semitism and the Abuse of History* (Berkeley and Los Angeles, CA: University of California Press, 2005), 26.

51 Andrew Barclay, Maria Sobolewska and Robert Ford, 'Political Realignment of British Jews: Testing Competing Explanations', *Electoral Studies* 61 (October 2019), https://doi.org/10.1016/j.electstud.2019.102063.

52 Pew Research Center, 'Jewish Americans in 2020', 11 May 2021, 159, https://www.pewresearch.org/religion/wp-content/uploads/sites/7/2021/05/PF_05.11.21_Jewish.Americans.pdf.

53 Philip Weiss, 'U.S. Jews Favor Return to Iran Deal, and Don't Care about Israel as a Political Issue', *Mondoweiss*, 14 April 2022, https://mondoweiss.net/2022/04/u-s-jews-favor-return-to-iran-deal-and-dont-care-about-israel-as-a-political-issue.

54 Philip Weiss, 'America's Whiteness Crisis, and Zionism's', *Mondoweiss*, 10 January 2021, https://mondoweiss.net/2021/01/americas-whiteness-crisis-and-zionisms.

55 Cypel, *The State of Israel vs. the Jews*, 175–202.

56 Ben Lorber, 'How the Israeli Flag Became a Symbol for White Nationalists', +972 *Magazine*, 22 January 2021, https://www.972mag.com/israeli-flag-white-nationalism-symbol.

57 Middle East Monitor, 'German News Agency Accused of "Weaponising" Anti-Semitism in Sacking of Journalists', *MEMO*, 8 February 2022, https://www.middleeastmonitor.com/20220208-german-news-agency-accused-of-weaponising-anti-semitism-in-sacking-of-journalists/.

58 Chesler, *The New Anti-Semitism*; selection of extracts cited in Finkelstein, *Beyond Chutzpah*, 37.

59 Nathan Perlmutter and Ruth Ann Perlmutter, *The Real Anti-Semitism in America*. (New York: Arbor House, 1982), 9.

60 Perlmutter and Perlmutter, *The Real Anti-Semitism in America*; selection of extracts cited in Finkelstein, *Beyond Chutzpah*, 27.

61 Jewish Virtual Library, 'Jewish Population in the United States by State', accessed 8 June 2023, https://www.jewishvirtuallibrary.org/jewish-population-in-the-united-states-by-state.

62 Dov Waxman, *Trouble in the Tribe: The American Jewish Conflict over Israel* (Princeton: Princeton University Press, 2016), 193ff.

63 Em Hilton, 'British Jews, We Cannot Afford to Align Ourselves with the Far Right', +972 *Magazine*, 16 November 2021, https://www.972mag.com/british-jews-far-right.

64 It is commonly claimed that Labour had an 'anti-Semitism problem' under Corbyn but not under his successor Keir Starmer, while those who insist that there was no such problem argue that Corbyn was targeted partly because of his sympathy with Palestinians. However, the IHRA definition was adopted by the Labour Party in 2018, when Corbyn was still its leader, in an attempt to deflect pressure that was being placed on him. This adds strength to the claim that Corbyn, not anti-Semitism, was the target. While Labour was roundly condemned by Zionist organisations and the British establishment for using the IHRA definition under Corbyn, it was praised for doing it under Starmer. This obviously implies that its problem was not anti-Semitism but who the Labour leader was. See Jonathan Cook, 'Labour Antisemitism Allegations: How Corbyn and Starmer Are Judged by Different Standards', *Middle East Eye*, 16 April 2021, https://www.middleeasteye.net/opinion/labour-antisemitism-allegations-how-corbyn-and-starmer-are-judged-different-standards.

65 Labour Party, 'The Shami Chakrabarti Inquiry', Report, 30 June 2016, 1, https://labour.org.uk/wp-content/uploads/2017/10/Chakrabarti-Inquiry-Report-30June16.pdf.

66 Jonathan Cook, 'How the EHRC Antisemitism Report Added Fire to Labour's Simmering Civil War', *Middle East Eye*, 5 November 2020, https://www.middleeasteye.net/opinion/ehrc-labour-antisemitism-civil-war-fire-added.

67 Equality and Human Rights Commission (EHRC), 'Investigation into Antisemitism in the Labour Party', Report, October 2020, 8, https://www.equalityhumanrights.com/sites/default/files/investigation-into-antisemitism-in-the-labour-party.pdf.

68 Robert Philpot, 'How Britain's Nazi-Loving Press Baron Made the Case for Hitler', *Times of Israel*, 5 August 2018, https://www.timesofisrael.com/how-britains-nazi-loving-press-baron-made-the-case-for-hitler.

69 Jon Stone, 'Boris Johnson Book Depicts Jews as Controlling the Media', *Independent*, 9 December 2019, https://www.independent.co.uk/news/uk/politics/boris-johnson-book-jews-control-media-general-election-a9239346.html.

70 JTA and Marty Oster, 'Former U.K. Parliament Speaker: Anti-Semitism Came from Own Conservative Party, Not Labour', *Haaretz*, 3 February 2020, https://www.haaretz.com/world-news/europe/former-u-k-parliament-speaker-anti-semitism-came-from-own-conservative-party-1.8492663.

71 David Broder, 'How Labour Became "Antisemitic": An Interview with Greg Philo', *Jacobin*, 5 October 2019, https://www.jacobinmag.com/2019/10/labour-party-antisemitism-claims-jeremy-corbyn.

72 Joseph Massad, 'Starmer's Apology Skipped over Britain's Long History of Antisemitism', *Middle East Eye*, 29 November 2021, https://www.middleeasteye.net/opinion/uk-antisemitism-starmer-apology-long-history.

73 Avi Shlaim, 'Labour Antisemitism Allegations: Are Left-Wing Jewish Party Members Being Targeted?', *Middle East Eye*, 14 March 2022, https://www.middleeasteye.net/opinion/uk-labour-antisemitism-allegations-left-wing-jewish-members-targeted.

74 Matti Bunzl, 'Between Anti-Semitism and Islamophobia: Some Thoughts on the New Europe', *American Ethnologist* 32, no. 4 (2005), 499–508, quoted in Lena Salaymeh and Shai Lavi, 'Secularism', in *Key Concepts in the Study of Anti-Semitism*, eds. Sol Goldberg, Scott Ury and Kalman Weiser (Cham: Palgrave Macmillan, 2021), 375.

75 Cypel, *The State of Israel vs. the Jews*, 186.

76 TOI Staff, 'White Nationalist Richard Spencer Tells Israelis That Jews Are "Over-Represented"', *Times of Israel*, 17 August 2017, https://www.timesofisrael.com/white-nationalist-richard-spencer-tells-israelis-that-jews-are-over-represented.

77 Spencer Sunshine, 'We Didn't Need More Evidence – Richard Spencer Has Always Been Anti-Semitic', *Jewish Telegraphic Agency*, 7 November 2019, https://www.jta.org/2019/11/07/opinion/we-didnt-need-more-evidence-richard-spencer-has-always-been-anti-semitic.

78 World Population Review, 'Muslim Population by Country 2022', https://worldpopulationreview.com/country-rankings/muslim-population-by-country.

79 Somdeep Sen, 'India's Deepening Love Affair with Israel', *Al Jazeera*, 9 September 2021, https://www.aljazeera.com/opinions/2021/9/9/indias-deepening-love-affair-with-israel.

80 Samaan Lateef, 'Why Is India's Government Celebrating an Antisemitic, Pro-Genocide Hitler Devotee?', *Haaretz*, 1 March 2021, https://www.haaretz.com/world-news/.premium-why-is-india-s-government-celebrating-an-antisemitic-pro-genocide-hitler-devotee-1.9579453.

81 Alain Badiou and Eric Hazan, 'Anti-Semitism: Real and Imagined', in *Reflections on Anti-Semitism*, by Alain Badiou, Eric Hazan and Ivan Segré, trans. David Fernbach (London and New York: Verso, 2013), 13.

82 Badiou and Hazan, 'Anti-Semitism', 14.

83 David Kaiser, 'What Hitler and the Grand Mufti Really Said', *Time*, 22 October 2015, https://time.com/4084301/hitler-grand-mufi-1941.

84 Cypel, *The State of Israel vs. the Jews*, 187.

85 Mahibul Hoque, 'The "Pro-Israel" Think Tank That Funds Antisemites across the World', *Palestine Chronicle*, 20 March 2021, https://www.palestinechronicle.com/middle-east-forum-a-pro-israel-think-tank-that-supports-and-funds-neo-nazis-and-antisemites-across-the-world.

86 Alana Lentin, *Why Race Still Matters* (Cambridge: Polity Press, 2020)

87 Cypel, *The State of Israel vs. the Jews*, 91.

88 Cypel, *The State of Israel vs. the Jews*, 190.

89 Edward W. Said, *Orientalism* (London: Penguin, 2003).

90 Cypel, *The State of Israel vs. the Jews*, 103.

91 Cypel, *The State of Israel vs. the Jews*, 104.

92 Cypel, *The State of Israel vs. the Jews*, 105.

93 Jeffrey Goldberg, 'Israel's Fears, Amalek's Arsenal', *New York Times*, 16 May 2009, https://www.nytimes.com/2009/05/17/opinion/17goldberg.html.

94 Yakov Hirsch, 'Israel Can't Be Faulted for Anything, Thanks to Hasbara Culture's Narrative of Jewish Victimhood', *Mondoweiss*, 20 September 2021, https://mondoweiss.net/2021/09/israel-cant-be-faulted-for-anything-thanks-to-hasbara-cultures-narrative-of-jewish-victimhood.

95 Avishai Margalit and Gabriel Motzkin, 'The Uniqueness of the Holocaust', *Philosophy & Public Affairs* 25, no. 1 (Winter 1996), 65–83.

96 The term 'self-hating Jew' has long been used by Zionists to vilify non- or anti-Zionist Jews. See Paul Reitter, *On the Origins of Jewish Self-Hatred* (Princeton, NJ: Princeton University Press, 2012).

CHAPTER 3 What Anti-Semitism Really Is

1 Robert H. Mnookin, *The Jewish American Paradox* (New York: Public Affairs, 2018), EPUB.

2 For the claim that anti-Semitism is the oldest human prejudice, see Robert S. Wistrich, *Antisemitism: The Longest Hatred* (New York: Pantheon Press, 1991).

3 Nasim Hasan Shah, 'The Concept of Al-Dhimmah and the Rights and Duties of Dhimmis in an Islamic State', *Institute of Muslim Minority Affairs Journal* 9, no. 2 (July 1988), 217–222.

4 Fordham University, 'Medieval Sourcebook: Abraham Ibd [sic] Daud: On Samuel Ha-Nagid, Vizier of Granada, 993-d after 1056', in *Internet Medieval Sourcebook*, ed. Paul Halsall, 1997 https://sourcebooks.fordham.edu/source/ha-nagid.asp.

5 James Carroll, *Constantine's Sword: The Church and the Jews* (Boston and New York: Houghton Mifflin, 2002), 237–267.

6 Madeleine Schwartz, 'The Origins of Blood Libel', *The Nation*, 28 January 2016, https://www.thenation.com/article/archive/the-origins-of-blood-libel.

7 Claire Bacha, Sue Einhorn and Sue Lieberman, '"If You Prick Me, Do I Not Bleed?": Antisemitism, Racism and Group Analysis – Some Thoughts', *Group Analysis* 54, no. 3 (2021), 388–401.

8 Kenneth R. Stow, *Catholic Thought and Papal Jewry Policy 1555–1593* (New York: The Jewish Theological Seminary Press, 2012).

9 Carroll, *Constantine's Sword*, 377; Malcolm V. Hay, *The Roots of Christian Anti-Semitism* (New York: Freedom Library Press, 1981), 164.

10 Carroll, *Constantine's Sword*, 374.

11 Carroll, *Constantine's Sword*, 374–375.

12 Robert Bernasconi, 'Racism', in *Key Concepts in the Study of Anti-Semitism*, eds. Sol Goldberg, Scott Ury and Kalman Weiser (Cham: Palgrave Macmillan, 2021), 353.

13 Bernasconi, 'Racism', 353.
14 Alana Lentin, *Why Race Still Matters* (Cambridge: Polity Press, 2020), 69.
15 Lentin, *Why Race Still Matters*, 68.
16 Bernasconi, 'Racism', 355.
17 Moshe Zimmerman, *Wilhelm Marr: The Patriarch of Anti-Semitism* (New York and Oxford: Oxford University Press, 1986), 21.
18 Zimmerman, *Wilhelm Marr*, 9.
19 Gerhard Rohringer, 'Foreword by the Translator', *The Victory of Judaism over Germanism: Viewed from a Nonreligious Point of View*, by Wilhem Marr, trans. Gerhard Rohringer, 2009 (Bern: Rudolph Costenoble, 1879), https://archive.org/details/marr-wilhelmthe-victory-of-judaism-over-germanism_202012
20 Marr, *The Victory of Judaism*, 8.
21 Marr, *The Victory of Judaism*, 12.
22 Marr, *The Victory of Judaism*, 6.
23 Marr, *The Victory of Judaism*, 34.
24 Zimmerman, *Wilhelm Marr*, 78.
25 Zimmerman, *Wilhelm Marr*, 78.
26 Gregory Blue, 'Gobineau on China: Race Theory, the "Yellow Peril", and the Critique of Modernity', *Journal of World History* 10, no. 1 (Spring 1999), 99.
27 Geoffrey Field, *Evangelist of Race: The Germanic Vision of Houston Stewart Chamberlain* (New York: Columbia University Press, 1981), 195.
28 Field, *Evangelist of Race,* 189.
29 Ian Buruma, *Anglomania: A European Love Affair* (New York: Vintage Books, 2000), 167.
30 Field, *Evangelist of Race*, 223.
31 Field, *Evangelist of Race*, 414.
32 Field, *Evangelist of Race*, 357.
33 Field, *Evangelist of Race*, 359.
34 Field, *Evangelist of Race*, 304.
35 Kalman Weiser, 'Introduction', in *Key Concepts in the Study of Anti-Semitism*, eds. Sol Goldberg, Scott Ury and Kalman Weiser (Cham: Palgrave Macmillan, 2021), 10.
36 Edward Said, 'Orientalism Reconsidered', *Cultural Critique* 1 (Autumn 1985), 99.
37 Quoted in Lena Salaymeh and Shai Lavi, 'Secularism', in *Key Concepts in the Study of Anti-Semitism,* eds. Sol Goldberg, Scott Ury and Kalman Weiser, (Cham: Palgrave Macmillan, 2021), 370.
38 Barnor Hesse, 'Raceocracy: How the Racial Exception Proves the Racial Rule', 7 March 2013, Webcast sponsored by Irving K. Barber Learning Centre and hosted by Green College, University of British Columbia, https://open.library.ubc.ca/cIRcle/collections/ubclibraryandarchives/67657/items/1.0076724.
39 Bernasconi, 'Racism', 353.
40 Doris Bergen, 'Nazism', in *Key Concepts in the Study of Anti-Semitism*, eds. Sol Goldberg, Scott Ury and Kalman Weiser, (Cham: Palgrave Macmillan, 2021), 259.
41 Richard C. Bush, 'Thoughts on the Nanjing Massacre', *Brookings*, 1 December 2007, https://www.brookings.edu/opinions/thoughts-on-the-nanjing-massacre.
42 Frantz Fanon, *Black Skin, White Masks,* trans. Charles Lam Markmann (London: Pluto Press, 1986), 122.
43 Alain Badiou and Eric Hazan, 'Anti-Semitism: Real and Imagined', in *Reflections on Anti-Semitism*, by Alain Badiou, Eric Hazan and Ivan Segré, trans. David Fernbach (London and New York: Verso, 2013), 11–12.

44 Lentin, *Why Race Still Matters*, 73.

45 Badiou and Hazan, 'Anti-Semitism', 15.

46 Lazar Berman, 'After Walling Itself in, Israel Learns to Hazard the Jungle Beyond', *Times of Israel*, 8 March 2021, https://www.timesofisrael.com/after-walling-itself-in-israel-learns-to-hazard-the-jungle-beyond.

47 Knesset, 'Full Text of Basic Law: Israel as the Nation State of the Jewish People', 19 July 2018, https://main.knesset.gov.il/EN/News/PressReleases/Pages/Pr13978_pg.aspx.

48 Jay Ruderman and Yedidia Z. Stern, 'Is "Israeli" a Nationality?', The Israel Democracy Institute, 9 March 2014, https://en.idi.org.il/articles/6516.

49 Steven Friedman, 'US Elections Expose Flaws in Western Democracy', *New Frame*, 12 November 2020, https://www.newframe.com/us-elections-expose-flaws-in-western-democracy.

50 Badiou and Hazan, 'Anti-Semitism', 30.

51 Badiou and Hazan, 'Anti-Semitism', 30.

52 Angelique Chrisafis, 'Jean-Marie Le Pen Convicted of Contesting Crimes Against Humanity', *The Guardian*, 16 February 2012, https://the guardian.com/world/2012/feb/16/jean-marie-le-pen-convicted.

53 Ali Abunimah, 'German Anti-Semitism Surges, from the Right', *Electronic Intifada*, 15 February 2021, https://electronicintifada.net/blogs/ali-abunimah/german-anti-semitism-surges-right.

54 Jonathan D. Sarna, 'The Long, Ugly Anti-Semitic History of "Jews Will Not Replace Us"', The Jewish Experience, Brandeis University, 19 November 2021, https://www.brandeis.edu/jewish-experience/jewish-america/2021/november/replacement-antisemitism-sarna.html.

55 Quoted in Sarna, 'The Long, Ugly Anti-Semitic History'.

56 Masha Gessen, 'Why the Tree of Life Shooter Was Fixated on the Hebrew Immigrant Aid Society', *New Yorker*, 27 October 2018, https://www.newyorker.com/news/our-columnists/why-the-tree-of-life-shooter-was-fixated-on-the-hebrew-immigrant-aid-society.

57 For a fictionalised account of this view, see Jean Raspail, *The Camp of the Saints*, trans. Norman Shapiro (New York: Scribner, 1975).

58 Mike Rothbaum (@Rav_Mike), 29 October 2021, 2:32 am, https://twitter.com/Rav_Mike/status/1453882336240623623.

59 Emad Moussa, 'Israel's Antisemitism Accusations Become More Meaningless Than Ever in Row over Amnesty Apartheid Report', *Mondoweiss*, 1 February 2022, https://mondoweiss.net/2022/02/israels-antisemitism-accusations-become-moremeaningless-than-ever-in-row-over-amnesty-apartheid-report/1.

60 Moussa, 'Israel's Antisemitism Accusations'.

61 Quoted in Em Hilton, 'British Jews, We Cannot Afford to Align Ourselves with the Far Right', *+972 Magazine*, 16 November 2021, https://www.972mag.com/british-jews-far-right.

62 Zubayr Alikhan, 'Israel's Erroneous Slurs Harm Jews and Threaten the Legitimate Battle Against Antisemitism', *Palestine Chronicle*, 12 February 2022, https://www.palestinechronicle.com/israels-erroneous-slurs-harm-jews-and-threaten-the-legitimate-battle-against-antisemitism.

63 Philip Weiss, 'Anti-Zionist Jews Are "Jews in Name Only" and "More Dangerous Than External Antisemitic Threat" – Chicago Reform Rabbi', *Mondoweiss*, 26 November 2021, https://mondoweiss.net/2021/11/anti-zionist-jews-are-jews-in-name-only-and-more-dangerous-than-external-antisemitic-threat-chicago-reform-rabbi.

CHAPTER 4 The Israeli State as a 'Cure' for Anti-Racism

1   David Ben-Gurion, 'The Imperatives of the Jewish Revolution', Speech to Youth Groups, Haifa, 1944, https://zionism-israel.com/hdoc/Ben-Gurion_Jewish_revolution.htm.

2   Shaul Magid, 'Savoring the Haterade: Why Jews Love Dara Horn's "People Love Dead Jews"', *Religion Dispatches*, 20 October 2021, https://religiondispatches.org/savoring-the-haterade-why-jews-love-dara-horns-people-love-dead-jews.

3   Salo Wittmayer Baron, 'Newer Emphases in Jewish History', *Jewish Social Studies* 25, no. 4 (1963), 235–248.

4   David Biale, *Power and Powerlessness in Jewish History* (New York: Schocken, 1986).

5   Hannah Arendt, *The Origins of Totalitarianism* (Cleveland, OH, New York: Harvest/HBJ, 1958), 8, cited in Biale, *Power and Powerlessness*, 5.

6   Michael Selzer, 'Introduction', in *Zionism Reconsidered: The Rejection of Jewish Normalcy*, ed. Michael Selzer (New York: Macmillan, 1970), x, cited in Biale, *Power and Powerlessness*, 5.

7   Jehuda Reinharz, 'The Conflict Between Zionism and Traditionalism Before World War I', *Jewish History* 7, no. 2 (Fall 1993), 59–78.

8   Shlomo Sand, *The Invention of the Jewish People*, trans. Yael Lotan (London and New York: Verso, 2009); Shaul Magid, 'Christian Supersessionism, Zionism, and the Contemporary Scene: A Critical Reading of Peter Ochs's Reading of John Howard Yoder', *Journal of Religious Ethics* 45, no. 1 (March 2017), 120.

9   Meir said this to Hannah Arendt who passed it on to the scholar Gershom Scholem. Marie Luise Knott, ed. *Der Briefwechsel: Hannah Arendt, Gershom Scholem* (Berlin: Jüdischer Verlag, 2010), 440, cited in Magid, 'Christian Supersessionism', 119.

10   Biale, *Power and Powerlessness*, 207.

11   Biale, *Power and Powerlessness*, 207.

12   Biale, *Power and Powerlessness*, 12.

13   Biale, *Power and Powerlessness*, 12.

14   Biale, *Power and Powerlessness*, 12.

15   Biale, *Power and Powerlessness*, 170.

16   John J. Mearsheimer and Stephen M. Walt, *The Israel Lobby and U.S. Foreign Policy* (New York: Farrar, Straus and Giroux, 2007).

17   Biale, *Power and Powerlessness*, 170.

18   Mearsheimer and Walt, *The Israel Lobby*.

19   Biale, *Power and Powerlessness*, 24.

20   Biale, *Power and Powerlessness*, 24.

21   Mahmood Mamdani, *Citizen and Subject: Contemporary Africa and the Politics of Late Colonialism* (Kampala: Fountain, 1995).

22   Biale, *Power and Powerlessness*, 53.

23   Biale, *Power and Powerlessness*, 54.

24   Biale, *Power and Powerlessness*, 54.

25   Biale, *Power and Powerlessness*, 59.

26   Biale, *Power and Powerlessness*, 62.

27   Meir ben Baruch of Rothenburg, *Responsa*, Prague edition no 1001, quoted in Biale, *Power and Powerlessness*, 63.

28   Mark R. Cohen, 'Prologue: The "Golden Age" of Jewish-Muslim Relations: Myth and Reality', in *A History of Jewish-Muslim Relations: From the Origins to the Present Day*,

eds. Abdelwahab Meddeb and Benjamin Stora (Princeton, NJ Princeton University Press, 2014), 37.

29   Giovanni da Anagni, *In librum quintum decretalium* (Milan, 1492), fol. 63, quoted in Biale, *Power and Powerlessness*, 63.

30   Bernard D. Weinryb, *The Jews of Poland: A Social and Economic History of the Jewish Community in Poland from 1100–1800*, trans. Jane Marie Todd and Michael B. Smith (Philadelphia: Jewish Publication Society of America, 1973), 150.

31   Biale, *Power and Powerlessness*, 77.

32   Biale, *Power and Powerlessness*, 78–79.

33   Salo Wittmayer Baron, *A Social and Religious History of the Jews*, vol. 11 (New York: Columbia University Press, 1957), 21.

34   Perry Anderson, *Lineages of the Absolutist State* (London and New York: Verso, 1974).

35   Biale, *Power and Powerlessness*, 91.

36   Clermont-Tonnerre, 'Speech on Religious Minorities and Questionable Professions (23 December 1789)', Liberté, Égalité, Fraternité: Exploring the French Revolution, https://revolution.chnm.org/d/284.

37   J. P. O'Malley, 'How Émile Zola's Role in the Dreyfus Affair Irrevocably Changed European Politics', *Times of Israel*, 9 March 2017, https://www.timesofisrael.com/how-emile-zolas-role-in-the-dreyfus-affair-irrevocably-changed-european-politics.

38   Michael Burns, *France and the Dreyfus Affair: A Documentary History* (Lexington: Plunkett Lake Press, 2014). Kindle.

39   Ben Sales, 'Harvard Once Capped the Number of Jews. Is It Doing the Same Thing to Asian Americans Now?', *Jewish Telegraphic Agency*, 17 October 2018, https://www.jta.org/2018/10/17/united-states/harvard-once-capped-the-number-of-jews-is-it-doing-the-same-thing-to-asians-now.

40   Biale, *Power and Powerlessness*, 170.

41   John Connelly, 'Nazis and Slavs: From Racial Theory to Racist Practice', *Central European History* 32, no. 1 (1999), 1–33.

CHAPTER 5 Zionism as an Escape from Jewishness

1   Sol Goldberg, 'Jewish Self-Hatred', in *Key Concepts in the Study of Anti-Semitism*, eds. Sol Goldberg, Scott Ury and Kalman Weiser (Cham: Palgrave Macmillan, 2021), 147–148.

2   Goldberg, 'Jewish Self-Hatred', 148–149.

3   W. M. L. Finlay, 'Pathologizing Dissent: Identity Politics, Zionism and the "Self-Hating Jew"', *British Journal of Social Psychology* 44, no. 2 (June 2005), 202, http://dx.doi.org/10.1348/014466604X17894.

4   Frantz Fanon, *Black Skin, White Masks*, trans. Charles Lam Markmann (London: Pluto Press, 1986), 69.

5   Daniel Boyarin, *Unheroic Conduct: The Rise of Heterosexuality and the Invention of the Jewish Man* (Berkeley, CA: University of California Press, 1997).

6   Boyarin, *Unheroic Conduct*, 276.

7   Marthe Robert, *From Oedipus to Moses: Freud's Jewish Identity* (New York: Anchor Books, 1976), 112, quoted in Boyarin, *Unheroic Conduct*, 276.

8   Sigmund Freud, *Moses and Monotheism*, trans. Katherine Jones (London: Hogarth Press and Institute of Psycho-analysis, 1939).

9   Quoted in Boyarin, *Unheroic Conduct*, 239.

10   Freud, *Moses and Monotheism*, 14.

11   Boyarin, *Unheroic Conduct*, 280.

12   Alana Lentin, *Why Race Still Matters* (Cambridge: Polity Press, 2020), 146.

13   For a full discussion, see Boyarin, *Unheroic Conduct*, 151–186.

14   Quoted in Boyarin, *Unheroic Conduct*, 280.

15   For a pioneering discussion of how dominated people respond in this way, see James C. Scott, *Weapons of the Weak: Everyday Forms of Peasant Resistance* (New Haven, CT: Yale University Press, 1985).

16   Boyarin, *Unheroic Conduct*, 277.

17   Quoted in Boyarin, *Unheroic Conduct*, 295.

18   Boyarin, *Unheroic Conduct*, 291.

19   Amos Perlmutter, 'A. D. Gordon: A Transcendental Zionist', *Middle Eastern Studies* 7, no. 1 (January 1971), 81–87.

20   A. D. Gordon, 'The Whole People of Israel', in *Writings, vol. 1: The Nation and Labour*, by A. D. Gordon, (Jerusalem: Zionist Library, 1952), quoted in Zeev Sternhell, *The Founding Myths of Israel: Nationalism, Socialism, and the Making of the Jewish State*, trans. David Maisel (Princeton, NJ: Princeton University Press, 1998).

21   Konstantin Azadovskii and Boris Egorov, 'From Anti-Westernism to Anti-Semitism: Stalin and the Impact of the "Anti-Cosmopolitan" Campaigns on Soviet Culture', *Journal of Cold War Studies* 4, no. 1 (Winter 2002), 66–80.

22   Shaul Magid, 'Christian Supersessionism, Zionism, and the Contemporary Scene: A Critical Reading of Peter Ochs's Reading of John Howard Yoder', *Journal of Religious Ethics* 45, no. 1 (March 2017), 126.

23   Sternhell, *Founding Myths*, 49–50.

24   Hebrew Bible, Isaiah, Chapter Two, Verse 8.

25   Jeff Halper, 'The Zionist Assault on Judaism', *Mondoweiss*, 2 July 2021, https://mondoweiss.net/2021/07/the-zionist-assault-on-judaism. See also: Justin Nortey, 'U.S. Jews Have Widely Differing Views on Israel', Pew Research Center, 21 May 2021, https://www.pewresearch.org/short-reads/2021/05/21/u-s-jews-have-widely-differing-views-on-israel.

26   Yair Wallach, 'The Global Right Is a Threat to US Jews – but a Natural Home for Israelis', *+972 Magazine*, 16 November 2020, https://www.972mag.com/israel-us-jewish-divide.

27   Philip Weiss, 'Israel Lobby Group Affirms Trend – 22% of Younger Jews Don't Want a Jewish State', *Mondoweiss*, 26 April 2022, https://mondoweiss.net/2022/04/israel-lobby-group-affirms-trend-22-of-younger-jews-dont-want-a-jewish-state.

28   Sylvain Cypel, *The State of Israel vs. the Jews*, trans. William Rodarmor (New York: Other Press, 2021), 210.

29   Anshel Pfeffer, 'Netanyahu Speaks for All Jews Whether They Like It or Not', *Haaretz*, 12 February 2015, https://www.haaretz.com/.premium-netanyahu-speaks-for-all-jews-1.5306070.

30   Richard Middleton-Kaplan, 'The Myth of Jewish Passivity', in *Jewish Resistance Against the Nazis*, ed. Patrick Henry (Washington, DC: Catholic University of America Press, 2014), 3.

31   Ethan Nechin, 'With the Nation-State Law, Israel's Religious Right Is Deciding Who Is a Jew', *+972 Magazine*, 20 December 2020, https://www.972mag.com/nation-state-law-judaism-religious-right.

32   Jonathan Lis, 'Israeli Minister Shaked: Progress on "Trump Heights" Settlement in Golan', *Haaretz*, 14 December 2021, https://www.haaretz.com/israel-news/.premium-israeli-minister-shaked-progress-on-trump-heights-settlement-in-golan-1.10465864.

33 David Smith, 'Donald Trump's Rhetoric Has Stoked Antisemitism and Hatred, Experts Warn', *The Guardian*, 29 October 2018, https://www.theguardian.com/us-news/2018/oct/29/donald-trumps-rhetoric-has-stoked-antisemitism-and-hatred-experts-warn.

34 Cypel, *The State of Israel vs. the Jews*, 295.

35 Cypel, *The State of Israel vs. the Jews*, 295.

36 Asa Winstanley, 'Israeli Ambassador Made Anti-Semitic Video', *Electronic Intifada*, 18 December 2020, https://electronicintifada.net/blogs/asa-winstanley/israeli-ambassador-made-anti-semitic-video.

37 Winstanley, 'Israeli Ambassador'.

38 Asa Winstanley, 'Netanyahu Advisers Hatched Anti-Semitic Conspiracy Against George Soros', *Electronic Intifada*, 19 March 2019, https://electronicintifada.net/blogs/asa-winstanley/netanyahu-advisers-hatched-anti-semitic-conspiracy-against-george-soros.

39 Dimi Reider, 'WATCH: The Most Anti-Semitic Israeli Cartoon Ever Made?', *+972 Magazine*, 14 February 2015, https://www.972mag.com/watch-the-most-anti-semitic-israeli-cartoon-ever-made.

40 Winstanley, 'Israeli Ambassador'.

41 Reider, 'Most Anti-Semitic Israeli Cartoon'.

42 Winstanley, 'Israeli Ambassador'.

43 Libby Lenkinski, 'How Trump and Netanyahu Made American Antisemitism Come Alive', *+972 Magazine*, 18 November 2020, https://www.972mag.com/how-trump-and-netanyahu-made-american-antisemitism-come-alive.

44 Boyarin, *Unheroic Conduct*, 279.

45 Boyarin, *Unheroic Conduct*, 279–280.

46 Jacques Kornberg, *Theodor Herzl: From Assimilation to Zionism* (Bloomington, IN: Indiana University Press, 1993), 24.

47 Boyarin, *Unheroic Conduct*, 276–277.

48 There are parallels between Herzl's and Freud's desire to escape Jewishness on the one hand, and the 'modernising' project of Kemal Ataturk, who governed Turkey from 1921 to 1934, on the other. Ataturk's regime sought to build a secular state by vilifying practising Muslims as 'uncivilised'. The intolerant secularism of Ataturk's state fuelled political Islam, currently represented by President Recep Tayyip Erdogan. See Binnaz Toprak, 'Secularism and Islam: The Building of Modern Turkey', *Macalester International* 15 (2005): Article 9, http://digitalcommons.macalester.edu/macintl/vol15/iss1/9.

49 Kornberg, *Theodor Herzl*, 24.

50 Peter Loewenberg, 'A Hidden Zionist Theme in Freud's "My Son, the Myops ..." Dream', *Journal of the History of Ideas* 31, no. 1 (January–March 1970), 129–132.

51 Quoted in Boyarin, *Unheroic Conduct*, 223.

52 Boyarin, *Unheroic Conduct*, 223.

53 Boyarin, *Unheroic Conduct*, 223.

54 Boyarin, *Unheroic Conduct*, 281.

55 Theodor Herzl, *Old New Land (Altneuland)*, trans. Lotta Levensohn (New York: Markus Wiener; Herzl Press, 1987).

CHAPTER 6 Mimicking the Oppressor

1 Quoted in Daniel Boyarin, *Unheroic Conduct: The Rise of Heterosexuality and the Invention of the Jewish Man* (Berkeley, CA: University of California Press, 1997), 285.

2   Marc Ellis, *Israel and Palestine – Out of the Ashes: The Search for Jewish Identity in the Twenty-First Century* (London: Pluto Press, 2002).

3   Max Weber, *Economy and Society*, eds. Guenther Roth and Claus Wittich (Berkeley: University of California Press, 1978), 54.

4   Boyarin, *Unheroic Conduct*, 33–80.

5   Boyarin, *Unheroic Conduct*, 53.

6   Michael Brenner, 'A State Like Any Other State or a Light unto the Nations?', *Israel Studies* 23, no. 3 (Fall 2018), 3.

7   Mahmood Mamdani, *Good Muslim, Bad Muslim: America, the Cold War and the Roots of Terror* (Johannesburg: Jacana, 2005), 35.

8   Mamdani, *Good Muslim, Bad Muslim*, 36.

9   Joseph Massad, 'Starmer's Apology Skipped over Britain's Long History of Antisemitism', *Middle East Eye*, 29 November 2021, https://www.middleeasteye.net/opinion/uk-antisemitism-starmer-apology-long-history.

10   Massad, 'Starmer's Apology'.

11   Shaul Magid, 'Christian Supersessionism, Zionism, and the Contemporary Scene: A Critical Reading of Peter Ochs's Reading of John Howard Yoder', *Journal of Religious Ethics* 45, no. 1 (March 2017), 132.

12   Magid, 'Christian Supersessionism', 132–133. The 1967 Six-Day War, which enabled Israel to occupy Palestinian and Syrian lands that had been outside its control until then – the West Bank (including Jerusalem), Gaza, and the Syrian Golan Heights – is regarded with almost religious veneration by Zionists.

13   Alana Lentin, *Why Race Still Matters* (Cambridge: Polity Press, 2020), 132. Lentin cites one example of a previous attempt to Westernise Jews – the 1870 French government decree that granted French citizenship to colonised Algerian Jews but not to Muslims.

14   Lewis Gordon, 'Rarely Kosher: Studying Jews of Color in North America', *American Jewish History* 100, no. 1 (January 2016), 105–116.

15   Tudor Parfitt, *The Lost Tribes of Israel: The History of a Myth* (London: Weidenfeld and Nicholson, 2002).

16   Lentin, *Why Race Still Matters*, 153.

17   Boyarin, *Unheroic Conduct*, 225.

18   Jacques Kornberg, *Theodor Herzl: From Assimilation to Zionism* (Bloomington, IN: Indiana University Press, 1993), 2.

19   This section is based on Steven Friedman, 'The Change Which Remains the Same: Towards a Decolonisation Which Does Not Recolonise', *The Thinker* 89, no. 4 (November 2021), 8–18.

20   Ashis Nandy, *The Intimate Enemy: Loss and Recovery of Self Under Colonialism*, in *Exiled at Home*, by Ashis Nandy (New Delhi: Oxford University Press, 2005).

21   Nandy, *The Intimate Enemy*, 64.

22   Nandy, *The Intimate Enemy*, 73.

23   Nandy, *The Intimate Enemy*, 100.

24   Nandy, *The Intimate Enemy*, 78–79.

25   Quoted in T. Dunbar Moodie, *The Rise of Afrikanerdom: Power, Apartheid, and the Afrikaner Civil Religion* (Berkeley, CA: University of California Press, 1975), 266.

26   Nandy, *The Intimate Enemy*, 85.

27   Nandy, *The Intimate Enemy*, 86.

28   Nandy, *The Intimate Enemy*, 86.

29   Nandy, *The Intimate Enemy*, 85–86.

30   Cornelia Aust, 'From Noble Dress to Jewish Attire: Jewish Appearances in the Polish-Lithuanian Commonwealth and the Holy Roman Empire', in *Dress and Cultural Difference in Early Modern Europe*, eds. Cornelia Aust, Denise Klein and Thomas Weller (Berlin and Boston: De Gruyter Oldenbourg, 2019), 90–112.

31   Beata Biedrońska-Słota and Maria Molenda, 'The Emergence of a Polish National Dress and Its Perception', in *Dress and Cultural Difference in Early Modern Europe*, eds. Cornelia Aust, Denise Klein and Thomas Weller (Boston, Berlin: De Gruyter Oldenbourg, 2019), 113–136.

32   Nandy, *The Intimate Enemy*, 73.

33   Nandy, *The Intimate Enemy*, 72.

34   Nandy, *The Intimate Enemy*, 73.

35   Nandy, *The Intimate Enemy*, 107–108.

36   Nandy, *The Intimate Enemy*, 110.

37   Nandy, *The Intimate Enemy*, 111.

38   Nandy, *The Intimate Enemy*, 107–111.

39   Nandy, *The Intimate Enemy*, 74.

40   Nandy, *The Intimate Enemy*, 108.

41   Nandy, *The Intimate Enemy*, 111.

42   Nandy, *The Intimate Enemy*, 72.

43   Nandy, *The Intimate Enemy*, 73–74.

44   Nandy, *The Intimate Enemy*, 73.

45   Nandy, *The Intimate Enemy*, 80.

46   Nandy, *The Intimate Enemy*, 103.

47   Rabindranath Tagore, *Gora* (New Delhi: Rupa, 2002).

48   Boyarin, *Unheroic Conduct*, 33–79.

49   Frustmanoos, 'Self-Hating Hindus: The Snakes amongst Us', *TFIpost*, 17 May 2016, https://tfipost.com/2016/05/self-hating-hindus.

50   Frustmanoos, 'Self-Hating Hindus'.

51   Pankaj Mishra, 'Modi's India Points to Perils of White Nationalism in U.S. and U.K', *Bloomberg*, 14 November 2021, https://www.bloomberg.com/opinion/articles/2021-11-14/modi-s-india-points-to-perils-of-white-nationalism-in-u-s-and-u-k.

52   Steve Biko, *I Write What I Like* (London: Bowerdean Press, 1978).

53   James C. Scott, *Weapons of the Weak: Everyday Forms of Peasant Resistance* (New Haven, CT: Yale University Press, 1985).

CHAPTER 7 Two Religions and the Nightmare the West Created

1   Brennan Center for Justice, 'Why Countering Violent Extremism Programs Are Bad Policy', New York University, 9 September 2019, https://www.brennancenter.org/our-work/research-reports/why-countering-violent-extremism-programs-are-bad-policy.

2   Mahmood Mamdani, *Good Muslim, Bad Muslim: America, the Cold War and the Roots of Terror* (Johannesburg: Jacana, 2005), 7.

3   Mamdani, *Good Muslim, Bad Muslim*, 6.

4   Philip Oltermann, 'Germany Agrees to Pay Namibia €1.1bn over Historical Herero-Nama Genocide', *The Guardian*, 28 May 2021, https://www.theguardian.com/

world/2021/may/28/germany-agrees-to-pay-namibia-11bn-over-historical-herero-nama-genocide.

5   Mamdani, *Good Muslim, Bad Muslim*, 7.

6   United Nations Office of the High Commissioner for Human Rights, 'Geneva Convention Relative to the Treatment of Prisoners of War, 1949', https://www.un.org/en/genocideprevention/documents/atrocity-crimes/Doc.32_GC-III-EN.pdf.

7   Johanna Jacques, 'A "Most Astonishing" Circumstance: The Survival of Jewish POWs in German War Captivity During the Second World War', *Social and Legal Studies* 30, no. 3 (2021), 362–383.

8   Jacques, '"Most Astonishing" Circumstance'.

9   Quoted in Mamdani, *Good Muslim, Bad Muslim*, 7.

10 Mamdani, *Good Muslim, Bad Muslim*, 7.

11 Aimé Césaire, *Discourse on Colonialism*, trans. Joan Pinkham (New York: Monthly Review Press, 2000), 36.

12 Frantz Fanon, *The Wretched of the Earth*, trans. Constance Farrington (New York: Grove Press, 1963)

13 Patrick Gathara, 'Covering Ukraine: A Mean Streak of Racist Exceptionalism', *Al Jazeera*, 1 March 2022, https://www.aljazeera.com/opinions/2022/3/1/covering-ukraine-a-mean-streak-of-racist-exceptionalism.

14 Josephine Harvey, 'CBS Journalist Apologizes for Saying Ukraine More "Civilized" Than Iraq, Afghanistan', *HuffPost*, 27 February 2022, https://www.huffpost.com/entry/media-racism-ukraine-conflict-coverage_n_621c08ffe4b0d1388f16a3dc.

15 Mamdani, *Good Muslim, Bad Muslim*, 8.

16 Mamdani, *Good Muslim, Bad Muslim*, 8.

17 Paul Hanebrink, *A Specter Haunting Europe: The Myth of Judeo-Bolshevism*, (Cambridge, MA, London: Belknap Press of Harvard University Press, 2018).

18 Mamdani, *Good Muslim, Bad Muslim*, 15.

19 Noa Landau, 'The Writing Has Been on the Wall for Yad Vashem's Schnorrer Culture', *Haaretz*, 28 February 2022, https://www.haaretz.com/opinion/.premium-the-writing-has-been-on-the-wall-for-yad-vashem-s-schnorrer-culture-1.10642584.

20 Orly Noy, 'For the Jewish State, the Holocaust Is a Tool to Be Manipulated', *+972 Magazine*, 20 November 2020, https://www.972mag.com/holocaust-antisemitism-israel-tool.

21 Soheir Asaad and Rania Muhareb, 'Dismantle What? Amnesty's Conflicted Messaging on Israeli Apartheid', *Mondoweiss*, 18 February 2022, https://mondoweiss.net/2022/02/dismantle-what-amnestys-conflicted-messaging-on-israeli-apartheid.

22 Mamdani, *Good Muslim, Bad Muslim*, 15.

23 Bernard Lewis, 'The Roots of Muslim Rage', *The Atlantic*, September 1990, https://www.theatlantic.com/magazine/archive/1990/09/the-roots-of-muslim-rage/304643.

24 Mamdani, *Good Muslim, Bad Muslim*, 23.

25 Mamdani, *Good Muslim, Bad Muslim*, 17.

26 Samuel Huntington, *The Clash of Civilizations and the Remaking of World Order* (New York: Simon and Schuster, 1996).

27 Mamdani, *Good Muslim, Bad Muslim*, 24.

28 Quoted by Edward W. Said, *Orientalism* (London: Penguin, 2003), 314.

29 See, for example, Allamah Abu al-'A'la Mawdudi, 'Human Rights in Islam', *al Tawhid Journal* IV, no. 3 (Rajab-Ramadhan 1407 (1987)), https://www.iium.edu.my/deed/articles/hr/hr.html. Mawdudi writes, 'In Islam human rights have been conferred by

God, no legislative assembly in the world, or any government on earth has the right or authority to make any amendment or change in the rights conferred by God.'

30 Mamdani, *Good Muslim, Bad Muslim*, 24–25.
31 Mamdani, *Good Muslim, Bad Muslim*, 26.
32 Mamdani, *Good Muslim, Bad Muslim*, 36.
33 Mark Silk, 'Steve Bannon and the Nationalist Roots of Trump's "Judeo-Christian" Vision', *Religion News Service*, 11 August 2019, https://religionnews.com/2019/08/11/our-latest-judeo-christian-civilizational-clash.
34 Mamdani, *Good Muslim, Bad Muslim*, 60–61.
35 Mamdani, *Good Muslim, Bad Muslim*, 61.
36 Mamdani, *Good Muslim, Bad Muslim*, 61.
37 Mamdani, *Good Muslim, Bad Muslim*, 61.
38 Azzam S. Tamimi, *Rachid Ghannouchi: A Democrat Within Islamism* (New York: Oxford University Press, 2001).
39 Mamdani, *Good Muslim, Bad Muslim*, 95.
40 Mamdani, *Good Muslim, Bad Muslim*, 97.
41 Mamdani, *Good Muslim, Bad Muslim*, 103.
42 Mamdani, *Good Muslim, Bad Muslim*, 120.
43 Mamdani, *Good Muslim, Bad Muslim*, 126.
44 Mamdani, *Good Muslim, Bad Muslim*, 157.
45 Mamdani, *Good Muslim, Bad Muslim*, 136.
46 Mamdani, *Good Muslim, Bad Muslim*, 138.
47 Mamdani, *Good Muslim, Bad Muslim*, 163.
48 John-Thor Dahlburg, 'Cold War Incursion Sows Seeds of Terror', *Los Angeles Times*, 4 August 1996, https://www.latimes.com/archives/la-xpm-1996-08-04-mn-31363-story.html.
49 Mamdani, *Good Muslim, Bad Muslim*, 140ff.
50 Mamdani, *Good Muslim, Bad Muslim*, 45ff. See also Karen Armstrong, *The Battle for God: Fundamentalism in Judaism, Christianity and Islam* (London: Harper Collins, 2000), 235ff.
51 Shlomo Sand, *The Invention of the Jewish People*, trans. Yael Lotan (London, New York: Verso, 2009).

CHAPTER 8 Colonising Anti-Racism

1 Harald Fischer-Tiné and Michael Mann, eds. *Colonialism as Civilizing Mission: Cultural Ideology in British India* (London: Anthem, 2004).
2 Richard Turner, 'Black Consciousness and White Liberals', *Reality: A Journal of Liberal Opinion* 4, no. 3 (July 1972), 20. See also Steven Friedman, 'The Ambiguous Legacy of Liberalism: Less a Theory of Society, More a State of Mind', in *Intellectual Traditions in South Africa: Ideas, Individuals and Institutions*, eds. Peter Vale, Lawrence Hamilton and Estelle Prinsloo (Pietermaritzburg: University of KwaZulu-Natal Press, 2014), 29–47.
3 Stanley Trapido, 'The Origins of the Cape Franchise Qualifications of 1853', *Journal of African History* 5, no. 1 (1964), 37–54.
4 Howard Ball, *The Bakke Case: Race, Education, and Affirmative Action* (Lawrence, KA: University of Kansas Press, 2000).

5   Alana Lentin, *Why Race Still Matters* (Cambridge: Polity Press, 2020), 60.

6   Lentin, *Why Race Still Matters*, 49.

7   Lentin, *Why Race Still Matters*, 89.

8   Lentin, *Why Race Still Matters*, 72.

9   Lawrence Glickman, '3 Tropes of White Victimhood', *The Atlantic,* 20 July 2021, https://www.theatlantic.com/ideas/archive/2021/07/three-tropes-white-victimhood/619463.

10   Anon, 'A Semi-Southern View of Reconstruction', *Hartford Courant*, 12 January 1875, https://www.newspapers.com/clip/75900894/hartford-courant/.

11   Correspondent, 'Friday, January 3, 1868', *The Courier-Journal*, 3 January 1868, https://www.newspapers.com/clip/81652857/the-courier-journal.

12   Jacey Fortin, 'Critical Race Theory: A Brief History', *New York Times*, 8 November 2021, https://www.nytimes.com/article/what-is-critical-race-theory.html.

13   Adam Gabbatt, 'Progressives Are Resisting Rightwing Book Banning Campaigns – and Are Winning', *The Guardian,* 22 March 2022, https://www.theguardian.com/education/2022/mar/22/educators-resisting-rightwing-book-banning.

14   Benjamin Butterworth, 'What Does "Woke" Mean? Origins of Term, and How the Meaning Has Changed', *iNews*, 26 June 2021, https://inews.co.uk/news/uk/woke-what-mean-meaning-origins-term-definition-culture-387962.

15   Douglas Blair, '12 People Canceled by the Left After Expressing Conservative Views', The Heritage Foundation, 20 September 2021, https://www.heritage.org/progressivism/commentary/12-people-canceled-the-left-after-expressing-conservative-views.

16   Ishaan Tharoor, 'The U.S. and British Right Ramp up the War on "Wokeness"', *Washington Post*, 9 April 2021, https://www.washingtonpost.com/world/2021/04/09/woke-wars-united-states-britain.

17   Steven Friedman, 'The DA Is Becoming the Poster Child of the Right', *New Frame,* 18 October 2021, https://www.newframe.com/the-da-is-becoming-the-poster-child-of-the-right.

18   Roger D. Petersen, *Understanding Ethnic Violence: Fear, Hatred, and Resentment in Twentieth-Century Eastern Europe* (Cambridge: Cambridge University Press, 2002).

19   Richard Dyer, *White: Essays on Race and Culture* (Abingdon: Routledge, 1997).

20   Steven Friedman, *Prisoners of the Past: South African Democracy and the Legacy of Minority Rule* (Johannesburg: Wits University Press, 2021).

21   Andile Zulu, 'Dissecting White Genocide: What Is to Be Feared and Why?', *Daily Maverick,* 1 April 2019, https://www.dailymaverick.co.za/opinionista/2019-04-01-dissecting-white-genocide-what-is-to-be-feared-and-why.

22   Michelle Peens and Bernard Dubbeld, 'Troubled Transformation: Whites, Welfare, and "Reverse-Racism" in Contemporary Newcastle', *Diversities* 15, no. 2 (2013), 7–22.

23   Zulu, 'Dissecting White Genocide'.

24   Gavin Silber and Nathan Geffen, 'Race, Class and Violent Crime in South Africa: Dispelling the "Huntley Thesis"', *South African Crime Quarterly* 30, no. 30 (March 2016), 35–43.

25   Murray Ingram, 'Let's Talk about the Meaning of "Merit Selection"', *Daily Maverick,* 4 May 2017, https://www.dailymaverick.co.za/opinionista/2017-05-04-lets-talk-about-the-meaning-of-merit-selection.

26   Anna Maree, 'South Africa: Democratic Alliance Turns Away from Black Leadership', *The Africa Report*, 25 May 2021, https://www.theafricareport.com/91149/south-africa-democratic-alliance-turns-away-from-black-leadership.

27   Qama Qukula, 'Mmusi Maimane Has Slammed Former DA Leader Tony Leon for Calling Him "an Experiment That Went Wrong"', *CapeTalk*, 4 April 2021, https://www.capetalk.co.za/articles/412955/watch-i-was-in-no-way-anyone-s-experiment-maimane-hits-back-at-tony-leon.

28   Jonathan Ofir, 'Israeli Government Crumbles (Again) on Apartheid Vote – as Its "Arab Experiment" Comes Apart', *Mondoweiss*, 7 June 2022, https://mondoweiss.net/2022/06/israeli-government-crumbles-again-on-apartheid-vote-as-its-arab-experiment-comes-apart.

29   Kevin Durrheim, 'White Opposition to Racial Transformation. Is It Racism?', *South African Journal of Psychology* 33, no. 4 (November 2003), 241–249.

30   Dineo Faku, 'Boardrooms Still Very Much White and Predominantly Male', *IOL*, 20 January 2021, https://www.iol.co.za/business-report/careers/boardrooms-still-very-much-white-and-predominantly-male-c6f4346c-4030-4067-bbb5-1dc61b298a3d.

31   Fred Khumalo, 'Phoenix Massacre: Let's Talk about Race', *City Press*, 29 November 2021, https://www.news24.com/citypress/columnists/fredkhumalo/close-up-phoenix-massacre-lets-talk-about-race-20211129.

32   South African History Online, '70. The Durban Riots, 1949', last modified 18 June 2019, https://www.sahistory.org.za/archive/70-durban-riots-1949.

33   Khumalo, 'Phoenix Massacre'.

34   Steven Friedman, *One Virus, Two Countries: What Covid-19 Tells Us about South Africa* (Johannesburg: Wits University Press, 2021).

35   Zimasa Matiwane, 'Mike Waters Resigns from DA Post over "Spineless" Poster Apology', *Business Live*, 11 October 2021, https://www.businesslive.co.za/bd/national/2021-10-11-mike-waters-resigns-from-da-post-over-spineless-poster-apology.

36   Steven Friedman, 'Seeing Ourselves as Others See Us: Racism, Technique and the Mbeki Administration', in *Mbeki and After: Reflections on the Legacy of Thabo Mbeki*, ed. Daryl Glaser (Johannesburg: Wits University Press, 2010), 163–186.

37   R. B. G. Choudree, 'Traditions of Conflict Resolution in South Africa', *African Journal on Conflict Resolution* 1, no. 1 (January 2000), 9–27.

38   Xolela Mangcu, 'Mobilise Communities Instead of Providing Houses of Cards', *Business Day*, 23 July 2009, 9, https://allafrica.com/stories/200907230375.html.; Richard Pithouse, 'Burning Message to the State in the Fire of the Poor's Rebellion', *Anarkismo.net*, 23 July 2009, https://www.anarkismo.net/article/13851.

39   Karen Heese and Kevin Allan, 'Urgent Messages in the Clattering Stones of Delivery Protests', *allAfrica*, republished from *Business Day*, 16 July 2009, https://allafrica.com/stories/200907160072.html.

40   Guillermo O'Donnell, 'Illusions About Consolidation', *Journal of Democracy* 7, no. 2 (April 1996), 34–51.

41   Steven Friedman, 'Getting Better Than "World Class": The Challenge of Governing Postapartheid South Africa', *Social Research* 72, no. 3 (Fall 2005), 757–784, http://www.jstor.org/stable/40971789.

42   Mandisa Mbali, *South African AIDS Activism and Global Health Politics* (New York: Palgrave Macmillan, 2013).

43   Staff Reporter, 'Mbeki Turns Aids Row into Race Issue', *Mail & Guardian*, 26 October 2004, https://mg.co.za/article/2004-10-26-mbeki-turns-aids-row-into-race-issue.

CONCLUSION The 'New Anti-Semitism' and Politics Today

1   Judith Butler, *Gender Trouble: Feminism and the Subversion of Identity* (New York: Routledge, 1990), 33.
2   Butler, *Gender Trouble*, 8.
3   Saul Dubow, 'Afrikaner Nationalism, Apartheid and the Conceptualization of "Race"', *Journal of African History* 33, no. 2 (1992), 209, https://www.jstor.org/stable/182999.
4   South African History Online, 'The History of Separate Development in South Africa', last updated 27 August 2019, https://www.sahistory.org.za/article/history-separate-development-south-africa.
5   Richard Steyn, *Churchill and Smuts: The Friendship* (Johannesburg: Jonathan Ball Publishers, 2017).
6   Anye Nyamnjoh, 'The Phenomenology of *Rhodes Must Fall*: Student Activism and the Experience of Alienation at the University of Cape Town', *Strategic Review for Southern Africa* 39, no. 1 (May 2017), 256–277, https://upjournals.up.ac.za/index.php/strategic_review/article/view/330.
7   Savo Heleta, 'Decolonisation of Higher Education: Dismantling Epistemic Violence and Eurocentrism in South Africa', *Transformation in Higher Education* 1, no. 1 (2016), a9, doi: https://doi.org/10.4102.
8   Steven Friedman, 'Speaking Power's Truth: South African Media in the Service of the Suburbs', in *Media and Citizenship: Between Marginalisation and Participation*, eds. Anthea Garman and Herman Wasserman (Cape Town: HSRC Press, 2017), 55–71.
9   Gareth van Onselen, 'Mmusi Maimane Presses the Self-Destruct Button', *Business Day*, 9 May 2018, https://www.businesslive.co.za/bd/opinion/columnists/2018-05-09-gareth-van-onselen-mmusi-maimane-presses-the-self-destruct-button.
10   See, for example, the heated debate on whether consensus decision-making is inherent to African political culture. Kwasi Wiredu, 'Democracy and Consensus in African Traditional Politics: A Plea for a Non-Party Polity', in *Postcolonial African Philosophy: A Critical Reader*, ed. Emmanuel Chukwudi Eze (Cambridge, MA, Oxford: Blackwell, 1997), 303–312; Paulin J. Hountondji, 'Knowledge of Africa, Knowledge by Africans: Two Perspectives on African Studies', *RCCS Annual Review* 1, no. 1 (September 2009), 121–131, http://journals.openedition.org/rccsar/174.
11   See comment by Nomboniso Gasa, quoted in Karen Breytenbach, 'Zuma Case "Highlights Misogynistic Culture"', *IOL*, 20 April 2006, https://www.iol.co.za/news/south-africa/zuma-case-highlights-misogynistic-culture-274707.
12   Ashis Nandy, *The Intimate Enemy: Loss and Recovery of Self Under Colonialism*, in *Exiled at Home,* by Ashis Nandy (New Delhi: Oxford University Press, 2005), 74.
13   Nandy, *The Intimate Enemy*, 82.
14   Idowu Omoyele, 'Arrested Decolonisation, Season 4', *Mail & Guardian*, 14 July 2017, https://mg.co.za/article/2017-07-14-00-arrested-decolonisation-season-4.
15   Ruth E. Gavison, 'The Jews' Right to Statehood: A Defense', *Azure* 15 (2003), 70–108.
16   Shlomo Sand, *The Invention of the Jewish People*, trans. Yael Lotan (London and New York: Verso, 2009).

17 Benedict Anderson, *Imagined Communities: Reflections on the Origin and Spread of Nationalism* (London and New York: Verso, 1983).

18 Pieter M. Judson, 'Nationalism in the Era of the Nation State, 1870–1945', in *The Oxford Handbook of Modern German History*, ed. Helmut Walser Smith (Oxford: Oxford University Press, 2011), 499–526.

19 Lowell W. Barrington, '"Nation" and "Nationalism": The Misuse of Key Concepts in Political Science', *PS: Political Science and Politics* 30, no. 4 (December 1997), 712–716.

20 David G. Mahal and Ianis G. Matsoukas, 'The Geographic Origins of Ethnic Groups in the Indian Subcontinent: Exploring Ancient Footprints with Y-DNA Haplogroups', *Frontiers in Genetics* 9 (23 January 2018), https://doi.org/10.3389/fgene.2018.00004.

21 Yun Zhou, 'Question of Ethnic Group Formulation in the Chinese Census', *China Population* and *Development Studies* 3, no. 1 (October 2019), 67–83.

22 know Botswana, 'Botswana Ethnic Groups and Tribes', accessed 8 June 2023, https://www.knowbotswana.com/botswana-ethnic-groups-and-tribes.html.

23 Sylvain Cypel, *The State of Israel vs. the Jews*, trans. William Rodarmor (New York: Other Press, 2021), 44.

24 See United Nations Human Rights Council, 'Independent International Fact-Finding Mission on Myanmar', accessed 8 June 2023, https://www.ohchr.org/en/hr-bodies/hrc/myanmar-ffm/index.

25 Madeline Roache, 'China Guilty of Uighur Genocide in Xinjiang, Tribunal Rules', *Al Jazeera*, 9 December 2021, https://www.aljazeera.com/news/2021/12/9/china-guilty-of-uighur-genocide-beyond-reasonable-doubt-report.

26 Reuters, 'Nancy Pelosi Says Trump Wants to "Make America White Again" – Video', *The Guardian*, 9 July 2019, https://www.theguardian.com/global/video/2019/jul/09/nancy-pelosi-says-trump-wants-to-make-america-white-again-video.

27 Jeremie Gilbert and David Keane, 'How French Law Makes Minorities Invisible', *The Conversation*, 13 November 2016, https://theconversation.com/how-french-law-makes-minorities-invisible-66723.

28 Nigel Rapport, 'Britain and Brexit: Imagining an Essentialist Sense of "Britishness" and Navigating amongst "the British"', *Anthropology Southern Africa* 43, no. 2 (2020), 94–106, https://doi.org/https://doi.org/10.1080/23323256.2020.1740604.

29 William H. Frey, 'The US Will Become "Minority White" in 2045, Census Projects', *Brookings*, 14 March 2018, https://www.brookings.edu/blog/the-avenue/2018/03/14/the-us-will-become-minority-white-in-2045-census-projects.

30 World Population Review, 'South Korea Population, 2023', accessed 8 June 2023, https://worldpopulationreview.com/countries/south-korea-population.

31 A Talmudic passage notes that some sources claim the injunction is mentioned 46 times. See Jonathan Sacks, 'Loving the Stranger Mishpatim 5779', The Rabbi Sacks Legacy Trust, 2019, https://www.rabbisacks.org/covenant-conversation/mishpatim/loving-the-stranger.

32 Lewis Gordon, 'Rarely Kosher: Studying Jews of Color in North America', *American Jewish History* 100, no. 1 (January 2016), 105–116.

33 Ivan David Kalmar and Derek Penslar, eds, *Orientalism and the Jews* (Chicago: University of Chicago Press, 2004), 284ff.

34 Haaretz, 'Balad: A Country of All Its Citizens, Cultural Autonomy for Arabs', 23 December 2002, https://www.haaretz.com/2002-12-23/ty-article/balad-a-country-of-all-its-citizens-cultural-autonomy-for-arabs/0000017f-e25b-d9aa-afff-fb5b591d0000.

35 A 'hyphenated citizen' is one who embraces multiple identities; for example, African-American, French-Muslim and Jewish-South African.

36 Michael Neocosmos, *From 'Foreign Natives' to 'Native Foreigners': Explaining Xeno-phobia in Post-Apartheid South Africa: Citizenship and Nationalism, Identity and Pol-itics* (Dakar: CODESRIA, 2010), 1ff.

37 South African History Online, 'The Freedom Charter', last updated 27 August 2019, https://www.sahistory.org.za/article/freedom-charter.

38 See comments on Steven Friedman, 'Anti-Migrant Sentiment Is a National Emer-gency', Facebook, 3 April 2022, https://www.facebook.com/steven.friedman.79274/posts/pfbid028LWzcQWePiUqhc7N86aHTSwpAEi6R2QXAszRrqsdSPXtxtMRywpNQNmsFx2hNCuXl.

39 Comments on Friedman, 'Anti-Migrant Sentiment'.

40 Muritala Dauda, Rauf Tunde Sakariyau and Abdullateef Ameen, 'Xenophobic Violence in South Africa and the Nigerians' Victimization: An Empirical Analysis', *Pertanika Journal of Social Science and Humanities* 26, no. 4 (December 2018), 2677–2700, http://www.pertanika.upm.edu.my/resources/files/Pertanika%20PAPERS/JSSH%20Vol.%2026%20(4)%20Dec.%202018/32.%20JSSH-2197-2017.pdf.

41 This view is discussed in theological terms (in which its application to the Israeli state's defenders is hinted at but never explicitly expressed) in Michael Goldberg, *Why Should Jews Survive? Looking Past the Holocaust Toward a Jewish Future* (New York and Oxford: Oxford University Press, 1995).

BIBLIOGRAPHY

Abunimah, Ali. 'German Anti-Semitism Surges, from the Right'. *Electronic Intifada*, 15 February 2021. https://electronicintifada.net/blogs/ali-abunimah/german-anti-semitism-surges-right.

Alikhan, Zubayr. 'Israel's Erroneous Slurs Harm Jews and Threaten the Legitimate Battle Against Antisemitism'. *Palestine Chronicle*, 12 February 2022. https://www.palestinechronicle.com/israels-erroneous-slurs-harm-jews-and-threaten-the-legitimate-battle-against-antisemitism/.

Anderson, Benedict. *Imagined Communities: Reflections on the Origin and Spread of Nationalism*. London, New York: Verso, 1983.

Anderson, Perry. *Lineages of the Absolutist State*. London, New York: Verso, 1974.

Anon. 'A Semi-Southern View of Reconstruction'. *Hartford Courant*, 12 January 1875. https://www.newspapers.com/clip/75900894/hartford-courant/.

Arendt, Hannah. *The Origins of Totalitarianism*. Cleveland, OH, New York: Harvest/HBJ, 1958.

Armstrong, Karen. *The Battle for God: Fundamentalism in Judaism, Christianity and Islam*. London: Harper Collins, 2000.

Armstrong, Karen. *The Lost Art of Scripture: Rescuing the Sacred Texts*. London: The Bodley Head, 2019.

Asaad, Soheir and Rania Muhareb. 'Dismantle What? Amnesty's Conflicted Messaging on Israeli Apartheid'. *Mondoweiss*, 18 February 2022. https://mondoweiss.net/2022/02/dismantle-what-amnestys-conflicted-messaging-on-israeli-apartheid/.

Aust, Cornelia. 'From Noble Dress to Jewish Attire: Jewish Appearances in the Polish-Lithuanian Commonwealth and the Holy Roman Empire'. In *Dress and Cultural Difference in Early Modern Europe*, edited by Cornelia Aust, Denise Klein and Thomas Weller, 90–112. Boston, Berlin: De Gruyter Oldenbourg, 2019.

Azadovskii, Konstantin and Boris Egorov. 'From Anti-Westernism to Anti-Semitism: Stalin and the Impact of the "Anti-Cosmopolitan" Campaigns on Soviet Culture'. *Journal of Cold War Studies* 4, no. 1 (2002): 66–80.

Bacha, Claire, Sue Einhorn and Sue Lieberman. '"If You Prick Me, Do I Not Bleed?": Antisemitism, Racism and Group Analysis – Some Thoughts'. *Group Analysis* 54, no. 3 (2021): 388–401.

Badiou, Alain and Eric Hazan, 'Anti-Semitism: Real and Imagined'. In *Reflections on Anti-Semitism*, edited by Alain Badiou, Eric Hazan and Ivan Segré. Translated from French by David Fernbach. London, New York: Verso, 2013.

Badiou, Alain, Eric Hazan and Ivan Segré. *Reflections on Anti-Semitism*. Translated from French by David Fernbach. London, New York: Verso, 2013.

Ball, Howard. *The* Bakke *Case: Race, Education, and Affirmative Action*. Lawrence, KA: University Press of Kansas, 2000.

Barclay, Andrew, Maria Sobolewska and Robert Ford. 'Political Realignment of British Jews: Testing Competing Explanations'. *Electoral Studies* 61 (October 2019). https://doi.org/10.1016/j.electstud.2019.102063.

Baron, Salo Wittmayer. *A Social and Religious History of the Jews*. New York: Columbia University Press, 1957.

Baron, Salo Wittmayer. 'Newer Emphases in Jewish History'. *Jewish Social Studies* 25, no. 4 (1963): 235–248.

Barrington, Lowell W. '"Nation" and "Nationalism": The Misuse of Key Concepts in Political Science'. *PS: Political Science and Politics* 30, no. 4 (1997): 712–716.

Beckert, Sven and Seth Rockman, eds. *Slavery's Capitalism: A New History of American Economic Development*. Philadelphia: University of Pennsylvania Press, 2016.

Ben-Gurion, David. 'The Imperatives of the Jewish Revolution'. Speech to Youth Groups, Haifa, 1944. https://zionism-israel.com/hdoc/Ben-Gurion_Jewish_revolution.htm.

Ben-Gurion, David. 'The Imperatives of the Jewish Revolution'. In *The Zionist Idea: A Historical Analysis and Reader*, edited by Arthur Hertzberg. Philadelphia, PA: University of Pennsylvania Press, 1959.

Ben-Gurion, David. 'Ben Gurion: Letter to His Son, October 5, 1937'. Translated from Hebrew by Institute of Palestine Studies. Jewish Voice for Peace, 6 April 2013. https://www.jewishvoiceforpeace.org/2013/04/the-ben-gurion-letter/.

Bergen, Doris. 'Nazism'. In *Key Concepts in the Study of Anti-Semitism*, edited by Sol Goldberg, Scott Ury and Kalman Weiser, 259. Cham: Palgrave Macmillan, 2021.

Berman, Lazar. 'After Walling Itself in, Israel Learns to Hazard the Jungle Beyond'. *Times of Israel*, 8 March 2021. https://www.timesofisrael.com/after-walling-itself-in-israel-learns-to-hazard-the-jungle-beyond.

Bernasconi, Robert. 'Racism'. In *Key Concepts in the Study of Anti-Semitism*, edited by Sol Goldberg, Scott Ury and Kalman Weiser, 245–252. Cham: Palgrave Macmillan, 2021.

Biale, David. *Power and Powerlessness in Jewish History*. New York: Schocken, 1986.

Biedrońska-Słota, Beata and Maria Molenda. 'The Emergence of a Polish National Dress and Its Perception'. In *Dress and Cultural Difference in Early Modern Europe*, edited by Cornelia Aust, Denise Klein and Thomas Weller, 113–136. European History Yearbook Volume 20. Berlin, Boston: De Gruyter, 2019.

Biko, Steve. *I Write What I Like*. London: Bowerdean Press, 1978.

Blair, Douglas. '12 People Canceled by the Left After Expressing Conservative Views'. The Heritage Foundation, 20 September 2021. https://www.heritage.org/progressivism/commentary/12-people-canceled-the-left-after-expressing-conservative-views.

Blue, Gregory. 'Gobineau on China: Race Theory, the "Yellow Peril", and the Critique of Modernity'. *Journal of World History* 10, no. 1 (1999): 93–139.

Booth, William. 'The Israeli General Who Compared the Jewish State to Nazi-Era Germany'. *Washington Post*, 8 May 2016. https://www.washingtonpost.com/news/

worldviews/wp/2016/05/08/the-israeli-general-who-compared-the-jewish-state-to-nazi-era-germany/.

Boyarin, Daniel. *Unheroic Conduct: The Rise of Heterosexuality and the Invention of the Jewish Man*. Berkeley, CA: University of California Press, 1997.

Brennan Center for Justice. 'Why Countering Violent Extremism Programs Are Bad Policy'. New York University, 9 September 2019. https://www.brennancenter.org/our-work/research-reports/why-countering-violent-extremism-programs-are-bad-policy.

Brenner, Michael. 'A State Like Any Other State or a Light unto the Nations?' *Israel Studies* 23, no. 3 (2018): 3–8.

Breytenbach, Karen. 'Zuma Case "Highlights Misogynistic Culture"'. *IOL*, 20 April 2006. https://www.iol.co.za/news/south-africa/zuma-case-highlights-misogynistic-culture-274707.

Broder, David. 'How Labour Became "Antisemitic": An Interview with Greg Philo'. *Jacobin*, 5 October 2019. https://jacobin.com/2019/10/labour-party-antisemitism-claims-jeremy-corbyn.

Brodkin, Karen. *How Jews Became White Folks and What That Says about Race in America*. London, New Brunswick, NJ: Rutgers University Press, 2000.

Brown, John. 'Rights Groups Demand Israel Stop Arming Neo-Nazis in Ukraine'. *Haaretz*, 9 July 2018. https://www.haaretz.com/israel-news/2018-07-09/ty-article/rights-groups-demand-israel-stop-arming-neo-nazis-in-the-ukraine/0000017f-e080-d7b2-a77f-e3870e1c0000.

Bunzl, Matti. 'Between Anti-Semitism and Islamophobia: Some Thoughts on the New Europe'. *American Ethnologist* 32, no. 4 (2005): 499–508.

Burns, Michael. *France and the Dreyfus Affair: A Documentary History*. Lexington: Plunkett Lake Press, 2014. Kindle.

Buruma, Ian. *Anglomania: A European Love Affair*. New York: Vintage Books, 2000.

Bush, Richard C. 'Thoughts on the Nanjing Massacre'. *Brookings*, 1 December 2007. https://www.brookings.edu/opinions/thoughts-on-the-nanjing-massacre.

Butler, Judith. *Gender Trouble: Feminism and the Subversion of Identity*. New York: Routledge, 1990.

Butterworth, Benjamin. 'What Does "Woke" Mean? Origins of Term, and How the Meaning Has Changed'. *iNews*, 26 June 2021. https://inews.co.uk/news/uk/woke-what-mean-meaning-origins-term-definition-culture-387962.

Carroll, James. *Constantine's Sword: The Church and the Jews*. Boston, New York: Houghton Mifflin, 2002.

Carroll, Lewis. *Through the Looking Glass and What Alice Found There*. Digital Scanning Inc., [1872] 2007.

Césaire, Aimé. *Discourse on Colonialism*. Translated from French by Joan Pinkham. New York: Monthly Review Press, 2000.

Chesler, Phyllis. *The New Anti-Semitism: The Current Crisis and What We Must Do about It*. San Francisco, CA: Jossey-Bass, 2003.

Choudree, Rajesh. 'Traditions of Conflict Resolution in South Africa'. *African Journal on Conflict Resolution* 1, no. 1 (2000): 9–27.

Chrisafis, Angelique. 'Jean-Marie Le Pen Convicted of Contesting Crimes Against Humanity'. *The Guardian*, 16 February 2012. https://www.theguardian.com/world/2012/feb/16/jean-marie-le-pen-convicted.

Clermont-Tonnerre. 'Speech on Religious Minorities and Questionable Professions (23 December 1789)'. Liberté, Égalité, Fraternité: Exploring the French Revolution. https://revolution.chnm.org/d/284.

Cohen, Mari. 'Deborah Lipstadt vs. "The Oldest Hatred"'. *Jewish Currents*, 28 April 2022. https://jewishcurrents.org/deborah-lipstadt-vs-the-oldest-hatred.

Cohen, Mark R. 'Prologue: The "Golden Age" of Jewish-Muslim Relations: Myth and Reality'. In *A History of Jewish-Muslim Relations: From the Origins to the Present Day*, edited by Abdelwahab Meddeb and Benjamin Stora, 28–38. Princeton, NJ: Princeton University Press, 2014.

Cohen, Robert A. H. 'We Need to Decolonise Our Understanding of Antisemitism'. *Patheos*, 6 March 2021. https://www.patheos.com/blogs/writingfromtheedge/2021/03/we-need-to-decolonise-our-understanding-of-antisemitism/.

Colbert, Noah. 'The Mythology of the "Black-Jewish Alliance"'. *Mondoweiss*, 22 December 2021. https://mondoweiss.net/2021/12/the-mythology-of-the-black-jewish-alliance/.

Connelly, John. 'Nazis and Slavs: From Racial Theory to Racist Practice'. *Central European History* 32, no. 1 (1999): 1–33.

Cook, Jonathan. 'How the EHRC Antisemitism Report Added Fire to Labour's Simmering Civil War'. *Middle East Eye*, 5 November 2020. https://www.middleeasteye.net/opinion/ehrc-labour-antisemitism-civil-war-fire-added.

Cook, Jonathan. 'Labour Antisemitism Allegations: How Corbyn and Starmer Are Judged by Different Standards'. *Middle East Eye*, 16 April 2021. https://www.middleeasteye.net/opinion/labour-antisemitism-allegations-how-corbyn-and-starmer-are-judged-different-standards.

Correspondent. 'Friday, January 3, 1868'. *The Courier-Journal*, 3 January 1868. https://www.newspapers.com/clip/81652857/the-courier-journal.

Cousin, Glynis and Robert Fine. 'A Common Cause: Reconnecting the Study of Racism and Antisemitism'. *European Societies* 14, no. 2 (2012): 166–185.

Cronin, David. 'EU Snubs Jews Who Criticize Israel'. *Electronic Intifada*, 21 January 2021. https://electronicintifada.net/blogs/david-cronin/eu-snubs-jews-who-criticize-israel.

Cypel, Sylvain. *The State of Israel vs. the Jews*. Translated from French by William Rodarmor. New York: Other Press, 2021.

Dahlburg, John-Thor. 'Cold War Incursion Sows Seeds of Terror'. *Los Angeles Times*, 4 August 1996. https://www.latimes.com/archives/la-xpm-1996-08-04-mn-31363-story.html.

Dauda, Muritala, Rauf Tunde Sakariyau and Abdullateef Ameen. 'Xenophobic Violence in South Africa and the Nigerians' Victimization: An Empirical Analysis'. *Pertanika Journal of Social Science and Humanities* 26, no. 4 (December 2018): 2677–2700. http://www.pertanika.upm.edu.my/resources/files/Pertanika%20PAPERS/JSSH%20Vol.%2026%20(4)%20Dec.%202018/32.%20JSSH-2197-2017.pdf.

Du Bois, W. E. B. *The Souls of Black Folk*. With an Introduction and Chronology by Jonathan Scott Holloway. New Haven, CT, and London: Yale University Press, 2015.

Dubow, Saul. 'Afrikaner Nationalism, Apartheid and the Conceptualization of "Race"'. *Journal of African History* 33, no. 2 (1992): 209–237. https://www.jstor.org/stable/182999.

Durrheim, Kevin. 'White Opposition to Racial Transformation. Is It Racism?' *South African Journal of Psychology* 33, no. 4 (2003): 241–249.

Dyer, Richard. *White: Essays on Race and Culture*. Abingdon: Routledge, 1997.

Eldar, Akiva. 'The Price of a Villa in the Jungle'. *Haaretz*, 30 January 2006. https://www.haaretz.com/2006-01-30/ty-article/the-price-of-a-villa-in-the-jungle/0000017f-eda5-d0f7-a9ff-efe5356e0000.

Ellis, Marc. *Israel and Palestine – Out of the Ashes: The Search for Jewish Identity in the Twenty-First Century*. London: Pluto Press, 2002.

Equality and Human Rights Commission (EHRC). 'Investigation into Antisemitism in the Labour Party', October 2020. https://www.equalityhumanrights.com/sites/default/files/investigation-into-antisemitism-in-the-labour-party.pdf.

Evans, Richard J. *The Coming of the Third Reich*. New York: Penguin Books, 2005.

Faku, Dineo. 'Boardrooms Still Very Much White and Predominantly Male'. *IOL*, 20 January 2021. https://www.iol.co.za/business-report/careers/boardrooms-still-very-much-white-and-predominantly-male-c6f4346c-4030-4067-bbb5-1dc61b298a3d.

Fanon, Frantz. *The Wretched of the Earth*. Translated from French by Constance Farrington. New York: Grove Press, 1963.

Fanon, Frantz. *Black Skin, White Masks*. Translated from French by Charles Lam Markmann. London: Pluto Press, 1986.

Feinstein, Andrew. 'Zille Is Wrong – There Is No Anti-Semitism in Reclaim the City's Opposition to the Tafelberg Sale'. *Daily Maverick*, 8 May 2017. https://www.dailymaverick.co.za/article/2017-05-08-op-ed-zille-is-wrong-there-is-no-anti-semitism-in-reclaim-the-citys-opposition-to-the-tafelberg-sale/.

Feldman, David. 'The Government Should Not Impose a Faulty Definition of Antisemitism on Universities'. *The Guardian*, 2 December 2020. https://www.theguardian.com/commentisfree/2020/dec/02/the-government-should-not-impose-a-faulty-definition-of-antisemitism-on-universities.

Fick, Marisa and Lawrence Schlemmer. 'Government Policy: Change or Stasis 1976–1982'. *Indicator* South Africa 1, no. 1 (1983): 7–9.

Field, Geoffrey. *Evangelist of Race: The Germanic Vision of Houston Stewart Chamberlain*. New York: Columbia University Press, 1981.

Finkelstein, Norman G. *Beyond Chutzpah: On the Misuse of Anti-Semitism and the Abuse of History*. Berkeley, Los Angeles, CA: University of California Press, 2005.

Finlay, W. M. L. 'Pathologizing Dissent: Identity Politics, Zionism and the "Self-Hating Jew"'. *British Journal of Social Psychology* 44, no. 2 (2005): 201–222. http://dx.doi.org/10.1348/014466604X17894.

Fischer-Tiné, Harald and Michael Mann, eds. *Colonialism as Civilizing Mission: Cultural Ideology in British India*. London: Anthem, 2004.

Fordham University. 'Medieval Sourcebook: Abraham Ibd [sic] Daud: On Samuel Ha-Nagid, Vizier of Granada, 993-d after 1056'. In *Internet Medieval Sourcebook*, edited by Paul Halsall, 1997. https://sourcebooks.fordham.edu/source/ha-nagid.asp.

Fortin, Jacey. 'Critical Race Theory: A Brief History'. *New York Times*, 8 November 2021. https://www.nytimes.com/article/what-is-critical-race-theory.html.

Foster, Arnold and Benjamin R. Epstein. *The New Anti-Semitism*. New York: McGraw Hill, 1974.

Freud, Sigmund. *Moses and Monotheism*. Translated from German by Katherine Jones. London: Hogarth Press and Institute of Psycho-analysis. 1939.

Frey, William H. 'The US Will Become "Minority White" in 2045, Census Projects'. Brookings, 14 March 2018. https://www.brookings.edu/blog/the-avenue/2018/03/14/the-us-will-become-minority-white-in-2045-census-projects/.

Friedman, Steven. 'Getting Better Than "World Class": The Challenge of Governing Postapartheid South Africa'. *Social Research* 72, no. 3 (2005): 757–784. http://www.jstor.org/stable/40971789.

Friedman, Steven. 'Seeing Ourselves as Others See Us: Racism, Technique and the Mbeki Administration'. In *Mbeki and After: Reflections on the Legacy of Thabo Mbeki*, edited by Daryl Glaser, 163–186. Johannesburg: Wits University Press, 2010.

Friedman, Steven. 'The Ambiguous Legacy of Liberalism: Less a Theory of Society, More a State of Mind?' In *Intellectual Traditions in South Africa: Ideas, Individuals and Institutions*, edited by Peter Vale, Lawrence Hamilton and Estelle Prinsloo. Pietermaritzburg: University of KwaZulu-Natal Press, 2014.

Friedman, Steven. *Class, Race and Power: Harold Wolpe and the Radical Critique of Apartheid*. Scottsville: University of KwaZulu-Natal Press, 2015.

Friedman, Steven. 'Speaking Power's Truth: South African Media in the Service of the Suburbs'. In *Media and Citizenship: Between Marginalisation and Participation*, edited by Anthea Garman and Herman Wasserman, 55–71. Cape Town: HSRC Press, 2017.

Friedman, Steven. 'US Elections Expose Flaws in Western Democracy'. *New Frame*, 12 November 2020. https://www.newframe.com/us-elections-expose-flaws-in-western-democracy/.

Friedman, Steven. 'The Change Which Remains the Same: Towards a Decolonisation Which Does Not Recolonise'. *The Thinker* 89, no. 4 (2021). https://doi.org/10.36615/thethinker.v89i4.685.

Friedman, Steven. 'The DA Is Becoming the Poster Child of the Right'. *New Frame*, 18 October 2021. https://www.newframe.com/the-da-is-becoming-the-poster-child-of-the-right/.

Friedman, Steven. *One Virus, Two Countries: What Covid-19 Tells Us about South Africa*. Johannesburg: Wits University Press, 2021.

Friedman, Steven. *Prisoners of the Past: South African Democracy and the Legacy of Minority Rule*. Johannesburg: Wits University Press, 2021.

Frustmanoos. 'Self-Hating Hindus: The Snakes amongst Us'. *TFIpost*, 17 May 2016. https://tfipost.com/2016/05/self-hating-hindus/.

Gabbatt, Adam. 'Progressives Are Resisting Rightwing Book Banning Campaigns – and Are Winning'. *The Guardian*, 22 March 2022. https://www.theguardian.com/education/2022/mar/22/educators-resisting-rightwing-book-banning.

Gannon, Megan. 'Race Is a Social Construct, Scientists Argue'. *Scientific American*, 5 February 2016. https://www.scientificamerican.com/article/race-is-a-social-construct-scientists-argue.

Gathara, Patrick. 'Covering Ukraine: A Mean Streak of Racist Exceptionalism'. *Al Jazeera*, 1 March 2022. https://www.aljazeera.com/opinions/2022/3/1/covering-ukraine-a-mean-streak-of-racist-exceptionalism.

Gavison, Ruth. 'The Jews' Right to Statehood: A Defense'. *Azure* 15 (2003): 70–108.

Gessen, Masha. 'Why the Tree of Life Shooter Was Fixated on the Hebrew Immigrant Aid Society'. *New Yorker*, 27 October 2018. https://www.newyorker.com/news/our-columnists/why-the-tree-of-life-shooter-was-fixated-on-the-hebrew-immigrant-aid-society.

Gilbert, Jeremie and David Keane. 'How French Law Makes Minorities Invisible'. *The Conversation*, 13 November 2016. https://theconversation.com/how-french-law-makes-minorities-invisible-66723.

Glickman, Lawrence. '3 Tropes of White Victimhood'. *The Atlantic*, 20 July 2021. https://www.theatlantic.com/ideas/archive/2021/07/three-tropes-white-victimhood/619463/.

Goldberg, Amos. 'Anti-Zionism and Antisemitism: How Right and Left Conflate Issues to Deny Palestinian Rights'. *Middle East Eye*, 28 April 2022. https://www.middleeasteye. net/opinion/israel-broad-coalition-conflates-anti-zionism-antisemitism.

Goldberg, Jeffrey. 'Israel's Fears, Amalek's Arsenal'. *New York Times*, 16 May 2009. https:// www.nytimes.com/2009/05/17/opinion/17goldberg.html.

Goldberg, Michael. *Why Should Jews Survive? Looking Past the Holocaust Toward a Jewish Future*. New York, Oxford: Oxford University Press, 1995.

Goldberg, Sol. 'Jewish Self-Hatred'. In *Key Concepts in the Study of Anti-Semitism*, edited by Sol Goldberg, Scott Ury and Kalman Weiser. Cham: Palgrave Macmillan, 2021.

Goldberg, Sol, Scott Ury and Kalman Weiser, eds. *Key Concepts in the Study of Anti-Semitism*. Cham: Palgrave Macmillan, 2021.

Goldin, Simha. *Apostasy and Jewish Identity in High Middle Ages Northern Europe: 'Are You Still My Brother?'* Translated by Jonathan Chipman. Manchester: Manchester University Press, 2014.

Gordon, Lewis R. 'Rarely Kosher: Studying Jews of Color in North America'. *American Jewish History* 100, no. 1 (2016): 105–116.

Gray, Aysa. 'The Bias of "Professionalism" Standards'. *Stanford Social Innovation Review*, 4 June 2019. https://doi.org/10.48558/TDWC-4756.

Greenspoon, Leonard J. 'Who Is a Jew? Reflections on History, Religion, and Culture'. *Studies in Jewish Civilization* 5 (2014). https://www.jstor.org/stable/j.ctt6wq61q.

Greenwald, Glenn and Andrew Fishman. 'Greatest Threat to Free Speech in the West: Criminalizing Activism Against Israeli Occupation'. *The Intercept*, 16 February 2016. https://theintercept.com/2016/02/16/greatest-threat-to-free-speech-in-the-west-criminalizing-activism-against-israeli-occupation.

Haaretz. 'Balad: A Country of All Its Citizens, Cultural Autonomy for Arabs'. *Haaretz*, 23 December 2002. https://www.haaretz.com/2002-12-23/ty-article/balad-a-country-of-all-its-citizens-cultural-autonomy-for-arabs/0000017f-e25b-d9aa-afff-fb5b591d0000.

Hall, Stuart. *The Fateful Triangle: Race, Ethnicity, Nation*. Cambridge, MA: Harvard University Press, 2017.

Halper, Jeff. 'The Zionist Assault on Judaism'. *Mondoweiss*, 2 July 2021. https://mondoweiss. net/2021/07/the-zionist-assault-on-judaism/.

Hannah Arendt Center, Bard College. Annual Fall Conference on Racism and Anti-Semitism. Annandale-on-Hudson, New York, October 2019. https://hac.bard.edu/ conference2019.

Hanau, Shira. 'Orthodox Jewish Trump Supporters Decry Violence but Not the Movement That Fueled the Mob'. *Jewish Telegraphic Agency*, 6 January 2021. https://www.jta. org/2021/01/06/politics/orthodox-jewish-trump-supporters-decry-violence-but-not-the-movement-that-fueled-the-mob.

Hanebrink, Paul. *A Specter Haunting Europe: The Myth of Judeo-Bolshevism*. Cambridge, MA, London: Belknap Press of Harvard University Press, 2018.

Harvey, Josephine. 'CBS Journalist Apologizes for Saying Ukraine More "Civilized" Than Iraq, Afghanistan'. *HuffPost*, 27 February 2022. https://www.huffpost.com/entry/ media-racism-ukraine-conflict-coverage_n_621c08ffe4b0d1388f16a3dc.

Hay, Malcolm V. *The Roots of Christian Anti-Semitism*. New York: Freedom Library Press, 1981.

Hearst, David and Peter Oborne. 'UK's Labour Accused of "Purging Jews" from Party over Antisemitism Claims'. *Middle East Eye*, 12 August 2021. https://www.middleeasteye. net/news/uk-labour-antisemitism-accused-purging-jews-over-claims.

Heese, Karen and Kevin Allan. 'Urgent Messages in the Clattering Stones of Delivery Protests'. *allAfrica*, republished from *Business Day*, 16 July 2009. https://allafrica.com/stories/200907160072.html.

Heleta, Savo. 'Decolonisation of Higher Education: Dismantling Epistemic Violence and Eurocentrism in South Africa'. *Transformation in Higher Education* 1, no. 1 (2016), a9. https://dx. doi.org/10.4102/the.v1i1.9.

Herzl, Theodor. *Zionistische Schriften*. Edited by Leon Kellner. Berlin: Judischer Verlag, 1905.

Herzl, Theodor. *Old New Land (Altneuland)*. Translated from German by Lotta Levensohn. New York: Markus Wiener and Herzl Press, 1987.

Hesse, Barnor. 'Raceocracy: How the Racial Exception Proves the Racial Rule'. 7 March 2013. Webcast sponsored by Irving K. Barber Learning Centre and hosted by Green College, University of British Columbia, https://open.library.ubc.ca/ cIRcle/collections/ubclibraryandarchives/67657/items/1.0076724.

Hilton, Em. 'British Jews, We Cannot Afford to Align Ourselves with the Far Right'. *+972 Magazine*, 16 November 2021. https://www.972mag.com/british-jews-far-right/.

Hirsch, Yakov. 'Bari Weiss Wants to Speak for the Jews'. *Mondoweiss*, 27 November 2020. https://mondoweiss.net/2020/11/bari-weiss-wants-to-speak-for-the-jews/.

Hirsch, Yakov. 'Israel Can't Be Faulted for Anything, Thanks to Hasbara Culture's Narrative of Jewish Victimhood'. *Mondoweiss*, 20 September 2021. https://mondoweiss.net/2021/09/israel-cant-be-faulted-for-anything-thanks-to-hasbara-cultures-narrative-of-jewish-victimhood.

Hirsch, Yakov. '"Never Again" Journalists Rosenberg, Stephens and Weiss Should Not Speak for the Jews on Colleyville and Antisemitism'. *Mondoweiss*, 27 January 2022. https://mondoweiss.net/2022/01/never-again-journalists-rosenberg-stephens-and-weiss-should-not-speak-for-the-jews-on-colleyville-and-antisemitism.

Hochschild, Adam. *King Leopold's Ghost: A Story of Greed, Terror and Heroism in Colonial Africa*. Boston, New York: Houghton Mifflin Harcourt, 1999.

Hoque, Mahibul. 'The "Pro-Israel" Think Tank That Funds Antisemites across the World'. *Palestine Chronicle*, 20 March 2021. https://www.palestinechronicle.com/middle-east-forum-a-pro-israel-think-tank-that-supports-and-funds-neo-nazis-and-antisemites-across-the-world/.

Hountondji, Paulin J. 'Knowledge of Africa, Knowledge by Africans: Two Perspectives on African Studies'. *RCCS Annual Review* 1, no. 1 (2009): 121–131. http://journals.openedition.org/rccsar/174.

Huntington, Samuel. *The Clash of Civilizations and the Remaking of World Order*. New York: Simon and Schuster, 1996.

Ignatiev, Noel. *How the Irish Became White*. New York, London: Routledge, 1995.

Ingram, Murray. 'Let's Talk about the Meaning of "Merit Selection"'. *Daily Maverick*, 4 May 2017. https://www.dailymaverick.co.za/opinionista/2017-05-04-lets-talk-about-the-meaning-of-merit-selection/.

International Holocaust Remembrance Alliance (IHRA). 'What Is Antisemitism?' https://www.holocaustremembrance.com/resources/working-definitions-charters/working-definition-antisemitism.

Jacques, Johanna. 'A "Most Astonishing" Circumstance: The Survival of Jewish POWs in German War Captivity During the Second World War'. *Social* and *Legal Studies* 30, no. 3 (2021): 362–383. https://doi.org/https://doi.org/10.1177/0964663920946468.

Jamal, Hebh. 'Germany Puts Artists, Academics in Its Anti-Palestinian Crosshairs'. *+972 Magazine*, 3 July 2022. https://www.972mag.com/germany-artists-academics-palestinian-antisemitism/.

Jeffery, Anthea. 'The State of Race Relations in SA 2019 – IRR'. *Politics Web*, 13 June 2019. https://www.politicsweb.co.za/documents/the-state-of-race-relations-in-sa-2019--irr.

Jerusalem Post Staff. 'After Chairman Controversy, Eitam Skipped over for Yad Vashem Role'. *Jerusalem Post*, 24 December 2020. https://www.jpost.com/israel-news/after-chairman-controversy-eitam-skipped-over-for-yad-vashem-role-653132.

Jewish Virtual Library. 'Jewish Population in the United States by State'. Accessed 8 June 2023. https://www.jewishvirtuallibrary.org/jewish-population-in-the-united-states-by-state.

Jones, Kenneth and Tema Okun. *Dismantling Racism: A Workbook for Social Change Groups*. Portland: Western States Center, 2001.

JTA/TOI Staff. 'Trump Praises Israel as "Your Country" to American Jews'. *Times of Israel*, 7 December 2018. https://www.timesofisrael.com/trump-praises-israel-as-your-country-to-american-jews/.

JTA and Marcy Oster. 'Former U.K. Parliament Speaker: Anti-Semitism Came from Own Conservative Party, Not Labour'. *Haaretz*, 3 February 2020. https://www.haaretz.com/world-news/europe/2020-02-03/ty-article/former-u-k-parliament-speaker-anti-semitism-came-from-own-conservative-party/0000017f-ea04-dea7-adff-fbffea2c0000.

Judaken, Jonathan. 'Introduction'. *The American Historical Review* 123, no. 4 (2018): 1122–1138. https://doi.org/10.1093/ahr/rhy024.

Judson, Pieter M. 'Nationalism in the Era of the Nation State, 1870–1945'. In *The Oxford Handbook of Modern German History*, edited by Helmut Walser Smith, 499–526. Oxford: Oxford University Press, 2012.

Kaiser, David. 'What Hitler and the Grand Mufti Really Said'. *Time*, 22 October 2015. https://time.com/4084301/hitler-grand-mufi-1941/.

Kalmar, Ivan David and Derek Penslar, eds. *Orientalism and the Jews*. Chicago: University of Chicago Press, 2004.

Keynan, Irit. 'Transforming Victimhood: From Competitive Victimhood to Sharing Superordinate Identity'. In *Victimhood Discourse in Contemporary Israel*, edited by Ilan Peleg, 137–152. Lanham, MD: Lexington Books, 2019.

Khumalo, Fred. 'Phoenix Massacre: Let's Talk about Race'. *City Press*, 29 November 2021. https://www.news24.com/citypress/columnists/fredkhumalo/close-up-phoenix-massacre-lets-talk-about-race-20211129.

Kingsley, Patrick. 'A Friend to Israel, and to Bigots: Viktor Orban's "Double Game" on Anti-Semitism'. *New York Times*, 14 May 2019. https://www.nytimes.com/2019/05/14/world/europe/orban-hungary-antisemitism.html.

Knesset. 'Full Text of Basic Law: Israel as the Nation State of the Jewish People', 19 July 2018. https://main.knesset.gov.il/en/news/pressreleases/pages/pr13978_pg.aspx.

Knott, Marie Luise, ed. *Der Briefwechsel: Hannah Arendt, Gershom Scholem*. Berlin: Jüdischer Verlag, 2010.

know Botswana. 'Botswana Ethnic Groups and Tribes'. Accessed 8 June 2023. https://www.knowbotswana.com/botswana-ethnic-groups-and-tribes.html.

Kornberg, Jacques. *Theodor Herzl: From Assimilation to Zionism*. Bloomington, IN: Indiana University Press, 1993.

Labour Party. 'The Shami Chakrabarti Inquiry'. Report, 30 June 2016. https://labour.org. uk/wp-content/uploads/2017/10/Chakrabarti-Inquiry-Report-30June16.pdf.

Landau, Noa. 'The Writing Has Been on the Wall for Yad Vashem's Schnorrer Culture'. *Haaretz*, 28 February 2022. https://www.haaretz.com/opinion/.premium-the-writing-has-been-on-the-wall-for-yad-vashem-s-schnorrer-culture-1.10642584.

Laqueur, Walter. *A History of Zionism: From the French Revolution to the Establishment of the State of Israel*. New York: Schocken, 2003.

Lateef, Samaan. 'Why Is India's Government Celebrating an Antisemitic, Pro-Genocide Hitler Devotee?' *Haaretz*, 1 March 2021. https://www.haaretz.com/world-news/2021-03-01/ty-article-opinion/.premium/why-is-indias-government-celebrating-an-antisemitic-pro-genocide-hitler-devotee/0000017f-e108-d804-ad7f-f1fa46980000.

Lenkinski, Libby. 'How Trump and Netanyahu Made American Antisemitism Come Alive'. *+972 Magazine*, 18 November 2020. https://www.972mag.com/how-trump-and-netanyahu-made-american-antisemitism-come-alive/.

Lentin, Alana. *Why Race Still Matters*. Cambridge: Polity Press, 2020.

Leonhard, Robert. *Visions of Apocalypse: What Jews, Christians and Muslims Believe about the End Times, and How Those Beliefs Affect Our World*. Laurel, MD: The Johns Hopkins University, 2010.

Lerman, Antony. *Whatever Happened to Anti-Semitism? Redefinition and the Myth of the 'Collective Jew'*. London: Pluto Press, 2022.

Levin, Bess. 'Trump Goes Full Anti-Semite, Unloads on American Jews in Wildly Bigoted Rant'. *Vanity Fair*, 17 December 2021. https://www.vanityfair.com/news/2021/12/donald-trump-anti-semitism-jews-israel.

Levy, Gideon. 'On This Holocaust Remembrance Day, Let Us Forget'. *Haaretz*, 2 May 2019. https://www.haaretz.com/opinion/2019-05-02/ty-article/.premium/let-us-forget/0000017f-f89e-d2d5-a9ff-f89ecc1a0000.

Lewis, Bernard. 'The Roots of Muslim Rage'. *The Atlantic,* September 1990. https://www.theatlantic.com/magazine/archive/1990/09/the-roots-of-muslim-rage/304643/.

Lis, Jonathan. 'Israeli Minister Shaked: Progress on "Trump Heights" Settlement in Golan'. *Haaretz*, 14 December 2021. https://www.haaretz.com/israel-news/2021-12-14/ty-article/.premium/israeli-minister-shaked-progress-on-trump-heights-settlement-in-golan/0000017f-e243-d568-ad7f-f36be1270000.

Loewenberg, Peter. 'A Hidden Zionist Theme in Freud's "My Son, the Myops ..." Dream'. *Journal of the History of Ideas* 31, no. 1 (1970): 129–132.

Lorber, Ben. 'Jewish Alternatives to Zionism: A Partial History'. Jewish Voice for Peace, 11 January 2019. https://www.jewishvoiceforpeace.org/2019/01/a-partial-history-of-jewish-alternatives/.

Lorber, Ben. 'How the Israeli Flag Became a Symbol for White Nationalists'. *+972 Magazine*, 22 January 2021. https://www.972mag.com/israeli-flag-white-nationalism-symbol/.

Magid, Shaul. 'Christian Supersessionism, Zionism and the Contemporary Scene: A Critical Reading of Peter Ochs's Reading of John Howard Yoder'. *Journal of Religious Ethics* 45, no. 1 (March 2017): 104–141. https://doi.org/https://doi.org/10.1111/jore.12170.

Magid, Shaul. *Piety and Rebellion: Essays in Hasidism*. Brighton, MA: Academic Studies Press, 2019.

Magid, Shaul. 'Savoring the Haterade: Why Jews Love Dara Horn's "People Love Dead Jews"'. *Religion Dispatches*, 20 October 2021. https://religiondispatches.org/savoring-the-haterade-why-jews-love-dara-horns-people-love-dead-jews/.

Mahal, David G. and Ianis G. Matsoukas. 'The Geographic Origins of Ethnic Groups in the Indian Subcontinent: Exploring Ancient Footprints with Y-DNA Haplogroups'. *Frontiers in Genetics* 9 (23 January 2018). https://doi.org/https://doi.org/10.3389/fgene.2018.00004.

Malik, Nesrine. 'Sometimes It's Hard to Remember What Life as a Muslim Was like before 9/11'. *The Guardian*, 13 September 2021. https://www.theguardian.com/commentisfree/2021/sep/13/life-as-a-muslim-before-911-islam.

Mamdani, Mahmood. *Citizen and Subject: Contemporary Africa and the Politics of Late Colonialism*. Kampala: Fountain, 1995.

Mamdani, Mahmood. *Good Muslim, Bad Muslim: America, the Cold War and the Roots of Terror*. Johannesburg: Jacana, 2005.

Mangcu, Xolela. 'Mobilise Communities Instead of Providing Houses of Cards'. *Business Day*, 23 July 2009. https://allafrica.com/stories/200907230375.html.

Maree, Anna. 'South Africa: Democratic Alliance Turns Away from Black Leadership'. *The Africa Report*, 25 May 2021. https://www.theafricareport.com/91149/south-africa-democratic-alliance-turns-away-from-black-leadership/.

Margalit, Avishai and Gabriel Motzkin. 'The Uniqueness of the Holocaust'. *Philosophy & Public Affairs* 25, no. 1 (1996): 65–83.

Marr, Wilhelm. *The Victory of Judaism over Germanism: Viewed from a Nonreligious Point of View*. Translated by Gerhard Rohringer, 2009. Bern: Rudolph Costenoble, 1879. https://archive.org/stream/marr-wilhelm-the-victory-of-judaism-over-germanism_202012/Marr%20Wilhelm%20-%20The%20Victory%20of%20Judaism%20over%20Germanism_djvu.txt.

Massad, Joseph. 'Starmer's Apology Skipped over Britain's Long History of Antisemitism'. *Middle East Eye*, 29 November 2021. https://www.middleeasteye.net/ opinion/uk-antisemitism-starmer-apology-long-history.

Matiwane, Zimasa. 'Mike Waters Resigns from DA Post over "Spineless" Poster Apology'. *Business Live*, 11 October 2021. https://www.businesslive.co.za/bd/national/2021-10-11-mike-waters-resigns-from-da-post-over-spineless-poster-apology.

Mawdudi, Allamah Abu al-'A'la. 'Human Rights in Islam'. *al Tawhid Journal* IV, no. 3 Rajab-Ramadhan 1407 (1987). https://doi.org/https://www.iium.edu.my/deed/articles/hr/hr.html.

Mbali, Mandisa. *South African AIDS Activism and Global Health Politics*. New York: Palgrave Macmillan, 2013.

Mearsheimer, John and Stephen Walt. *The Israel Lobby and U.S. Foreign Policy*. New York: Farrar, Straus and Giroux, 2007.

Middle East Monitor. 'Corbyn Critic Claims Anti-Capitalism Is Also Anti-Semitism'. *MEMO*, 4 March 2019. https://www.middleeastmonitor.com/20190304-corbyn-critic-claims-anti-capitalism-is-also-anti-semitism/.

Middle East Monitor. 'German News Agency Accused of "Weaponising" Anti-Semitism in Sacking of Journalists'. *MEMO*, 8 February 2022. https://www.middleeastmonitor.com/20220208-german-news-agency-accused-of-weaponising-anti-semitism-in-sacking-of-journalists/.

Middle East Monitor. 'Labour Drops Case Against "Anti-Zionist" Jewish Woman for Alleged Anti-Semitism'. *MEMO*, 8 February 2022. https://www.middleeastmonitor.com/20220208-labour-drops-case-against-anti-zionist-jewish-woman-for-alleged-anti-semitism.

Middleton-Kaplan, Richard. 'The Myth of Jewish Passivity'. In *Jewish Resistance Against the Nazis*, edited by Patrick Henry, 3–26. Washington, DC: Catholic University of America Press, 2014.

Mishra, Pankaj. 'Modi's India Points to Perils of White Nationalism in U.S. and U.K.'. *Bloomberg*, 14 November 2021. https://www.bloomberg.com/opinion/articles/2021-11-14/modi-s-india-points-to-perils-of-white-nationalism-in-u-s-and-u-k#xj4y7vzkg.

Mnookin, Robert H. *The Jewish American Paradox*. EPUB. New York: Public Affairs, 2018.

Moodie, T. Dunbar. *The Rise of Afrikanerdom: Power, Apartheid, and the Afrikaner Civil Religion*. Berkeley, CA: University of California Press, 1975.

Morris, Andrea. 'Texas Becomes 4th US State Taking Action Against Ben & Jerry's Unilever over Israel Move'. *CBN News*, 1 October 2021. https://www1.cbn.com/cbnnews/israel/2021/september/texas-becomes-4th-us-state-taking-action-against-ben-and-jerrys-unilever-over-israel-move.

Moussa, Emad. 'Israel's Antisemitism Accusations Become More Meaningless Than Ever in Row over Amnesty Apartheid Report'. *Mondoweiss*, 1 February 2022. https://mondoweiss.net/2022/02/israels-antisemitism-accusations-become-more-meaningless-than-ever-in-row-over-amnesty-apartheid-report/1.

Nahmias, Omri. '10 US States Adopt IHRA Definition of Antisemitism on Holocaust Remembrance Day'. *Jerusalem Post*, 27 January 2022. https://www.jpost.com/diaspora/antisemitism/article-694812.

Nandy, Ashis. *The Intimate Enemy: Loss and Recovery of Self Under Colonialism*. In *Exiled at Home,* by Ashis Nandy. New Delhi: Oxford University Press, 2005.

Narunsky, Gareth and Zeddy Lawrence. 'NSW Adopts IHRA Definition'. *Australian Jewish News*, 16 December 2021. https://www.australianjewishnews.com/nsw-adopts-ihra-definition/.

Nechin, Etan. 'With the Nation-State Law, Israel's Religious Right Is Deciding Who Is a Jew'. *+927 Magazine*, 20 December 2020. https://www.972mag.com/nation-state-law-judaism-religious-right/.

Nelson Mandela Foundation. 'Freedom Charter 60th Anniversary'. 26 June 2015. https://www.nelsonmandela.org/news/entry/freedom-charter-60th-anniversary.

Neocosmos, Michael. *From 'Foreign Natives' to 'Native Foreigners': Explaining Xenophobia in Post-Apartheid South Africa: Citizenship and Nationalism, Identity and Politics.* Dakar: CODESRIA, 2010.

Nortey, Justin. 'U.S. Jews Have Widely Differing Views on Israel'. Pew Research Center, 21 May 2021. https://www.pewresearch.org/short-reads/2021/05/21/u-s-jews-have-widely-differing-views-on-israel/.

Noy, Orly. 'For the Jewish State, the Holocaust Is a Tool to Be Manipulated'. *+927 Magazine*, 20 November 2020. https://www.972mag.com/holocaust-antisemitism-israel-tool/.

Nyamnjoh, Anye. 'The Phenomenology of *Rhodes Must Fall*: Student Activism and the Experience of Alienation at the University of Cape Town'. *Strategic Review for Southern Africa* 39, no. 1 (2017): 256–277. https://upjournals.up.ac.za/index.php/strategic_review/article/view/330.

O'Donnell, Guillermo. 'Illusions about Consolidation'. *Journal of Democracy* 7, no. 2 (April 1996): 34–51.

Ofir, Jonathan. 'Israeli Government Crumbles (Again) on Apartheid Vote – as Its "Arab Experiment" Comes Apart'. *Mondoweiss*, 7 June 2022. https://mondoweiss.

net/2022/06/israeli-government-crumbles-again-on-apartheid-vote-as-its-arab-experiment-comes-apart/.

Oltermann, Philip. 'Germany Agrees to Pay Namibia €1.1bn over Historical Herero-Nama Genocide'. *The Guardian*, 28 May 2021. https://www.theguardian.com/world/2021/may/28/germany-agrees-to-pay-namibia-11bn-over-historical-herero-nama-genocide.

O'Malley, J. P. 'How Émile Zola's Role in the Dreyfus Affair Irrevocably Changed European Politics'. *Times of Israel*, 9 March 2017. https://www.timesofisrael.com/how-emile-zolas-role-in-the-dreyfus-affair-irrevocably-changed-european-politics.

Omoyele, Idowu. 'Arrested Decolonisation, Season 4'. *Mail & Guardian*, 14 July 2017. https://mg.co.za/article/2017-07-14-00-arrested-decolonisation-season-4/.

Open Letter. 'Statement on the IHRA Definition and the Question of Palestine'. *Mondoweiss*, 1 December 2020. https://mondoweiss.net/2020/12/statement-on-the-ihra-definition-and-the-question-of-palestine/.

Palestinian BDS National Committee. 'Israel's Legal Warfare on BDS Fosters Repression and McCarthyism across the World'. BDS Movement, 17 March 2016. https://bdsmovement.net/news/israel's-legal-warfare-bds-fosters-repression-and-mccarthyism-across-world.

Parfitt, Tudor. *The Lost Tribes of Israel: The History of a Myth*. London: Weidenfeld and Nicholson, 2002.

Parr, Chris. 'Eighteen Universities Yet to Adopt IHRA Antisemitism Definition'. *Research Professional News*, 11 November 2021. https://www.researchprofessionalnews.com/rr-news-uk-universities-2021-11-eighteen-universities-yet-to-adopt-ihra-antisemitism-definition/.

Peens, Michelle and Bernard Dubbeld. 'Troubled Transformation: Whites, Welfare, and "Reverse-Racism" in Contemporary Newcastle'. *Diversities* 15, no. 2 (2013): 7–22.

Perlmutter, Amos. 'A. D. Gordon: A Transcendental Zionist'. *Middle Eastern Studies* 7, no. 1 (January 1971): 81–87.

Perlmutter, Nathan and Ruth Ann Perlmutter. *The Real Anti-Semitism in America*. New York: Arbor House, 1982.

Petersen, Roger D. *Understanding Ethnic Violence: Fear, Hatred, and Resentment in Twentieth Century Eastern Europe*. Cambridge: Cambridge University Press, 2002.

Pew Research Center. 'Jewish Americans in 2020'. 11 May 2021. https://www. pewresearch.org/religion/wp-content/uploads/sites/7/2021/05/PF_05.11.21_ Jewish.Americans.pdf.

Pfeffer, Anshel. 'Netanyahu Speaks for All Jews Whether They Like It or Not'. *Haaretz*, 12 February 2015. https://www.haaretz.com/2015-02-12/ty-article/.premium/netanyahu-speaks-for-all-jews/0000017f-db84-db22-a17f-ffb5ec230000.

Phelps, Jordyn. 'Trump Defends 2017 "Very Fine People" Comments, Calls Robert E. Lee "a Great General"'. *ABC News*, 26 April 2019. https://abcnews.go.com/Politics/trump-defends-2017-fine-people-comments-calls-robert/story?id=62653478.

Philpot, Robert. 'How Britain's Nazi-Loving Press Baron Made the Case for Hitler'. *Times of Israel*, 5 August 2018. https://www.timesofisrael.com/how-britains-nazi-loving-press-baron-made-the-case-for-hitler/.

Pierce, Andrew. 'They Raised a Beetroot in the Air and Shouted F*** Capitalism: Minute by Minute, Andrew Pierce Reconstructs Jeremy Corbyn's Four-Hour Meeting with Hate-Filled Group That Mocks Judaism'. *Daily Mail*, 3 April 2018. https://www.dailymail.co.uk/news/article-5575579/They-raised-beetroot-air-shouted-f-capitalism.html.

Pithouse, Richard. 'Burning Message to the State in the Fire of Poor's Rebellion'. *Anarkismo. net*, 23 July 2009. https://www.anarkismo.net/article/13851.

Qukula, Qama. 'Mmusi Maimane Has Slammed Former DA Leader Tony Leon for Calling Him "an Experiment That Went Wrong"'. *CapeTalk*, 4 April 2021. https://www.capetalk.co.za/articles/412955/watch-i-was-in-no-way-anyone-s-experiment-maimane-hits-back-at-tony-leon.

Rao, Anees. 'I Don't Want to Belong to Any Club That Will Accept Me as a Member'. *Medium*, 19 September 2016. https://medium.com/@aneesrao/i-dont-want-to-belong-to-any-club-that-will-accept-me-as-a-member-1210a65e49e9.

Rapport, Nigel. 'Britain and Brexit: Imagining an Essentialist Sense of "Britishness" and Navigating amongst "the British"'. *Anthropology Southern Africa* 43, no. 2 (2020): 94–106. https://doi.org/https://doi.org/10.1080/23323256.2020.1740604.

Raspail, Jean. *The Camp of the Saints*. Translated from French by Norman Shapiro. New York: Scribner, 1975.

Ravitzky, Aviezer. *Messianism, Zionism, and Jewish Religious Radicalism*. Chicago, London: University of Chicago Press, 1996.

Reider, Dimi. 'WATCH: The Most Anti-Semitic Israeli Cartoon Ever Made?' *+927 Magazine*, 14 February 2015. https://www.972mag.com/watch-the-most-anti-semitic-israeli-cartoon-ever-made/.

Reinharz, Jehuda. 'The Conflict Between Zionism and Traditionalism Before World War I'. *Jewish History* 7, no. 2 (1993): 59–78.

Reitter, Paul. *On the Origins of Jewish Self-Hatred*. Princeton, NJ: Princeton University Press, 2012.

Reuters. 'Nancy Pelosi Says Trump Wants to "Make America White Again" – Video'. *The Guardian*, 9 July 2019. https://www.theguardian.com/global/video/2019/jul/09/nancy-pelosi-says-trump-wants-to-make-america-white-again-video.

Roache, Madeline. 'China Guilty of Uighur Genocide in Xinjiang, Tribunal Rules'. *Al Jazeera*, 9 December 2021. https://www.aljazeera.com/news/2021/12/9/china-guilty-of-uighur-genocide-beyond-reasonable-doubt-report.

Robert, Marthe. *From Oedipus to Moses: Freud's Jewish Identity*. New York: Anchor Books, 1976.

Rohringer, Gerhard. 'Foreword by the Translator'. In *The Victory of Judaism over Germanism: Viewed from a Nonreligious Point of View*, by Wilhelm Marr, 4–5, 2009. Bern: Rudolph Costenoble, 1879. https://archive.org/stream/marr-wilhelm-the-victory-of-judaism-over-germanism_202012/Marr%20Wilhelm%20-%20The%20Victory%20of%20Judaism%20over%20Germanism_djvu.txt.

Roodt, Marius. 'Mboweni Plays the Race Card to South Africa's Detriment'. *Daily Friend*, 13 February 2021. https://dailyfriend.co.za/2021/02/13/mboweni-plays-the-race-card-to-south-africas-detriment/.

Ruderman, Jay and Yedidia Z. Stern. 'Is "Israeli" a Nationality?' The Israel Democracy Institute, 9 March 2014. https://en.idi.org.il/articles/6516.

Sabbagh, Dan. 'Labour Adopts IHRA Antisemitism Definition in Full'. *The Guardian*, 4 September 2018. https://www.theguardian.com/politics/2018/sep/04/labour-adopts-ihra-antisemitism-definition-in-full.

Sacks, Jonathan. 'Loving the Stranger Mishpatim 5779'. The Rabbi Sacks Legacy Trust, 2019. https://www.rabbisacks.org/covenant-conversation/mishpatim/loving-the-stranger/.

Sagir, Ceren. 'Labour Criticised After Motion of No Confidence in Starmer Branded Anti-Semitic'. *Morning Star*, 13 March 2021. https://morningstaronline.co.uk/article/b/labour-criticised-after-motion-no-confidence-starmer-branded-anti-semitic?.

Said, Edward W. 'Orientalism Reconsidered'. *Cultural Critique* no. 1 (1985): 89–107.

Said, Edward W. *Orientalism*. London: Penguin, 2003.

Salaymeh, Lena and Shai Lavi. 'Secularism'. In *Key Concepts in the Study of Anti-Semitism*, edited by Sol Goldberg, Scott Ury and Kalman Weiser, 375. Cham: Palgrave Macmillan, 2021.

Sales, Ben. 'Harvard Once Capped the Number of Jews. Is It Doing the Same Thing to Asian Americans Now?' *Jewish Telegraphic Agency*, 17 October 2018. https://www.jta.org/2018/10/17/united-states/harvard-once-capped-the-number-of-jews-is-it-doing-the-same-thing-to-asians-now.

Sales, Ben. 'Right Anti-Semite, Wrong Trump Protest: Tweets of Racist T-Shirt May Help Bigots'. *Times of Israel*, 12 January 2021. https://www.timesofisrael.com/right-anti-semite-wrong-trump-protest-tweets-of-racist-t-shirt-may-help-bigots/.

Sand, Shlomo. *The Invention of the Jewish People*. Translated by Yael Lotan. London, New York: Verso, 2009.

Sanders, Richard. '"The Wrong Sort of Jew": How Labour Pursued Complaints Against Elderly Jewish Opponents of Israel'. *Middle East Eye*, 24 September 2020. https://www.middleeasteye.net/big-story/labour-antisemitism-jewish-opponents-israel-targeted.

Sarna, Jonathan D. 'The Long, Ugly Anti-Semitic History of "Jews Will Not Replace Us"'. The Jewish Experience, Brandeis University, 19 November 2021. https://www.brandeis.edu/jewish-experience/jewish-america/2021/november/replacement-antisemitism-sarna.html.

Sayarer, Julian. 'The Antisemitic Face of Israel's Evangelical Allies'. *Jacobin*, 20 February 2022. https://www.jacobinmag.com/2022/02/israeli-us-evangelical-alliance-zionism-antisemitism.

Schoenfeld, Gabriel. *The Return of Anti-Semitism*. San Francisco, CA: Encounter Books, 2004.

Schwartz, Madeleine. 'The Origins of Blood Libel'. *The Nation*, 28 January 2016. https://www.thenation.com/article/archive/the-origins-of-blood-libel/.

Scott, James C. *Weapons of the Weak: Everyday Forms of Peasant Resistance*. New Haven, CT: Yale University Press, 1985.

Seabrook, Jeremy. 'Racism Is Our Socialism of Fools'. *The Guardian*, 26 February 2004. https://www.theguardian.com/politics/2004/feb/26/eu.immigrationandpublicservices4.

Selzer, Michael, ed. *Zionism Reconsidered: The Rejection of Jewish Normalcy*. New York: Macmillan, 1970.

Selzer, Michael. 'Introduction'. In *Zionism Reconsidered: The Rejection of Jewish Normalcy*, edited by Michael Selzer. New York: Macmillan, 1970.

Sen, Somdeep. 'India's Deepening Love Affair with Israel'. *Al Jazeera*, 9 September 2021. https://www.aljazeera.com/opinions/2021/9/9/indias-deepening-love-affair-with-israel.

Shah, Nasim Hasan. 'The Concept of Al-Dhimmah and the Rights and Duties of Dhimmis in an Islamic State'. *Institute of Muslim Minority Affairs Journal* 9, no. 2 (1988): 217–222. https://doi.org/https://doi.org/10.1080/02666958808716075.

Shlaim, Avi. 'On British Colonialism, Antisemitism, and Palestinian Rights'. *Middle East Eye*, 1 March 2021. https://www.middleeasteye.net/big-story/uk-palestine-israel-policy-balfour-johnson-anitsemitism-colonialism.

Shlaim, Avi. 'Labour Antisemitism Allegations: Are Left-Wing Jewish Party Members Being Targeted? *Middle East Eye*, 14 March 2022. https://www.middleeasteye.net/opinion/uk-labour-antisemitism-allegations-left-wing-jewish-members-targeted.

Silber, Gavin and Nathan Geffen. 'Race, Class and Violent Crime in South Africa: Dispelling the "Huntley Thesis"'. *South African Crime Quarterly* 30, no. 30 (March 2016), 35–43. https://doi.org/10.17159/2413-3108/2009/i30a897.

Silk, Mark. 'Steve Bannon and the Nationalist Roots of Trump's "Judeo-Christian" Vision'. *Religion News Service*, 11 August 2019. https://religionnews.com/2019/08/11/our-latest-judeo-christian-civilizational-clash/.

Simon Wiesenthal Center. 'Understand Simon Wiesenthal Center's Mission'. Accessed 8 June 2023. https://www.wiesenthal.com/about/about-the-simon-wiesenthal-center/.

Sizer, Stephen. 'Christian Zionism: Justifying Apartheid in the Name of God'. *Churchman* 115, no. 2 (2001): 147–171.

Skwawkbox (SW). 'Attacks on Corbyn for Spending Passover with the "Wrong" Jews – and What They Might Mean'. *Skwawkbox*, 3 April 2018. https://skwawkbox.org/2018/04/03/attacks-on-corbyn-for-spending-passover-with-the-wrong-jews-and-what-they-might-mean/.

Smith, David. 'Donald Trump's Rhetoric Has Stoked Antisemitism and Hatred, Experts Warn'. *The Guardian*, 29 October 2018. https://www.theguardian.com/us-news/2018/oct/29/donald-trumps-rhetoric-has-stoked-antisemitism-and-hatred-experts-warn.

Solomon, Abba. 'Why Jewish Organizations Reflexively Defend Israel – Even When Not Asked'. *Mondoweiss*, 8 February 2022. https://mondoweiss.net/2022/02/why-jewish-organizations-reflexively-defend-israel-even-when-not-asked/.

South African History Online. '70. The Durban Riots, 1949'. Last modified 18 June 2019. https://www.sahistory.org.za/archive/70-durban-riots-1949.

South African History Online. 'The Freedom Charter'. Last updated 27 August 2019. https://www.sahistory.org.za/article/freedom-charter.

South African History Online. 'The History of Separate Development in South Africa'. Last updated 27 August 2019. https://www.sahistory.org.za/article/history-separate-development-south-africa.

Staff Reporter. 'Mbeki Turns Aids Row into Race Issue'. *Mail & Guardian*, 26 October 2004. https://mg.co.za/article/2004-10-26-mbeki-turns-aids-row-into-race-issue/.

Staff Writers. 'Israel May Be Eighth-Ranked in Global Power, but It's Really Not Much Fun'. *Haaretz*, 1 March 2016. https://www.haaretz.com/israel-news/israel-is-the-eighth-ranked-global-powe-1.5411241.

Staples, Brent. 'How Italians Became "White"'. *New York Times*, 12 October 2019. https://www.nytimes.com/interactive/2019/10/12/opinion/columbus-day-italian-american-racism.html.

Stern, Kenneth. 'I Drafted the Definition of Antisemitism. Rightwing Jews Are Weaponizing It'. *The Guardian*, 13 December 2019. https://www.theguardian.com/commentisfree/2019/dec/13/antisemitism-executive-order-trump-chilling-effect.

Sternhell, Zeev. *The Founding Myths of Israel: Nationalism, Socialism, and the Making of the Jewish State*. Translated by David Maisel. Princeton, NJ: Princeton University Press, 1998.

Stern-Weiner, Jamie. 'The Politics of a Definition: How the IHRA Working Definition of Antisemitism Is Being Misrepresented'. Free Speech on Israel, April 2021. https://www.documentcloud.org/documents/20689366-stern-weiner-j-fsoi-the-politics-of-a-definition.

Steyn, Richard. *Churchill and Smuts: The Friendship*. Johannesburg: Jonathan Ball Publishers, 2017.

Stone, Jon. 'Boris Johnson Book Depicts Jews as Controlling the Media'. *Independent*, 9 December 2019. https://www.independent.co.uk/news/uk/politics/boris-johnson-book-jews-control-media-general-election-a9239346.html.

Stow, Kenneth R. *Catholic Thought and Papal Jewry Policy, 1555–1593*. New York: The Jewish Theological Seminary Press, 2012.

Sunshine, Spencer. 'We Didn't Need More Evidence – Richard Spencer Has Always Been Anti-Semitic'. *Jewish Telegraphic Agency*, 7 November 2019. https://www.clevelandjewishnews.com/jta/we-didn-t-need-more-evidence-richard-spencer-has-always-been-anti-semitic/article_8d74e3c6-9168-5057-a80b-d782c21efc8d.html.

Tagore, Rabindranath. *Gora*. New Delhi: Rupa, 2002.

Tamimi, Azzam S. *Rachid Ghannouchi: A Democrat Within Islamism*. New York: Oxford University Press, 2001.

Tharoor, Ishaan. 'The U.S. and British Right Ramp up the War on "Wokeness"'. *Washington Post*, 9 April 2021. https://www.washingtonpost.com/world/2021/04/09/ woke-wars-united-states-britain.

TOI Staff. 'White Nationalist Richard Spencer Tells Israelis That Jews Are "Over-Represented"'. *Times of Israel*, 17 August 2017. https://www.timesofisrael.com/white-nationalist-richard-spencer-tells-israelis-that-jews-are-over-represented/.

Toprak, Binnaz. 'Secularism and Islam: The Building of Modern Turkey'. *Macalester International* 15 (2005): Article 9. http://digitalcommons.macalester.edu/macintl/vol15/iss1/9.

Trapido, Stanley. 'The Origins of the Cape Franchise Qualifications of 1853'. *Journal of African History* 5, no. 1 (1964): 37–54.

Turner, Richard. 'Black Consciousness and White Liberals'. *Reality: A Journal of Liberal Opinion* 4, no. 3 (July 1972): 20–22.

United Nations Human Rights Council. 'Independent International Fact-Finding Mission on Myanmar'. Accessed 8 June 2023. https://www.ohchr.org/en/hr-bodies/hrc/myanmar-ffm/index.

United Nations Office of the High Commissioner for Human Rights. 'Geneva Convention Relative to the Treatment of Prisoners of War, 1949'. https://www.un.org/en/genocideprevention/documents/atrocity-crimes/Doc.32_GC-III-EN.pdf.

Van Onselen, Gareth. 'Mmusi Maimane Presses the Self-Destruct Button'. *Business Day*, 9 May 2018. https://www.businesslive.co.za/bd/opinion/columnists/2018-05-09-gareth-van-onselen-mmusi-maimane-presses-the-self-destruct-button/.

Varshney, Ashutosh. *Battles Half Won: India's Improbable Democracy*. New Delhi: Penguin Viking, 2013.

Wadi, Ramona. 'Defeating the IHRA Witch Hunt: An Interview with Palestinian Activist and Scholar Shahd Abusalama'. *Mondoweiss*, 7 February 2022. https://mondoweiss.net/2022/02/defeating-the-ihra-witch-hunt-an-interview-with-palestinian-activist-and-scholar-shahd-abusalama/.

Wallach, Yair. 'The Global Right Is a Threat to US Jews – but a Natural Home for Israelis'. *+972 Magazine*, 16 November 2020. https://www.972mag.com/israel-us-jewish-divide/.

Waxman, Dov. *Trouble in the Tribe: The American Jewish Conflict over Israel*. Princeton: Princeton University Press, 2016.

Weber, Max. *Economy and Society*. Edited by Guenther Roth and Claus Wittich. Berkeley: University of California Press, 1978.

Weinryb, Bernard D. *The Jews of Poland: A Social and Economic History of the Jewish Community in Poland* from *1100–1800*. Translated by Jane Marie Todd and Michael B. Smith. Philadelphia: Jewish Publication Society of America, 1973.

Weiss, Philip. 'Capitol Riot Provides Shock to Netanyahu, Friedman … and American Exceptionalism'. *Mondoweiss*, 8 January 2021. https://mondoweiss.net/2021/01/capitol-riot-provides-shock-to-netanyahu-friedman-and-american-exceptionalism/.

Weiss, Philip. 'America's Whiteness Crisis, and Zionism's'. *Mondoweiss*, 10 January 2021. https://mondoweiss.net/2021/01/americas-whiteness-crisis-and-zionisms/.

Weiss, Philip. 'Anti-Zionist Jews Are "Jews in Name Only" and "More Dangerous Than External Antisemitic Threat" – Chicago Reform Rabbi'. *Mondoweiss*, 26 November 2021. https://mondoweiss.net/2021/11/anti-zionist-jews-are-jews-in-name-only-and-more-dangerous-than-external-antisemitic-threat-chicago-reform-rabbi/.

Weiss, Philip. 'Israel Lobby Is in New Territory – Mounting "Apartheid" Allegations – and Showing Some Cracks'. *Mondoweiss*, 2 February 2022. https://mondoweiss.net/2022/02/israel-lobby-is-in-new-territory-mounting-apartheid-allegations-and-showing-some-cracks/.

Weiss, Philip. 'U.S. Jews Favor Return to Iran Deal, and Don't Care about Israel as a Political Issue'. *Mondoweiss*, 14 April 2022. https://mondoweiss.net/2022/04/u-s-jews-favor-return-to-iran-deal-and-dont-care-about-israel-as-a-political-issue/.

Weiss, Philip. 'Israel Lobby Group Affirms Trend – 22% of Younger Jews Don't Want a Jewish State'. *Mondoweiss*, 26 April 2022. https://mondoweiss.net/2022/04/israel-lobby-group-affirms-trend-22-of-younger-jews-dont-want-a-jewish-state/.

Winstanley, Asa. 'Netanyahu Advisers Hatched Anti-Semitic Conspiracy Against George Soros'. *Electronic Intifada*, 19 March 2019. https://electronicintifada.net/blogs/asa-winstanley/netanyahu-advisers-hatched-anti-semitic-conspiracy-against-george-soros.

Winstanley, Asa. 'Israeli Ambassador Made Anti-Semitic Video'. *Electronic Intifada*, 18 December 2020. https://electronicintifada.net/blogs/asa-winstanley/israeli-ambassador-made-anti-semitic-video.

Winstanley, Asa. 'David Miller's Sacking Is Just the Start'. *Middle East Monitor*, 12 October 2021. https://www.middleeastmonitor.com/20211012-david-millers-sacking-is-just-the-start/.

Wiredu, Kwasi. 'Democracy and Consensus in African Traditional Politics: A Plea for a Non-Party Polity'. In *Postcolonial African Philosophy: A Critical Reader*, edited by Emmanuel Chukwudi Eze, 303–312. Cambridge, MA, Oxford: Blackwell, 1997.

Wistrich, Robert S. *Antisemitism: The Longest Hatred*. New York: Pantheon Press, 1991.

World Population Review. 'Muslim Population by Country, 2022'. Accessed 8 June 2023. https://worldpopulationreview.com/country-rankings/muslim-population-by-country.

World Population Review. 'South Korea Population, 2023'. Accessed 8 June 2023. https://worldpopulationreview.com/countries/south-korea-population.

Zhou, Yun. 'Question of Ethnic Group Formulation in the Chinese Census'. *China Population and Development Studies* 3, no. 1 (2019): 67–83. https://doi.org/https://doi.org/10.1007/s42379-019-00034-5.

Zimmerman, Moshe. *Wilhelm Marr: The Patriarch of Anti-Semitism*. New York, Oxford: Oxford University Press, 1986.

Zulu, Andile. 'Dissecting White Genocide: What Is to Be Feared and Why?' *Daily Maverick*, 1 April 2019. https://www.dailymaverick.co.za/opinionista/2019-04-01-dissecting-white-genocide-what-is-to-be-feared-and-why/.

Printed in the USA
CPSIA information can be obtained
at www.ICGtesting.com
JSHW021716140624
64814JS00002B/114